Organizational Stress

FOUNDATIONS FOR ORGANIZATIONAL SCIENCE
A Sage Publications Series

Series Editor
David Whetten, *Brigham Young University*

Editors
Peter J. Frost, *University of British Columbia*
Anne S. Huff, *University of Colorado* and *Cranfield University* (UK)
Benjamin Schneider, *University of Maryland*
M. Susan Taylor, *University of Maryland*
Andrew Van de Ven, *University of Minnesota*

The FOUNDATIONS FOR ORGANIZATIONAL SCIENCE series supports the development of students, faculty, and prospective organizational science professionals through the publication of texts authored by leading organizational scientists. Each volume provides a highly personal, hands-on introduction to a core topic or theory and challenges the reader to explore promising avenues for future theory development and empirical application.

Cary L. Cooper / Philip J. Dewe
Michael P. O'Driscoll

Organizational Stress

A Review and Critique of Theory, Research, and Applications

Foundations for
Organizational
Science
A Sage Publications Series

Sage Publications
International Educational and Professional Publisher
Thousand Oaks ■ London ■ New Delhi

For information:

Sage Publications, Inc.
2455 Teller Road
Thousand Oaks, California 91320
E-mail: order@sagepub.com

Sage Publications Ltd.
6 Bonhill Street
London EC2A 4PU
United Kingdom

Sage Publications India Pvt. Ltd.
M-32 Market
Greater Kailash I
New Delhi 110 048 India

Printed in the United States of America

Library of Congress Cataloging-in-Publication Data

Cooper, Cary L.
 Organizational stress: A review and critique of theory, research, and applications / by Cary L. Cooper, Philip J. Dewe, and Michael P. O'Driscoll
  p. cm.
Includes bibliographical references and index.
 ISBN 0-7619-1480-3 (c)—ISBN 0-7619-1481-1 (p)
 1. Job stress. I. Dewe, Philip. II. O'Driscoll, Michael P. III. Title.
 HF5548.85 .C656 2001
 158.7′2—dc21   00–011071

This book is printed on acid-free paper.

01 02 03 04 05 06 07 7 6 5 4 3 2 1

Acquisition Editor:	Marquita Flemming
Editorial Assistant:	MaryAnn Vail
Production Editor:	Diane S. Foster
Editorial Assistant:	Victoria Cheng
Typesetter:	Siva Math Setters, Chennai, India
Indexer:	Will Ragsdale
Cover Designer:	Michelle Lee

Contents

Introduction to the Series

The title of this series, **Foundations for Organizational Science** (FOS), denotes a distinctive focus. FOS books are educational aids for mastering the core theories, essential tools, and emerging perspectives that constitute the field of organizational science (broadly conceived to include organizational behavior, organizational theory, human resource management, and business strategy). Our ambitious goal is to assemble the "essential library" for members of our professional community.

The vision for the series emerged from conversations with several colleagues, including Peter Frost, Anne Huff, Rick Mowday, Benjamin Schneider, Susan Taylor, and Andy Van de Ven. A number of common interests emerged from these sympathetic encounters, including enhancing the quality of doctoral education by providing broader access to the master teachers in our field, "bottling" the experience and insights of some of the founding scholars in our field before they retire, and providing professional development opportunities for colleagues seeking to broaden their understanding of the rapidly expanding subfields within organizational science.

Our unique learning objectives are reflected in an unusual set of instructions to FOS authors. They are encouraged to (a) "write the way they teach"—framing their book as an extension of their teaching notes, rather than as the expansion of a handbook chapter; (b) pass on their "craft knowledge" to the next generation of scholars—making them wiser, not just smarter; (c) share with their "virtual students and colleagues" the insider tips and best bets for research that are normally reserved for one-on-one mentoring sessions; and (d) make the complexity of their subject matter comprehensible to nonexperts so that readers can share their puzzlement, fascination, and intrigue.

We are proud of the group of highly qualified authors who have embraced the unique educational perspective of our "Foundations" series. We encourage your suggestions for how these books can better satisfy your learning needs—as a newcomer to the field preparing for prelims or developing a dissertation proposal, or as an established scholar seeking to broaden your knowledge and proficiency.

—DAVID A. WHETTEN
SERIES EDITOR

Preface

The last half-century has seen an enormous change in the nature of society and of the workplace in particular (Cooper, 1998). The 1960s epitomized the limitless possibilities of change, with the British prime minister of the time proclaiming that the "white heat of technology" was about to transform our lives, producing a leisure age of 20-hour working weeks. This was followed by a period of industrial strife and conflict during the 1970s in much of the developed world. The workplace became a battleground between employers and workers, highlighted by Studs Terkel's observation, in his acclaimed 1972 book, *Working:*

> This book, being about work, is, by its very nature, about violence—to the spirit as well as to the body. It is about ulcers as well as accidents, about shouting matches as well as fistfights, about nervous breakdowns as well as kicking the dog around. It is, above all, about daily humiliations. (p. xi)

Out of the industrial relations turmoil of the 1970s came the "enterprise culture" of the 1980s, a decade of privatization, merger mania, joint ventures, process reengineering, and the like, transforming workplaces into free-market, hothouse cultures. Although this entrepreneurial period on both sides of the Atlantic improved economic competitiveness in international markets, there were also the first signs of strain, as "stress" and "burnout" became concepts in the everyday vocabulary of many working people.

By the end of the 1980s and into the early 1990s, the sustained recession, the move toward the privatization of the public sector, and the information technology revolution laid the groundwork for potentially the most profound changes in the workplace since the industrial revolution. The early 1990s were dominated by the effects of recession and efforts to get out of it, as organizations downsized and flattened their structures. There were fewer people doing more work and feeling more job insecure. The rapid expansion of information technology also meant the added burden of information overload and the accelerating pace of work, with people demanding more and more information coming in faster and faster. From the middle 1980s throughout the 1990s, we also saw a dramatic increase in the number of women in the workplace, with a noticeable pushing of the "glass ceiling" further upward. The changing role of men and women at work, and at home, added another dimension to the large changes taking place in the world.

The downsizing and the rapidity of change had certainly taken its toll in the 1990s. Although this scenario is cause enough for concern, the underlying trend toward "outsourcing" is leading toward a new form of employment arrangement, the "short-term contract" or "freelance" culture. This has led to what employers refer to euphemistically as "the flexible workforce," although in family-friendly terms it can at times be anything but flexible. The psychological contract between employer and employee in terms of "reasonably permanent employment for work well done" is truly being undermined, as more and more employees no longer regard their employment as secure and many more are engaged in part-time working and short-term contracts. Indeed, the British Institute of Management survey (Worrall & Cooper, 1997-1999) has generated some disturbing results among Britain's managers. In particular, organizations at the end of the 1990s were found to be in a state of constant change, with over 60% of this national sample of managers having undergone a major restructuring over the previous 12 months. Furthermore, and of specific relevance in the context of the present book, these changes led directly to increased job insecurity, lowered morale, and the erosion of motivation and loyalty. Most of these changes involved downsizing, cost reduction, delayering, and outsourcing. The perception of managers in this research was that although inevitably these changes led to a slight increase in profitability and productivity, decision making was slower and, more importantly, the organization was deemed to have lost the right mix of human resource skills and experience in the process (Worrall & Cooper, 1997-1999).

So what are the consequences of this change? First, as more and more people work from their homes, whether part time or on a short-term contract, we will be increasingly creating "virtual organizations." The big corporate question here is: How will the virtual organization of the future manage this dispersed workforce, along with the communication difficulties already apparent in existing organizational structures? Second, with two out of three families/couples engaged in two-earner or dual-career employment, how will working from home affect the delicate balance between home and work, or indeed the roles between men and women? Third, since the industrial revolution, many white-collar, managerial and professional workers have not experienced high levels of job insecurity, and even many blue-collar workers who were laid off in heavy manufacturing industries of the past were frequently reemployed when times got better. This situation has clearly changed. The question that society has to ask itself is: Can human beings cope with permanent job insecurity, without the safety and security of organizational structures, which in the past provided training development and careers?

The purpose of the present book is to review research in the field of organizational stress in order to reflect upon what this research can tell us about the current and future state of the workplace and its impact on the health of all employees. It helps to focus our efforts on the future of work, where it is going, and the role industrial and organizational psychologists can play in better understanding the dynamics of occupational stress. Hopefully, this book will provide the groundwork for PhD students and academics alike in their efforts to identify future areas of fertile research in the field of workplace stress, stress management interventions, and what can be done to minimize or eliminate the sources of stress that are so poignantly represented in Studs Terkel's insightful observations about working.

References

Cooper, C. L. (1998). The Psychological Implications of the Changing Nature of Work. *Royal Society of Arts Journal, 1,* 71-84.

Terkel, S. (1972). *Working.* New York: Avon.

Worrall, L., & Cooper, C. L. (1997–1999). *IM/UMIST Quality of Working Life Survey.* London: Institute of Management.

Acknowledgments

The authors wish to acknowledge Ben Schneider, Arthur Brief, and David Whetten for their feedback and comments on earlier versions of this volume and also to thank Dan Ganster, Tom Kalliath, Arie Shirom, and Paul Spector for comments on specific chapters. Appreciation is extended to Sue Cartwright, Lyn Davidson, Valerie Sutherland, and Brian Faragher, along with all of our graduate and postgraduate students who have worked with us over the years in conducting research on job stress, burnout, and coping. Finally, we wish to express our deep appreciation to our wives (Rachel Davies Cooper, Linda Trenberth, and Elizabeth O'Driscoll) for their ongoing support and encouragement throughout the writing and production of this book.

1 What Is Stress?

To the individual whose health or happiness has been ravaged by an inability to cope with the effects of job-related stress, the costs involved are only too clear. Whether manifested in minor complaints of illness, serious ailments such as heart disease, or social problems such as alcoholism and drug abuse, stress-related problems exact a heavy toll on individuals' lives (Watts & Cooper, 1998). In addition, it has long been recognized that families suffer directly or indirectly from the stress problems of their members—suffering that can be manifested in unhappy marriages, divorces, and spouse and child abuse. But what price do organizations and nations pay for a poor fit between people and their environments? Only recently has stress been seen as a contributory factor to the productivity and health costs of companies and countries, but, as studies of stress-related illnesses and deaths show, stress imposes a high cost on individual health and well-being as well as organizational productivity (Cooper, Liukkonen, & Cartwright, 1996; Sutherland & Cooper, 1990).

This book examines the concept of stress and its application in organizational contexts. In the following chapters, we review the sources and outcomes of job-related stress, the methods used to assess levels and consequences of occupational stress, and the strategies that might be used by individuals and organizations to confront stress and its associated problems. We also devote one chapter to examining a very extreme form of occupational stress—burnout, which has been found to have severe consequences for individuals and their organizations. Finally, we discuss scenarios for jobs and work in the new millennium, as well as the potential sources of stress that these scenarios may generate.

The major focus of this volume is research on stress arising in job-related, organizational contexts. In each chapter, we examine critical issues concerning stress research and some of the challenges facing researchers in this broad and complex field. Our aim is not to provide a total review of all relevant studies on job stress but to stimulate awareness and critical thinking about significant theoretical and empirical issues. The present chapter begins with a brief overview of the historical origins and early approaches to the study of stress, discusses the strengths and weaknesses of these early approaches, and describes the evolution of the contemporary *transactional* model of stress. We conclude the chapter with an exploration of emerging themes in the delineation of stress and related concepts.

Overview of Stress Definitions

One difficulty in conducting research on stress is that wide discrepancies exist in the way that stress is defined and operationalized. For instance, the concept of stress has variously been defined as both an independent and a dependent variable (Cox, 1985) and as a "process." This confusion over terminology is compounded by the broad application of the stress concept in medical, behavioral, and social science research over the past 50 to 60 years. Each discipline has investigated stress from its own unique perspective, adopting as a guideline either a stimulus-based model (stress as the "independent" variable) or a response-based model (stress as the "dependent" variable). The approach taken is dictated by the objectives of the research and the intended action resulting from the findings. What is clear from the different ways in which stress has been defined is that there has been considerable debate and discussion as to what is really meant by stress.

As we discuss in this chapter, the importance of this debate can be established by way of two points. First, theoretical definitions of concepts determine the nature and direction of research, as well as the possible explanations that can be proffered for research findings. Definitions provide researchers with theoretical boundaries that need to be constantly extended and reviewed to ensure that what is being defined reflects the nature of the experience itself (Newton, 1995). Second, the definitional debate gives a sense of time and historical perspective, shedding light on why a certain focus or approach prevails, and a mechanism for considering the explanatory potential of current research.

Almost all research on stress begins by pointing to the difficulties associated with and the confusion surrounding the way in which the term *stress* has been used. As has already been noted, stress has been defined as a stimulus, a response, or the result of an interaction between the two, with the interaction described in terms of some imbalance between the person and the environment (Cox, 1978). As empirical knowledge has developed, particularly that surrounding the person-environment (P-E) interaction, researchers have considered the nature of that interaction and, more importantly, the psychological processes through which it takes place (Dewe, 1992).

From this debate has emerged a belief that traditional approaches to defining stress (i.e., stimulus, response, interaction) have, by directing attention toward external events, diverted researchers away from considering the processes within the individual through which such events are appraised (Duckworth, 1986). This is not to say that such ideas have gone unresearched or that earlier definitional approaches are necessarily inadequate. However, as knowledge and understanding of stimulus, response, and interaction definitions and their associated meaning have advanced, the debate about how stress should be defined has shifted ground. Rather than singling out and focusing separately on the different elements of the stress process, we suggest that it is now time to examine more comprehensively the nature of that process itself and to integrate stimulus and response definitions within an overall conceptual framework that acknowledges the dynamic linkages between all elements of the stress process.

Contemporary views on how stress should be defined require researchers to think of stress as being relational (Lazarus & Launier, 1978): the result of a *transaction* between the individual and the environment (Lazarus, 1990). The transactional approach draws researchers toward identifying those processes that link the individual to the environment. What distinguishes this approach from earlier approaches is the emphasis on "transaction"—identifying the processes that link the different components, recognizing that stress does not reside solely in the individual or solely in the environment but in the conjunction between the two, and accepting that no one component (i.e., stimulus, response) can be said to be stress (Lazarus, 1990) because each is part of, and must be understood within, the context of a process.

One last point before considering the different stress definitions in more detail. It should not be assumed that different approaches to defining stress have followed in some logical sequence. A range of factors, including the discipline of the researcher, the direction of the research, and the research questions asked, will influence whether a particular definitional approach is adopted. Furthermore, at the conceptual level many researchers agree that stress should be defined in transactional terms, but empirical research has often adopted definitions that emphasize a particular part of the stress process rather than the nature of the process itself. Despite the confusion in terminology, the important message to emerge is that defining stress is not just an exercise in semantics: The way in which stress is defined has a fundamental impact on how research is conducted and results are explained, and definitions must capture the essence of the stress experience rather than simply reflect a rhetoric (Newton, 1995).

Response-Based Definitions of Stress

The phrase "being under stress" is one that most people can identify with, although it can mean different things to different individuals. This expression focuses not so much on the nature of stress itself but on its outcomes or consequences. A response-based approach (see Figure 1.1) views stress as a dependent variable (i.e., a response to disturbing or threatening stimuli).

The origins of response-based definitions can be found in medicine and are usually viewed from a physiological perspective—a logical stance for a discipline trained to diagnose and treat symptoms but not necessarily their causes. The work of Hans Selye in the 1930s and 1940s marks the beginning of this approach to the study of stress. In 1936, Selye introduced the notion of stress-related illness in terms of the *general adaptation syndrome* (GAS), suggesting that stress is a nonspecific

ENVIRONMENT   PERSON

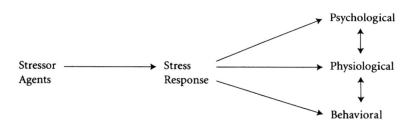

STIMULUS ⟶ RESPONSE

Figure 1.1. A Response-Based Model of Stress

SOURCE: Reproduced from *Understanding Stress*, Sutherland and Cooper, 1990, Nelson Thornes Ltd.

response of the body to any demand made upon it (Selye, 1956). Selye's focus was medical: General malaise was characterized by loss of motivation, appetite, weight, and strength. Evidence from animal studies also indicated internal physical degeneration and deterioration. Responses to stress were considered to be invariant to the nature of the stressor and therefore to follow a universal pattern.

Three stages of response were described within the GAS (see Figure 1.2). The alarm reaction is the immediate psychophysiological response, when the initial "shock" phase of lowered resistance is followed by "countershock." At this time, defense mechanisms are activated, forming the emergency reaction known as the "fight or flight" response (Cannon, 1935). Increased sympathetic activity results in the secretion of catecholamines, which prepare the body physiologically for action: For example, heart rate and blood pressure increase, the spleen contracts, and blood supplies are redirected to the brain and skeletal muscles. The second stage is resistance to a continued stressor, in which the adaptation response and/or return to equilibrium replace the alarm reaction. However, resistance cannot continue indefinitely, and if the alarm reaction is elicited too intensely or too frequently over an extended period, the energy needed for adaptation becomes depleted, and the third stage (exhaustion, collapse, or death) occurs (Selye, 1983).

Stimulus-Based Definitions of Stress

Identification of potential sources of stress is the central theme of the stimulus-based model of stress (Goodell, Wolf, & Rogers, 1986). The rationale of this approach is that some external forces impinge on the organism in a disruptive way. Stimulus-based definitions of stress have their roots in physics and engineering, the analogy being that stress can be defined as a force exerted, which in turn results in a demand or load reaction, hence creating distortion. If the organism's tolerance level is exceeded, temporary or permanent damage occurs. The aphorism "the straw that breaks the camel's back" encapsulates the essence of stimulus-based definitions of stress. An individual is perpetually bombarded with potential sources of stress (which are typically referred to as *stressors*), but just one more apparently minor or innocuous event can alter the delicate balance between coping and the total breakdown of coping behavior. In short, this model of stress treats stress as an independent variable that elicits some response from the person.

Rapid industrialization provided the initial impetus for this approach, and much of the early research into blue-collar stress aimed to identify sources of stress in the work environment in order to provide optimal working conditions (Cooper & Smith, 1985). Considerable attention was paid to physical and task circumstances (such as heat, cold, noise, and social density). However, it is now realized that focusing solely on objective measures of environmental conditions is inadequate. Individual differences, such as variability in tolerance levels and expectations, can account for the fact that two individuals exposed to exactly the same situation might react in completely different ways. This is a major weakness of the stimulus model. In fact, Lazarus (1966) stated that no objective criterion is sufficient to describe a situation as "stressful" and that only the person experiencing the event can do this. Nevertheless, although the stimulus model has limitations, it is useful in identifying common stressor themes or patterns that might affect the majority of the workforce. In Chapter 3, we provide an overview of some of the more prevalent and pervasive stressors that are encountered in organizational contexts. However, as we shall discuss in more detail in later chapters (see especially Chapter 6), attention to the individual's perceptions and appraisal of the stressors is essential for determining whether the person is experiencing distress or "strain."

Shortcomings of Response and Stimulus Definitions

Both the response and stimulus definitions of stress are set conceptually within a relatively simple stimulus-response paradigm. It is now recognized that they largely ignore individual differences and the perceptual and cognitive processes that might underpin these differences (Cox, 1990; Sutherland & Cooper, 1990). In short, response and stimulus definitions have proved to be taxonomic in nature, providing researchers with an opportunity to establish what are essentially lists of responses and situations (or events) that may fall under each definitional heading. Such definitions are important and necessary; however, as research into stress has advanced, approaches to defining stress have often failed because they are unable to provide a comprehensive "theory of stress" or a context for considering the nature of the stress experience itself.

Specifically, three criticisms can be leveled at stimulus-response definitions. The first has already been mentioned—they reflect only one component of the stress process and say little about the process itself. Embedded within this criticism are concerns that, in an attempt to explore the range of situations and responses that may give rise to stress, little attention (at least at the empirical level) has been given to the inherent properties of the different stimuli and responses themselves. For example, stimulus definitions have been important in identifying different categories of events that have the potential for causing stress (e.g., "acts of God," "critical life events," and "daily hassles"). As a result, properties of the events themselves (such as their frequency, duration, demand, intensity, and severity) have been somewhat overlooked in the understandable drive to explore relationships between the mere occurrence of these different events and a range of stress responses.

Much the same can be said for response-based definitions. Because almost any response can be classified as a "stress response," often responses are regarded as homogeneous, and little consideration has been given to the duration of the response or its pattern. Nor, for that matter, has much attention been paid to the idea that certain events may give rise to very specific responses. Therefore, to suggest that an event is not stressful may overlook the fact that researchers must pay more attention to the specificity of responses and their nature rather than simply concluding (perhaps erroneously) that no stress is present in such an encounter. Because stimulus-response definitions each focus on a single aspect of a relationship, it is only ever possible to conclude that an event has *the potential* to be stressful or that a response *may be* a stress response. We believe that a stimulus or a response can be declared as "stressful" or a "stress response" only when the two components are considered in relation to one another and the impact of one on the other has been determined. For this reason, as we shall see later in this chapter, contemporary stress definitions have focused first on the *interaction* between the stimulus and response and then on the *transactional* nature of stress itself.

The second problem that emerges when stress is defined simply in terms of a stimulus or response has also been alluded to. It is that these frameworks fail to account for individual differences. This criticism stems from the argument that knowledge of a stimulus condition, for example, does not necessarily allow exact prediction of a response because whether a stimulus is likely to produce a response depends on the moderating influences of individual differences (e.g., personality attributes, expectations, values, and goals), the context (e.g., levels of social support, control, and appraisal), and the person's role and status within the organization (e.g., tenure, function, level in the hierarchy, and job attributes). Much of this criticism can be summed up in the view that what is stressful for one individual may not be stressful for another. Chapter 5 further discusses potential moderators of job-related stress, including individual differences.

The third criticism is directed more toward the impact that such definitions have on understanding the stress process. This criticism is best expressed by the view that arbitrarily limiting the definition of stress to only one dimension of a process draws attention away from the nature of the process itself. As we have already discussed, stress involves both a stimulus and a response in relation to one another, and it is the relational nature of stress that should be the focus of any definition (Lazarus & Launier, 1978). When considered in these terms, the aim should be to point researchers toward those processes that link the individual with the environment. To accept that stress resides, not in any one component, but in the nature of the relationship itself should be the integrating point of any definition. Early efforts to examine this relationship built upon the notion of *interaction* between environmental stimuli and individuals' responses.

Stress as an Interaction

The interactional approach to defining stress focuses on the statistical interaction between the stimulus and the response. This approach, described as "structural" (Stahl, Grim, Donald, & Neikirk, 1975) and "quantitative" (Straus, 1973), is one where a relationship, usually correlational, is hypothesized between a stimulus and a response. This approach is essentially static (cause and effect), with any consideration of process being limited to inferential explanations when the interaction fails to materialize or is different from that predicted. This is where, according to Lazarus and Launier (1978), description has taken a back seat to simple cause-effect formulations. A definition like this, which focuses only on the interaction between two variables, means that attempts to explain the complexity of such a relationship are limited to "structural manipulations," such as the influence of a third (moderator) variable, which again do not provide an explication of the stress process.

The above comments are not intended to imply that moderator analysis is not worth pursuing. However, as we shall see in Chapter 5, job stress research has investigated a very large array of moderator variables, sometimes with little theoretical rationale for their inclusion in a study's design, resulting in inconsistent (and frequently ambiguous) findings about the role of these variables. We suggest that it is important now to move beyond the simple identification of potential moderator variables to more comprehensive theories that attempt to explain the mechanisms by which all relevant factors interact. Furthermore, even when moderators are selected on a theoretical basis, empirical findings often simply demonstrate a moderator effect rather than explicating the role that the moderator plays in the stress process.

Taking this argument a stage further, job stress should now be viewed as a transaction—an ongoing relationship between the individual and the environment. The *interactional* approach is limited in its ability to expose the causal pathways inherent in that relationship. In contrast, the *transactional* model of stress endeavors to explore the essential nature of stressor-response-outcome relationships and to encapsulate an understanding of the dynamic stress process itself, not merely the statistical relationship between variables.

Stress as a Transaction

Whereas the interactional definition of stress focuses on the structural features of the person's interaction with his or her environment, transactional definitions are more concerned with the dynamics of the psychological mechanisms of cognitive appraisal and coping that underpin a stressful encounter. There are two types of appraisal. From a transactional perspective (Lazarus, 1966), the experience of stress is defined first by the person's realization that something is at stake (*primary appraisal*). In the primary appraisal process, the individual gives meaning to an encounter. The meanings that best express this appraisal process are those involving *harm*, the *threat* of harm, or *challenge*. Once an encounter is appraised as being in some way a threat to the person's well-being, the *secondary appraisal* process begins. This process is concerned with the identification and availability of coping resources to deal with the threat, harm, or challenge (Lazarus, 1991). These two appraisals are the key to the stress-coping process (Dewe, Cox, & Ferguson, 1993).

Stress is, therefore, not a factor that resides in the individual or the environment; rather, it is embedded in an ongoing process that involves individuals transacting with their environments, making appraisals of those encounters, and attempting to cope with the issues that arise. At the heart of the transactional definition is the idea that stress is a dynamic cognitive state. It is a disruption in *homeostasis* or an *imbalance* that gives rise to a requirement for resolution of that imbalance or restoration of homeostasis (Dewe et al., 1993). What distinguishes this approach from other definitions is its emphasis on the process—on meaning, adjustment, and coping as core defining elements—and its focus on understanding the adaptive process itself.

As already stated, the term *transaction* implies that stress is neither in the person nor in the environment but in the relationship between the two (Lazarus, 1990). Stress arises when the demands of a particular encounter are appraised by the individual as about to tax or exceed the resources available, thereby threatening well-being (Lazarus, 1991) and necessitating a change in individual functioning to "manage" the encounter. The transactional definition points to three important themes—a dynamic cognitive state, a disruption or imbalance in normal functioning, and the resolution of that disruption or imbalance (Dewe et al., 1993; Holroyd & Lazarus, 1982; Newton, 1989). As will be discussed later, these themes provide the framework for modeling stress and for capturing what is believed to be the essence of the stress experience.

Thinking of stress in this way reveals a "number of profound implications" (Lazarus, 1991, p. 6) for the way stress is researched and stress interventions are designed. It requires researchers to consider which research methods are appropriate for understanding the complexities of the stress process, how such knowledge should be applied, and the responsibilities we have to those whose working lives we research. Although the application of the transactional perspective to work settings is not without its critics (Brief & George, 1991), and although it is not free of methodological concerns, job stress research "can only benefit from the careful and thoughtful application" of this approach (Harris, 1991, p. 28).

It is clear that there is a gap between interactional and transactional approaches to defining stress and that the transactional perspective requires a fundamental shift in how stress is conceptualized and researched. From an interactional standpoint (see Coyne & Gottlieb, 1996), constructs such as causes (stimuli) and consequences (responses) are "detachable entities" capable of being described independently of each other and, when entered into a causal relationship, maintain a conceptual distinctiveness. From a transactional perspective, on the other hand, such constructs are defined relationally and ultimately become inseparable from the context within which the stressful encounter takes place. As Lazarus (1990) has illustrated, no one variable can be said to be "stress," as they are all part of the transaction process, and an independent variable at one time may (as the encounter unfolds) be considered at another time as a dependent variable. For example, trying to predict what factors influence how people cope at one time makes coping a dependent variable, whereas other research may explore coping as a predictor of an individual's well-being and hence treat coping as an independent variable.

As noted above, there is still considerable confusion over the actual meaning of *stress*, which is reflected in the variety of ways in which this term has been defined (O'Driscoll & Cooper, 1996). Following the transactional model of the stress process and the terminology suggested by Beehr and colleagues (Beehr, 1998; Beehr & Franz, 1987), in this book we adopt the following conceptualizations:

- *Stress:* the overall transactional process
- *Stressors:* the events or properties of events (stimuli) that are encountered by individuals
- *Strain:* the individual's psychological, physical, and behavioral responses to stressors
- *Outcomes:* the consequences of strain at both the individual and the organizational level

Stressors, therefore, are the antecedent conditions, and strain is the person's response(s) to those conditions. We agree with Beehr that the term stress should be used not to describe specific elements of the transaction between the individual and his or her environment but rather to denote the overall process incorporating stressors, strains, and coping responses.

Theoretical Models of Job-Related Stress

As early as 1970, McGrath (1987) urged researchers to approach the investigation of stress using theoretical models that would reflect the sequence of events in stress transactions as well as their interrelationships. The first step in determining how robust current models of work stress are in aiding our understanding of the stress process requires that we consider the context—the theoretical frameworks—out of which such models have emerged. These frameworks should provide not only a platform upon which research can be built but also a stimulus to research and theory building as we differentiate and elaborate the relevant constructs (Leventhal, 1997).

Much of the research on work stress has been carried out using an *interactional* framework, even though, as we will see later, attempts have been made to at least recognize within this context the dynamic-adaptational nature of stress. The issue here is the same as has already been discussed in relation to defining stress: that is, that the interactional perspective may not provide a sufficiently comprehensive framework to enable a full understanding of the stress process (Lazarus, 1990). Nevertheless, this approach has clearly been important in drawing attention to the separate constructs that play a significant role in understanding stress. Indeed, many of the studies described in this volume have been based upon this interactional perspective.

As outlined by Tetrick and LaRocco (1987), the work stress model that best characterizes the interactional framework postulates that the perceived presence of certain work conditions (see Chapter 2) may be associated with a number of stress responses (Chapter 3). This model also predicts that various organizational characteristics, situational factors, and individual differences can influence (moderate) this stimulus-response relationship (see Chapter 5). Generally, the model has resulted in three types of research applications (Dewe, 1991). These include (a) identifying, describing, and categorizing different stimuli; (b) demonstrating a relationship between the different categories of stimuli and responses; and (c) exploring the nature of that relationship by investigating the moderating effects of different organizational, job-specific, and individual-difference variables.

As we shall illustrate in later chapters, the information provided by the interactional approach on stress-related constructs is not in dispute. However, the model itself and the findings that have emerged from the model have exposed a number of limitations in its ability to explain the dynamic nature of the stress *process,* leading researchers to question its efficacy. Nor is there doubt that future frameworks, if they are to advance our understanding of stress, will need to focus on the sequence of events in addition to the relationship between stimuli and responses (Kaplan, 1996). This is not to say that the significance of the stress process has been ignored. However, the first priority for many researchers has been the identification of stressful work conditions and structures, along with determination of their relationship with different measures of strain, rather than exploration of the stress process itself (Duckworth, 1986).

Despite the above limitations, models of work stress have long contained elements of the stress process. Similarly, researchers have for some time accepted the transactional nature of stress, at least at the theoretical level, even though empirical research has predominantly been conducted from an interactional perspective. This state of affairs may well account for the observation of Lazarus (1991) that, although work stress researchers recognize the importance of process considerations, they continue to pay only "lip service to the most advanced theories about the stress process" (p. 2).

The aim of the discussion that follows is to briefly review a number of these models and to examine their contribution to our understanding of the stress process. Whether they can be categorized as "interactional" or "transactional" models is not of concern in the present context. Rather, we hope to illustrate the major thrust of each theory, the ways in which it has enhanced our knowledge of job-related stress, and whether it incorporates elements of the transactional nature of stress. Our selection of models is not exhaustive, but it does draw attention to a number of common features that reflect the domain within which work stress research takes place. Similarly, the intention here is not to engage in a detailed critique of these models but rather to consider the notion of P-E fit, which is either implicitly or explicitly common to most models of work stress, and to consider how far the notion of fit can be taken as embodying the "transactional" nature of the stress process.

Reviewers (e.g., Cummings & Cooper, 1979; Edwards & Cooper, 1988; Eulberg, Weekley, & Bhagat, 1988; Kahn & Byosiere, 1992) have identified a number of specific models that they believe have played an important role in developing the theoretical context for investigating work stress. These include McGrath's (1976) stress cycle model, the P-E fit approach (French, Caplan, & Van Harrison, 1982), Karasek's (1979) job demands-control model, the general systems approach of Cox and McKay (1981), and Cummings and Cooper's (1979) cybernetic model for studying work stress. Kahn and Byosiere (1992) noted that there are several points of convergence among different frameworks, in particular the notion that stress entails a sequence of events that includes (a) the presence of a demand, (b) a set of evaluative processes through which that demand is perceived as significant and taxing in terms of its impact on individual resources or requiring from the individual something other than normal functioning, and (c) the generation of a response that typically affects the well-being of the individual.

Despite general consensus on the above issues, there is less than complete agreement about the conceptualization and measurement of even the most well-established and researched constructs, such as demands and responses. Where there is agreement, however, it is most likely to be along the lines that (a) demands and responses can now be understood only within the context of the evaluative processes that give significance and meaning to encounters; (b) it is through these processes that the individual and the environment are linked; (c) it is these processes that best express the relational-transactional nature of work stress; and (d) strain occurs when there is an imbalance between the demands of the encounter and the resources of the individual to manage those demands. Unfortunately, agreement on these points occurs mainly at the conceptual level, and there is considerable wrangling among researchers over how these evaluative processes should be defined and measured, how they should be incorporated into a work setting, and whether current methodologies can ever adequately capture their transactional qualities.

The idea of a sequence of events and the concept of "fit" can best be understood by considering the approaches adopted by the different models. McGrath (1976), for example, proposed a sequence of events where the demands of an encounter and its outcome(s) are linked through three processes: appraisal, decision making, and performance. The first of these (appraisal) concerns how the encounter is interpreted, the second (decision making) involves the selection of a response, and the third (performance) involves how well the encounter is managed. McGrath also referred to an "outcomes process," which he described as the feedback mechanism through which the encounter is reappraised. In this model, "imbalance" or "misfit" occurs as a result of the individual's appraisal of events and occurs when the consequences of not meeting the demands are perceived as being significant.

The *P-E fit* model of stress is perhaps the one that has been most widely discussed in the literature (Edwards, 1991; Edwards & Cooper, 1988; Eulberg et al., 1988). In brief, this model proposes that strain occurs when the relationship between the person and the environment is out of equilibrium. That is, a lack of fit between the characteristics of the person (e.g., abilities, values) and the environment (e.g., demands, supplies) can lead to unmet individual needs or unmet job demands. These unmet needs or demands can in turn result in strain. The main point is that *subjective* P-E misfit—that is, how individuals perceive the encounter—increases the likelihood that strain will occur. Implicit in the notion of misfit is the individual's ability to manage an encounter, and elements like values, supplies, demands, and abilities, all of which help to determine the perceived misfit, could be described as representing aspects of a transactional process. The difficulty is that there is little in the way of empirical evidence to support this model, due to problems in clarifying the exact nature of misfit and appropriately measuring the constructs involved (Edwards & Cooper, 1988).

The *job demands-control* model (Karasek, 1979) is based on the proposition that the interaction between job demands and job control (referred to as *job decision latitude,* and defined in terms of decision authority and skill level) is the key to explaining strain-related outcomes. In this model, strain occurs when high job demands (or pressures) are combined with low decision latitude (a perceived inability to influence tasks and procedures at work). The concept of control has long been recognized as an important facet of the stress process. However, debate over how control should be operationalized and questions about how the interaction should best be measured have meant that attempts to replicate Karasek's findings have generated mixed results (Fox, Dwyer, & Ganster, 1993). (Refer to Chapter 5 for further discussion of evidence concerning Karasek's model and the role of control in stressor-strain relationships.)

In their *general systems* model of stress, Cox and McKay (1981) described strain as the psychological state that occurs when there is a personally significant imbalance or lack of fit between an individual's perceptions of environmental demands and his or her ability to cope with those demands. According to these theorists, imbalance occurs via a five-stage sequence that includes the source of the demand, the perception of that demand in relation to coping resources, the recognition of changes in well-being, the evaluation of coping activities, and, finally, the feedback or reappraisal of the event. It is, as Cox (1993) suggested, useful to "think of stress as embedded in an on-going process which involves individuals interacting with their environment, making appraisals of that interaction and attempting to cope with, and sometimes failing to cope with, the problems that arise" (p. 18).

Whereas the Cox and McKay model is based on a general systems approach, the model offered by Cummings and Cooper (1979) is based on a cybernetic approach, which the authors believe is consistent with frameworks for investigation already being used by work stress researchers. The usefulness of a cybernetic framework lies, according to these authors, in the fact that it focuses on the stress cycle—"the sequential events that represent the continuous interaction between person and environment" (p. 415). The basic premise of this model is that behavior is directed toward reducing deviations from a specific goal state and that it involves (a) the detection of strain through the presence of a perceived mismatch between the person's actual and preferred states; (b) the selection of an adjustment process; (c) the implementation of the adjustment process—that is, coping behaviors; and (d) the effect of those coping behaviors on the stressful encounter. Another advantage of the cybernetic framework is that it, like some of the other models, draws attention to the temporal nature of stressful encounters and hence the need to consider the impact of time on P-E transactions.

Other researchers (e.g., Beehr & Franz, 1987; Ivancevich & Matteson, 1980; Payne, Jick, & Burke, 1982) have also developed models that incorporate transactional elements. These models, like those discussed above, draw attention to a number of themes that may provide a common pathway for research and a better understanding of the stress process and its application to work settings. The first theme is that of a misfit, mismatch, or imbalance between the person and the environment. All of the above models are based upon a fundamental premise that strain occurs when there is a misfit, mismatch, or imbalance between the demands of the situation and the resources of the individual. The issue facing researchers is agreeing on what exactly the nature of that misfit is. Three factors are crucial: The misfit must be perceived (by the individual) as salient and significant, it must represent a threat to the person's well-being, and it must require actions over and above normal functioning. One criticism that can be aimed at many of these models is that although they identify some of the structural components that precipitate a misfit, they frequently fail to identify those elements that characterize the nature of the misfit and that link the person and the environment.

Agreeing on the nature of that mismatch is important because it forces researchers to focus on process issues. More particularly, it shifts attention to the evaluative-appraisal process (Lazarus, 1990) that individuals undergo in determining the significance of an encounter (primary appraisal), along with its impact and what can be done to deal with it (secondary appraisal). Identification of the different aspects of the appraisal process provides the context for exploring the transactional nature of any encounter. Accepting the need to consider stress in transactional-process terms has dramatic consequences for stress measurement because it requires the development of a framework that directs research toward such questions as "How can we capture the changing person-environment relationship?" and "Where in this transaction is the stress of the stress process and what needs to be measured?" (Lazarus, 1990, p. 4). This approach requires consideration not only of how structural components of the appraisal process should be defined and measured, but also of the adequacy of contemporary measurement practices in capturing the transactional process itself.

Stress: Third-Wave Epidemic or Scapegoat?

Although the pervasiveness of references to stress in the popular media as well as in academic publications may help in drawing attention to the issues involved, some of the discussion and suggestions that have emerged have made it almost impossible at times to separate findings from fiction and research from anecdote, to the extent that to the casual observer it is questionable whether being under stress is any different from simply being alive. For those engaged in research, it is not difficult to identify a sense of frustration growing out of the fact that it always seems necessary to spend so much time defining stress when there are far more important issues to confront (Beehr & Franz, 1987). Some researchers have even contended that stress is too large a phenomenon and too all-encompassing to investigate (Schuler, 1980).

This has not deterred research interest in the phenomenon. However, it is also clear that the current level of interest and popularity that surrounds the idea of stress is not always helpful. Defining stress is not meant to be a tortuous academic exercise in semantics far removed from the "real world," nor should it be viewed as some sort of initiation process that all researchers have to go through. Definitions provide a context, a sense of coherence, and a framework for understanding research findings. More importantly, as researchers we have a moral obligation to those whose working lives we wish to explore. This obligation requires that we give thought to how stress can best be defined so that research captures the reality of the stressful encounter and is relevant to and reflects the experience of those who are being researched. In short, to fail to give careful consideration to what we mean by stress may well trivialize encounters that "affect adversely the psychological well being of most persons exposed to them" (Brief & George, 1991, p. 16).

It is important to tread a middle ground, where stress is not regarded as causally linked to all ills and is not seen as the root cause of all social problems. When it does occur, however, stress can leave individuals emotionally drained and often more vulnerable to other illness and disease. The real issue is not whether there is too much or too little stress in people's lives but how we can understand the stress process and its implications for the management of stress. The complexities involved in developing this understanding should not be oversimplified by inadequate consideration of what we are trying to research, nor should they be trivialized by exaggeration of the issues involved.

There is an extensive body of research working to redress this balance. Sophisticated techniques have been developed to obtain data on biochemical, neuroendocrine, and electrical systems of the body, and computer-based statistical analysis enables simultaneous investigation of many parameters and variables. As we shall discuss further in Chapter 9, researchers should now explore both the subjective and objective measurement of stress. Understanding the explanatory potential that resides in both types of methodologies would allow a more balanced approach to emerge that aims to establish the most appropriate methods for unraveling the stress process. Longitudinal analysis may also become a feature of future research. Continual refinement of traditional research methods and exploration of the utility of new methods will enable job stress researchers to evaluate the appropriateness of different methodologies for understanding and exploring the totality of the stress process.

Emerging Themes in Stress Research

How stress should be defined should by now be recognized as important. Definitions provide a framework for understanding why different approaches have been adopted, the results that have emerged, and, as knowledge has accumulated, their relative strengths and weaknesses and how future research may be directed. Contemporary definitions now point to the idea of a *transaction* where the emphasis is on identifying those processes that link the individual with the environment. This approach, though accepted at the theoretical level, has yet to receive a more complete treatment at the empirical level.

Adopting a transactional perspective means that no one variable can be said to be stress (as in the more traditional approach to defining stress) because, as Lazarus (1990) has articulated, stress "has been defined as a continually changing relationship between person and environment" (p. 4). This book draws attention to critical issues in the conceptualization, measurement, and understanding of job stress in the context of people's working lives and their lives overall. In particular, when considering stress research, contemporary practice and procedures may need to be reviewed, taking into account the following issues.

What is being measured? Two questions stem from consideration of this issue. The first is, "Whose reality is being assessed?" and the second asks,

"Do measures actually assess what they purport to?" By considering these questions, attention is drawn not just to how adequate current measures are in expressing the transactional nature of stress but also to whether existing methods can capture the complexities of the stress process. As we shall discuss later (see Chapter 8 in particular), there is a need to reflect on whether stress research has relied too heavily on psychometric assessments of measurement validity, perhaps at the expense of determining whether the measures actually reflect the reality and experience of those being asked to complete them. Following from this is the more complex (and perplexing!) question of how the stress process *should* be investigated.

How appropriate are current methodologies? This, as will be discussed later, is not about whether one methodology is better than another but rather about what methods should be used to best capture the stress process. This issue inevitably requires some discussion of the roles of qualitative and quantitative methodologies. Here we need to consider two questions (which are raised again in Chapter 8): "Where are current methodologies taking us?" and "What can alternative methodologies provide?" (see Van Maanen, 1979). For instance, qualitative methods reflect a richness in their approach to data gathering and analysis and should be viewed as offering a number of insights into interpretation and understanding separate from those provided by quantitative methods. If a distinction is made between description (quantitative) and meaning (qualitative), then the convergence of both approaches offers a balance and draws on the strengths of both approaches to unravel the complexities of the stress process.

What does all this mean in practice? Specifically, what are the measurement implications of considering stress research from a transactional perspective? This question can be answered in a number of different ways. At the *construct level*, there is a need to develop measures that capture important facets of the stress process and to ensure that all key facets of that process are assessed appropriately. At the *systems level*, the question is, "How can we capture the changing person-environment relationship?" (Lazarus, 1990, p. 4). Although we will address these two issues in more detail later, they are raised here to draw attention to the need for a two-phased strategy in stress research. Phase 1 entails getting the construct measurement right. Researchers should resist the temptation of wanting to measure the process before adequate consideration has been given to construct measurement. Phase 2 requires consideration of the role that a construct plays within a complex system that encompasses reciprocal causality and contains changing moderating and mediating relationships. This is a much more difficult task. In the following chapters, we reflect upon some of the critical issues involved.

In summary, adopting a transactional perspective requires reconsideration of traditional measurement practices and research designs. At the heart of the matter is the need for theory-based measurement (Lazarus, 1990) aimed at capturing the nature of the stress process itself. Researchers must acknowledge that this aim may be achieved only following a period of "quiet reconstruction" during which accepted traditions are critically examined in terms of how best they express that process. They must also consider how appropriate different methodologies are in describing the subtleties of the stress process. This consideration may differ depending on whether the focus of the research is at the construct or the systems level, whether the aim is to describe events or determine their meaning. Whatever the level of analysis, stress research can no longer stand apart from such issues if advances are to be made in our understanding of the stress process. With this view in mind, the remaining chapters are designed to stimulate thought about what needs to be done and how best that may be achieved.

We begin in Chapter 2 with a review of environmental factors that may function as sources of stress. As noted above, these variables are referred to as stressors, and it is important to be aware of the impact of various kinds of stressors on individuals in the workplace. Equally important, however, is an understanding of individuals' reactions or responses to these stressors, which we discuss in Chapter 3. Following other theorists (e.g., Beehr and his colleagues), we refer to these reactions as *strains*. They represent the physiological, psychological, and behavioral response of individuals to threats upon their well-being. In Chapter 4, we outline the phenomenon of burnout, a special form of strain that has been studied particularly in relation to human service occupations, although in recent years it has also been investigated in other occupational groups. Factors that induce burnout and potential consequences of burnout are examined in this chapter.

Chapter 5 identifies several variables that may serve as either buffers (alleviators) or exacerbators of stressor-strain relationships. Job stress research has explored a number of these moderator variables, and in Chapter 5 we review the findings of this research and discuss mechanisms that may be responsible for moderator effects. We emphasize that a complete understanding of these effects can be obtained only if they are studied within the context of the transactional model of stressor-strain relations.

In Chapters 6 and 7, we turn to the issue of stress management. Chapter 6 analyzes the stress-coping behaviors of individuals, again from the transactional perspective, and reviews research that has been conducted on the use and effectiveness of coping strategies. Chapter 7 is based on the premise that organizations share the responsibility for stress management and that interventions at the organizational level may be needed to address the effects of certain kinds of stressors, especially those over which individuals may have little control. Methodologies for evaluating the effectiveness of stress management interventions are discussed in this chapter.

Chapter 8 focuses attention on a range of methodological issues that confront researchers of job-related stress. We review various research designs, their strengths and limitations, and examine whether existing methodologies are capable of providing a satisfactory assessment of the stress-coping process as it is represented within the transactional framework. In this chapter, we also raise suggestions on how the outcomes of job stress research may be optimized.

The final chapter in this volume, entitled "The Changing Nature of Work," reflects upon the ever-changing context in which individuals function, in particular how technological, environmental, economic, political, and sociocultural forces shape the way in which work arrangements (and hence jobs) are being restructured. Here we posit that changes in workplace environments have tended to be dominated by technological and economic imperatives and that there is a need for greater application of perspectives that also emphasize psychological and sociocultural dimensions of work experiences. Ultimately, the design and maintenance of workplace environments that enhance individual well-being, as well as contribute to organizational productivity, is a major challenge that confronts practitioners and researchers alike.

We hope that this volume, and the issues explored within it, will stimulate debate and discussion among the community of stress researchers. Job stress research is embarking upon an exciting period in its history as we move into a century that promises to open up new, and perhaps very different, workplace arrangements. We do not purport to hold all the answers—rather, our aim is to raise some significant questions about research in this field and to challenge researchers to reflect upon their theories, frameworks, and empirical activities.

References

Beehr, T. (1998). An organizational psychology meta-model of occupational stress. In C. Cooper (Ed.), *Theories of organizational stress* (pp. 6-27). New York: Oxford University Press.

Beehr, T., & Franz, T. (1987). The current debate about the meaning of job stress. *Journal of Organizational Behavior Management, 8,* 5-18.

Brief, A. P., & George, J. M. (1991). Psychological stress and the workplace: A brief comment on Lazarus' outlook. *Journal of Social Behavior and Personality, 6,* 15-20.

Cannon, W. (1935). Stresses and strain of homeostasis. *American Journal of Medical Science, 189*(1), 1-14.

Christian, P., & Lolas, F. (1985). The stress concept as a problem for a theoretical pathology. *Social Science and Medicine, 2,* 363-365.

Cooper, C., Liukkonen, P., & Cartwright, S. (1996). *Stress prevention in the workplace: Assessing the costs and benefits to organisations.* Luxembourg: Office for Official Publications of the European Communities.

Cooper, C., & Smith, M. (1985). *Job stress and blue collar work.* New York: John Wiley.

Cox, T. (1978). *Stress.* New York: Macmillan.

Cox, T. (1985). *Stress* (2nd ed.). New York: Macmillan.

Cox, T. (1990). The recognition and measurement of stress: Conceptual and methodological issues. In N. Corlett & J. Wilson (Eds.), *Evaluation of human work.* London: Taylor & Francis.

Cox, T. (1993). *Stress research and stress management: Putting theory to work* (Health and Safety Executive Contract Research Rep. No. 61). Suffolk, UK: HSE Books.

Cox, T., & McKay, C. (1981). A transactional approach to occupational research. In E. N. Corlett & J. Richardson (Eds.), *Stress, work design and productivity* (pp. 91-115). New York: John Wiley.

Coyne, J., & Gottlieb, B. (1996). The mismeasure of coping by checklist. *Journal of Personality, 64,* 959-991.

Cummings, T. G., & Cooper, C. L. (1979). A cybernetic framework for studying occupational stress. *Human Relations, 32,* 395-418.

Dewe, P. J. (1991). Primary appraisal, secondary appraisal and coping: Their role in stressful work encounters. *Journal of Occupational Psychology, 64,* 331-351.

Dewe, P. J. (1992). The appraisal process: Exploring the role of meaning, importance, control and coping in work stress. *Anxiety, Stress and Coping, 5,* 95-109.

Dewe, P., Cox, T., & Ferguson, E. (1993). Individual strategies for coping with stress and work: A review. *Work and Stress, 7,* 5-15.

Duckworth, D. (1986). Managing without stress. *Personnel Management, 16*(1), 40-43.

Edwards, J. R. (1991). Person-job fit: A conceptual integration, literature review, and methodological critique. *International Review of Industrial and Organizational Psychology, 6,* 283-357.

Edwards, J. R., & Cooper, C. L. (1988). Research in stress, coping and health: Theoretical and methodological issues. *Psychological Medicine, 18,* 15-20.

Eulberg, J. R., Weekley, J. A., & Bhagat, R. S. (1988). Models of stress in organisational research: A metatheoretical perspective. *Human Relations, 41,* 331-350.

Fox, M., Dwyer, D., & Ganster, D. (1993). Effects of stressful job demands and control of physiological and attitudinal outcomes in a hospital setting. *Academy of Management Journal, 36,* 289-318.

French, J., Caplan, R., & Van Harrison, R. (1982). *The mechanisms of job stress and strain.* New York: John Wiley.

Goodell, H., Wolf, S., & Rogers, F. B. (1986). Historical perspective. In S. Wolf & A. J. Finestone (Eds.), *Occupational stress, health and performance at work.* Littleton, MA: PSG Inc.

Grinker, R. (1953). *Psychosomatic concepts.* New York: Norton.

Harris, J. R. (1991). The utility of the transactional approach for occupational stress research. *Journal of Social Behaviour and Personality, 6,* 21-29.

Holroyd, K. A., & Lazarus, R. S. (1982). Stress, coping and somatic adaptation. In L. Goldberger & S. Breznitz (Eds.), *Handbook of stress: Theoretical and clinical aspects* (pp. 21-35). New York: Free Press.

Ivancevich, J. M., & Matteson, M. T. (1980). *Stress and work.* Glenview, IL: Scott, Foresman.

Kahn, R. L., & Byosiere, P. (1992). Stress in organizations. In M. D. Dunnette (Ed.), *Handbook of industrial and organizational psychology* (pp. 571-648). Chicago: Rand McNally.

Kaplan, H. B. (1996). Themes, lacunae, and directions in research on psychosocial stress. In H. B. Kaplan (Ed.), *Psychosocial stress: Perspectives on structures, theory, life courses and methods* (pp. 369-401). New York: Academic Press.

Karasek, R. A. (1979). Job demands, job decision latitude, and mental strain: Implications for job redesign. *Administrative Science Quarterly, 24,* 285-308.

Lazarus, R. L., & Launier, R. (1978). Stress-related transactions between person and environment. In L. A. Pervin & M. Lewis (Eds.), *Perspectives in international psychology* (pp. 287-327). New York: Plenum.

Lazarus, R. S. (1966). *Psychological stress and the coping process.* New York: McGraw-Hill.

Lazarus, R. S. (1990). Theory-based stress measurement. *Psychological Inquiry, 1,* 3-13.

Lazarus, R. S. (1991). Psychological stress in the workplace. *Journal of Social Behavior and Personality, 6,* 1-13.

Leventhal, H. (1997). Systems as frameworks, theories and models: From the abstract to the concrete instance. *Journal of Health Psychology, 2,* 160-162.

McGrath, J. E. (1976). Stress and behavior in organizations. In M. D. Dunnette (Ed.), *Handbook of industrial and organizational psychology* (pp. 1351-1395). Chicago: Rand McNally.

McGrath, J. E. (1987). Stress and behavior in organizations. In M. D. Dunnette (Ed.), *Handbook of industrial and organizational psychology.* Chicago: Rand McNally.

Newton, T. J. (1989). Occupational stress and coping with stress: A critique. *Human Relations, 42,* 441-461.

Newton, T. J. (1995). *Managing stress: Emotion and power at work.* Thousand Oaks, CA: Sage.

O'Driscoll, M. P., & Cooper, C. L. (1996). Sources and management of excessive job stress and burnout. In P. Warr (Ed.), *Psychology at work* (4th ed., pp. 188-223). New York: Penguin.

Payne, R. A., Jick, T. D., & Burke, R. J. (1982). Whither stress research? An agenda for the 1980s. *Journal of Occupational Behaviour, 3,* 131-145.

Pearlin, L. I., Lieberman, M. A., Menaghan, E. G., & Mullan, J. T. (1981). The stress process. *Journal of Health and Social Behavior, 22,* 337-356.

Schuler, R. S. (1980). Definition and conceptualization of stress in organizations. *Organizational Behavior and Human Performance, 25,* 184-215.

Selye, H. (1956). *The stress of life.* New York: McGraw-Hill.

Selye, H. (1976). *Stress in health and disease.* Oxford, UK: Butterworths.

Selye, H. (1983). The stress concept: Past, present and future. In C. L. Cooper (Ed.), *Stress research.* New York: John Wiley.

Stahl, S., Grim, C., Donald, C., & Neikirk, A. (1975). A model for the social sciences and medicine: The case for hypertension. *Social Science and Medicine, 9,* 31-38.

Straus, M. A. (1973). A general systems theory approach to a theory of violence between family members. *Social Science Information, 12,* 105-125.

Sutherland, V., & Cooper, C. L. (1990). *Understanding stress.* London: Chapman & Hall.

Tetrick, L., & LaRocco, J. (1987). Understanding, prediction, and control as moderators of the relationships between perceived stress, satisfaction, and psychological well-being. *Journal of Applied Psychology, 72,* 538-543.

Van Maanen, J. (1979). Reclaiming qualitative methods for organisational research: A preface. *Administrative Science Quarterly, 24,* 520-526.

Watts, M., & Cooper, C. L. (1998). *Stop the world: Finding the way through the pressures of life.* London: Hodder & Stoughton.

2 Job-Related Sources of Strain

_____

A s discussed in Chapter 1, contemporary approaches to understanding stress are based on a transactional perspective. One core element of this model of stress-coping is awareness of the events, issues, and objects (including people) that may function as *stressors* (sources of strain) for individuals. Lazarus and Folkman (1984) have argued that strain occurs when environmental demands or constraints are perceived by a person to exceed his or her resources or capacities. Research on job-related stressors has built upon this perspective, as well as on Karasek's (1979) job demands-control model, which will be discussed in further detail in Chapter 5. These and other theoretical accounts of the stress-coping process emphasize the importance of thoroughly exploring the nature and scope of environmental factors that have the potential to create strain for individuals in the workplace.

Determinants of strain can generally be grouped into three major categories: job-specific sources, organizational sources, and individual (personal) sources. In this chapter, we focus on environmental rather than individual (within-person) factors, but this does not imply that the latter are not important. Indeed, there is an extensive literature, especially in social and clinical psychology, that highlights the salience of dispositional traits and states (such as Type A behavior disposition and neuroticism) for the experience of strain, and in Chapter 5 we consider some of these variables as potential moderators of stressor-strain relationships. For the present, however, we concentrate on factors that lie external to the individual and that can impinge upon his or her experience of workplace-related strain.

Under the rubric of "environmental" sources of strain, Cartwright and Cooper (1997) have further differentiated six primary work-related stressors:

1. Factors intrinsic to the job itself
2. Roles in the organization
3. Relationships at work, such as those with supervisors, colleagues, and subordinates
4. Career development issues
5. Organizational factors, including the structure and climate of the organization as well as its culture and political environment
6. The home-work interface

The first five of these categories relate to stressors within the workplace environment, whereas the sixth focuses on the interplay between the job and life off the job. Our intention here is not to provide an exhaustive description of all potential stressors within each category but to highlight some of the critical factors that have been explored in research and to illustrate the relationship between these factors and worker experiences of strain. Each category will be reviewed separately, but it is important to note that they are not necessarily discrete and that people's responses to stressors are part of a dynamic process. Nevertheless, the above classification offers a useful framework for identifying physical and psychosocial sources of job-related strain.

The order of discussion that follows does not imply that, across occupational groups, certain forms of stressors are uniformly more salient than others. Early research on job stress tended to focus predominantly on aspects of the physical environment, with a prevalence of research on jobs where these factors were likely to have a significant impact upon individuals. During the 1960s, particularly in the wake of research conducted by Kahn, Wolfe, Quinn, and Snoek (1964), interest shifted somewhat away from physical factors to role stressors, and this emphasis has continued. In the 1990s, however, changing employment and labor market conditions, along with changes in workforce demographics, have fueled interest in issues surrounding the nature of the job and job security, the virtual disappearance of lifetime career paths in many sectors, and the balance between job or career demands and family commitments and responsibilities. We reflect upon some of these trends later in this chapter.

Intrinsic Job Characteristics

These stressors are associated with the performance of specific tasks that make up an individual's job, sometimes referred to as *task content* factors (Kahn & Byosiere, 1990), as well as work environment and work-scheduling factors. They include variables such as the level of job complexity, the variety of tasks performed, the amount of discretion and control that individuals have over the pace and timing of their work, and the physical environment in which the work is performed. Here we will survey some of the physical demands and environmental stressors that workers may have to contend with and that may influence their levels of strain. Chapter 5 examines the role of lack of discretion and control as a major predictor of job-related strain.

Early investigations of blue-collar workers aimed to identify the links between physical conditions and productivity (Munsterberg, 1913; Roethlisberger & Dickson, 1939), and the importance of relationships between environmental factors and health was soon realized. The significance of "subjective reactivity" to the physical environment also evolved from the Hawthorne studies (Roethlisberger & Dickson, 1939). Kornhauser (1965) observed that factors related to poor mental health included unpleasant working conditions and the requirements to operate at a fast pace, expend considerable physical effort for long periods, and work excessive and inconvenient hours.

The physical demands of work surroundings and the distress caused by noise, vibration, and extremes of temperature will be briefly reviewed first, as they represent some of the earliest forms of stressors that were investigated by organizational psychologists and other researchers in the field. Then we examine workload (both quantitative and qualitative), work hours (including shift work), the effects of technological changes, and exposure to risks and hazards as potential agents of job-related strain.

Noise

Poor working conditions (including excessive temperature or noise) can have a serious detrimental impact on worker physical health and psychological well-being (Cooper, 1987). Jones (1983) suggested that the importance of sound to individual health and well-being cannot be overstated. Although certain kinds of sound (for instance, language and music) enrich people's lives and underpin culture and society, unwanted sound is referred to as *noise*. Ivancevich and Matteson (1980) argued that excessive noise (approximately 80 decibels) on a recurring, prolonged basis can cause strain, predominantly by reducing worker tolerance to other stressors and adversely influencing motivation (Smith, Cohen, Cleveland, & Cohen, 1978). However, noise operates less as a stressor in situations where it is excessive but expected than in those circumstances where it is unpredictable or unexpected. In addition, a change in noise levels can be potentially more stressful than absolute noise levels (Jewell, 1998).

Noise has been reported by many groups of workers as a harmful stressor, particularly in manufacturing and similar industries. For example, in the U.K. steel industry, Kelly and Cooper (1981) observed a relationship between perceptions of noise and levels of strain, and unpleasant working conditions due to noise (and other factors intrinsic to the job) were found to be a significant predictor of job dissatisfaction among workers on drilling rigs and platforms in the North Sea (Sutherland & Cooper, 1986) and on an offshore installation in Norwegian waters (Hellesoy, 1985).

Vibration and Temperature

Along with noise, vibration and temperature are acknowledged as major environmental sources of strain, producing elevated catecholamine levels and alterations to psychological and neurological functioning (Selye, 1976). Health hazards include nausea, loss of balance, and fatigue. Vibration from rotary or impacting machines is particularly problematic in industries such as steel casting (Kelly & Cooper, 1981); in occupations that use machinery such as pneumatic drills, riveting hammers, aircraft propellers, and helicopters; and on offshore drilling rigs and platform installations (Sutherland & Cooper, 1986). Vibrations that transfer from physical objects to the body may adversely affect performance; hands and feet are particularly vulnerable, but the annoyance factor is also a major psychological consideration. Vibration was reported as a substantial stressor by 37% of workers in Sutherland and Cooper's (1986) study, even though many claimed that they had habituated to it. Unfortunately, the long-term effects of this exposure are not known, and further longitudinal studies are needed to ascertain the full range of vibration effects on physical and psychological well-being.

Temperature is another characteristic of the physical environment that may have a significant impact on workers. Physiological responses to thermal conditions vary greatly between workers and even within the same individual from one occasion to the next (Ramsey, 1983). Nevertheless, extreme temperatures (hot or cold) can induce physiological responses that might have undesirable effects on both work performance and individual health and well-being (Jewell, 1998). Work that demands critical decisions, fine discrimination, and performance of fast or skilled action can be impaired by thermal stressors. In a cold environment, manual dexterity is reduced and may be a factor in accident occurrence due to reduced sensitivity, slowed movement, and interference from protective clothing rather than to loss of impaired cognitive ability (Surry, 1968). Similarly, performance of perceptual and motor tasks deteriorates in very high temperatures (Jewell, 1998). As with vibration, there is a need for more controlled research that examines the range of effects of extreme temperatures, as well as exploring individual differences in temperature tolerance.

Workload

The amount of work that has to be performed is another significant stressor for many workers. Both overload and underload can generate psychological (and physical) strain. In 1908, Yerkes and Dodson proposed their now well-known Yerkes-Dodson Law, which states that there is an inverted-U relationship between the amount of work required of a person and his or her health and performance. Each individual therefore has an optimal band of workload. Substantial deviations above or below this optimal band are likely to induce strain.

It is also important to distinguish between quantitative and qualitative overload/underload. *Quantitative workload* refers to the sheer amount of work required and the time frame in which work must be completed. Having to work under time pressure to meet deadlines is a major source of quantitative overload (Narayanan, Menon, & Spector, 1999) and has been related to high levels of strain, anxiety, and depression, as well as to job performance (Cooper & Roden, 1985; Kushmir & Melamed, 1991; Westman & Eden, 1992). Quantitative underload has also been identified as a stressor, with boredom and lack of challenge from monotonous, routine work predicting anxiety, depression, and job dissatisfaction (Kelly & Cooper, 1981). Lack of stimulation may be particularly damaging at night, when the individual could have difficulty adjusting to the change in sleep pattern but does not have enough stimulation in the work setting to keep alert (Poulton, 1978).

Work overload and underload may also result from an irregular flow of work that is not under the control of the worker. This is not restricted to paced assembly lines; many outdoor occupations are paced by climatic conditions, and a variety of jobs are controlled by the dictates of seasonal demands or market needs. Certain workers, such as air traffic controllers, firefighters, and pilots, must deal with long periods of inactivity and the need to spring into action when a crisis occurs. This is potentially hazardous if the employee fails to respond appropriately in an emergency (Davidson & Veno, 1980).

Qualitative overload and underload can also be potent sources of psychological strain and are associated with workers' affective reactions to their jobs. Qualitative overload occurs when individuals believe they do not have the skills or capacities to satisfactorily perform job tasks, and it has been linked to low levels of self-esteem (Udris, 1981, cited in International Labour Office [ILO], 1986). An example of this would be a line worker who has been promoted to a supervisory capacity on the grounds of superior work performance but who has no past experience of supervision of others or work delegation. This situation may be exacerbated by the person's having to assume responsibility for the performance outputs of other workers.

Qualitative underload may be as damaging as overload in that the individual is not given the opportunity to use acquired skills or to develop full potential ability. For example, Hall (1976) demonstrated that graduate recruits are likely to suffer qualitative underload. Following a stimulating university environment, they often enter employment with high expectations that are not realized. This manifests itself in reported job dissatisfaction, poor motivation, and high labor turnover (Hall, 1976). As with quantitative underload, boredom and shifts or lapses in attention may have serious consequences. Also, the individual feels that he or she is not getting anywhere and is unable to demonstrate his or her full potential. Udris (1981, cited in ILO, 1986) suggested that qualitative overload is associated with dissatisfaction, tension, and low self-esteem, whereas qualitative underload is linked to dissatisfaction, depression, irritation, and psychosomatic complaints.

New technology and the increasing automation of industry can lead to the simplification of work and repetitive jobs that are potentially stressful in terms of workload (Martin & Wall, 1989). Although a hectic work pace is stressful, work that is dull, repetitive, and monotonous is equally detrimental to the individual's physical and psychological well-being (Warr, 1994). Lack of stimulation, underutilization of skills, and boredom characterize many blue-collar occupations and may also be dangerous. For instance, Cheliot (1979) found a high incidence of deactivation episodes among electronic assemblers (monitored by continuous electroencephalography over the entire day). The theta rhythm observed, referred to as microsleep, is indicative of the boredom and tedium experienced by the workers and may be responsible for the occurrence of accidents. Melamed, Ben-Avi, Luz, and Green (1995) also found that repetitive work and work underload were linked with subjective monotony, which in turn was associated with lower job satisfaction and higher levels of psychological distress.

An important issue to consider in research on workload is the distinction between perceived and actual (or objective) demands. The transactional model of stress-coping emphasizes that the individual's perception of his or her environment is critical for the experience of strain and the activation of coping responses. From this perspective, objectively defined characteristics of the work environment do not necessarily contribute to strain, because these may be perceived as a threat to well-being by one individual but not by another. Research on job design, for instance, has indicated that perceptions of job characteristics may be salient for individuals' reactions but that actual job characteristics are also important to assess (Melamed et al., 1995). From an organizational intervention standpoint, it is relevant to determine whether certain environmental factors are consistently reported by a large proportion of the workforce as being stressful, for such consensus would indicate that the effects of these factors could not be explained by differential perceptions.

From the above overview, it is evident that optimal matching between work demands and individual capabilities is required to prevent strain from developing. This may necessitate greater flexibility in the design of jobs to tailor them more directly to the skills and interests of individual workers. In many current workplace contexts, this may not be easy to achieve, given the relatively fixed job structures that are established. One of the major challenges is to create job designs that promote the achievement of organizational goals, while at the same time providing individuals with the opportunity to engage in satisfying and fulfilling job tasks that do not create unmanageable strain.

Work Hours

The sheer number of hours that a person works can produce strain. Numerous studies have found a significant correlation between the overall number of hours worked and various indices of health and well-being. A recent meta-analysis of research in this field (Sparks, Cooper, Fried, & Shirom, 1997) obtained small but statistically significant correlations between hours of work and overall health, as well as both physiological and psychological health symptoms. Individuals who worked excessive hours showed more symptoms of ill health than their counterparts who worked fewer hours. Sparks et al. (1997) noted, however, that there may be a nonlinear relationship between number of hours worked and strain-related symptoms, with individuals working more than 48 hours a week being most susceptible to health problems.

Recent years have witnessed the emergence of an increasing variety of different patterns of working hours or weeks, generically referred to as work *schedules*. There are many social and economic reasons for the utilization of alternatives to the typical 9 a.m. to 5 p.m., 40-hour working week, but there can be no doubt that they have significantly affected quite a large proportion of the workforce. The most frequently studied alternative work schedule is shift work, which is typically defined as a changing pattern of work hours (although some workers are employed on so-called permanent shifts). Given the increasing demand for 24-hour provision of services, changing technologies that facilitate continuous plant operation, and ever-increasing competition within the marketplace, more and more organizations are using shift work as an approach to increasing their productivity and efficiency. In some industries, particularly transport and communication sectors, shift workers constitute up to 40% of the labor force (Folkard, 1996).

In the past 20 years, a great deal of research has been carried out to determine the effects of shift work on workers' job performance (especially efficiency), work attitudes, and overall psychological and physical well-being. As noted by Folkard (1996), there is now considerable evidence that shift work can lead to a variety of difficulties for shift workers and their families, primarily because of disturbances in circadian rhythms (the "body clock") and disruptions to family and social life. In many cases, these effects have been associated with a decline in physical health, satisfaction, and overall subjective well-being (Folkard, 1996; Seymour & Buscherhof, 1991).

However, problems with shift work are not uniform across all shift work schedules, nor do all individuals experience the same kinds of problems or to the same extent, and further investigations are needed to determine the factors that mediate and moderate the effects of shift work. For instance, it has been long known that fixed shifts are less harmful to employees than rotating shifts, especially backward rotating (Jamal & Baba, 1992). For instance, Toterdell, Spelten, Smith, Barton, and Folkard (1995) found that night shift work can cause additional problems for workers because they need to adjust to two different routines: a nocturnal work shift schedule and a diurnal pattern on their days off work. These researchers also suggested that more attention needs to be given to the timing and duration of rest days, particularly for night-shift workers.

Another form of alternative work schedule that has received some attention recently is the compressed shift schedule. Again for enhanced flexibility and productivity, and also to reduce travel costs where workers must be transported to a workplace that is some distance from where they live (e.g., an offshore oil rig), many organizations have extended the working hours per day, sometimes (but not always) accompanied by a shorter working week. Pierce and Dunham (1992) explored the impact of changing from a forward-rotating 8-hour shift schedule to a 12-hour compressed-shift schedule. Their findings indicated that compressing the shift schedule may in fact mitigate some of the negative effects typically found with shift work, especially because it permits better matching between the job and off-the-job (e.g., family) activities.

New Technology

In a rapidly changing occupational environment, skills may quickly become obsolete. However, the need to constantly become familiar with new equipment and systems may pose a threat to some individuals. Unless adequate training and preparation are provided, potentially stressful situations may develop when new technology is introduced into the workplace and the individual feels unable to cope with the innovations. Korunka, Weiss, Huemer, and Karetta (1995) observed, for instance, that the introduction of new technologies is related to changes in employee job satisfaction and physical health. Similarly, the pressures of keeping up with new technology are also experienced by business executives and managers (Cartwright & Cooper, 1997). Although computer utilization at all levels of organizations has increased dramatically in recent years, often managers are the most wary of advances in computer technology and the least inclined to adopt new systems (Beatty & Lee, 1992; Hall & Torrington, 1986). This may create problems not only for managers themselves but also for their (perhaps more computer-literate) subordinates, who can feel thwarted in their efforts to "modernize" work processes by a lack of expertise and even interest to update on the part of their superiors. Subordinates may also experience overload if they do not receive adequate guidance and supervision from their supervisors.

Exposure to Risk and Hazards

Various occupational groups have been identified as high risk in terms of physical danger: for example, police officers, mine workers, soldiers, prison personnel, firefighters, and workers on oil and gas exploration and production installations (Cartwright & Cooper, 1997; Davidson & Veno, 1980; Elliot, 1985; Fisher & Cooper, 1990; Kalimo, 1980). These workers may be in a constant state of arousal, ready to react immediately. The resulting adrenaline rush, muscle tension, and respiration changes may be a threat to long-term health. However, it is not known if the special risks associated with these occupations are necessarily perceived as sources of strain by individuals engaged in them. It is possible that a continued emphasis on the need for safety in a hazardous environment may be a greater source of strain than the hazards themselves. Bohemier (1985) suggested that it is human nature to avoid thinking about danger or death in a hazardous or risky environment and that it is necessary to block out some of the realities that the worker must otherwise continually face.

Nevertheless, studies indicate that some workers do perceive the risks and hazards associated with the job as a source of strain. For instance,

Kelly and Cooper (1981) and Cooper and Kelly (1984) found that casters in the steel industry and crane operators acknowledged the dangers of their job and that awareness of the dangers and the consequences of making a mistake were significant predictors of depression and anxiety among crane operators. In a Norwegian study, 36% of offshore platform personnel felt unsafe with regard to helicopter transport, 34% felt unsafe with regard to evacuation facilities, and 24% were concerned about the risk of fire and explosion (Hellesoy, 1985). Finally, the risk of exposure to certain chemicals, including the inhalation of vapors, dust, and exposure to chemicals that are irritants to the skin, is frequently reported as one to the most harmfully perceived stressors among workers in the chemical industry (ILO, 1986).

To summarize this overview of the impact of job-related environmental factors on workers' experience of strain, two overarching issues should be noted. First, as noted earlier, it is important to investigate both objective and subjective work conditions to develop a comprehensive profile of physical stressors in the workplace, as well as to understand workers' reactions to these stressors. Although some research has explored both, the predominant focus has been on subjective perceptions of the work environment, although researchers do not always make clear the distinction between subjective and objective aspects. (We address this issue again toward the end of this chapter.) Second, it is evident that stressors do not operate in isolation from each other and that there can be additive (and perhaps interactive!) effects where several stressors are experienced concurrently. Unfortunately, however, and perhaps due to the constraints on conducting multivariable research within organizations, many studies have examined individual stressors (such as those identified above) in isolation, rather than considering their combined impact.

As with research on the other forms of stressors outlined in this chapter, more systematic assessment of the differential salience of environmental factors for worker strain and well-being needs to be conducted to determine which factors serve as the most potent stressors for various occupational groups.

Organizational Roles

Roles encompass the behaviors and demands that are associated with the job an individual performs. The importance of role-related strain was first underlined by Kahn et al. (1964), whose early investigations in this area have provided a platform and a framework for most subsequent research on role strain. According to Kahn et al., dysfunction in roles can occur in two primary ways: role *ambiguity* (lack of clarity about the role) and role *conflict* (competing or conflicting job demands). These two role stressors have been the most frequently investigated sources of job-related strain.

Role Ambiguity

As defined by Kahn et al. (1964), *role ambiguity* refers to unpredictability of the consequences of one's role performance. Later conceptualizations have extended the definition to include a lack of information needed to perform the role, and the typical measure of this construct assesses both unpredictability of consequences and information deficiency regarding expected role behaviors (Pearce, 1981). Numerous studies have demonstrated a consistent link between substantial role ambiguity in the job and high levels of psychological strain (see, e.g., O'Driscoll & Beehr, 1994; Schaubroeck, Cotton, & Jennings, 1989).

Role Conflict

Similarly, role conflict, which reflects incompatible demands on the person (either within a single role or between multiple roles occupied by the individual), can induce negative emotional reactions due to perceived inability to be effective on the job (Schaubroek et al., 1989). Several studies have confirmed this detrimental effect of role conflict on both self-reported strain (O'Driscoll & Beehr, 1994) and physiological indicators of strain (Kahn & Byosiere, 1990). Typically, however, the association between role conflict and psychological strain is not as strong as that between ambiguity and strain (Jackson & Schuler, 1985), and further research is needed to tease out the impact of different forms of role conflict on worker attitudes and experiences. Quick and Quick (1984) differentiated four kinds of role conflict:

1. *Intrasender role conflict:* for example, when a supervisor or manager communicates expectations that are mutually incompatible
2. *Intersender role conflict:* when two or more people (e.g., supervisors, managers, colleagues, clients) communicate expectations that are incompatible

3. *Person-role conflict*: when an individual perceives a conflict between his or her expectations and values and those of the organization or key people in the work environment
4. *Inter-role conflict*: when a person occupies two or more roles that may have conflicting expectations or requirements (See the section "The Home-Work Interface" later in this chapter.)

Although each of these forms of conflict has negative consequences, the nature of their effects, as well as mechanisms for alleviating them, will differ markedly.

Role Overload

A third role variable is overload, which refers to the number of different roles a person has to fulfill (see the above discussion on work overload). Not only can role overload lead to excessive demands on an individual's time, but it also may create uncertainty about his or her ability to perform these roles adequately. Along with role ambiguity and conflict, overload has been found to be a major correlate of job-related strain (Cooper, 1987). In fact, Narayanan et al. (1999) found that work overload was mentioned more frequently by respondents as a source of strain than either role ambiguity or role conflict.

One potential explanation for the negative effects of these role variables on employee physical and psychological well-being is that they create uncertainty, which in itself is psychologically uncomfortable and, if persistent and at high levels, can result in emotional disturbance in the individual. Beehr and colleagues (Beehr, 1987; Beehr & Bhagat, 1985) adapted the expectancy theory of motivation to explain the diverse forms of uncertainty that may arise from role stressors. Specifically, role ambiguity, conflict, and overload may be linked with reduced effort-to-performance expectancy ($E \rightarrow P$) because they create uncertainty among employees that their efforts will lead to satisfactory job performance, and with performance-to-outcome expectancy ($P \rightarrow O$) because employees are unsure of the link between rewards and successful job performance.

O'Driscoll and Beehr (1994) found that these forms of uncertainty were significantly related to workers' affective experiences, including dissatisfaction and psychological strain. In this study, job satisfaction functioned as a mediator of the effects of role stressors (especially ambiguity)

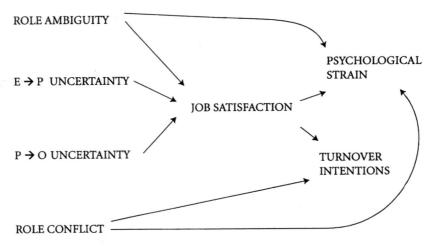

ROLE AMBIGUITY

E → P UNCERTAINTY

P → O UNCERTAINTY

JOB SATISFACTION

PSYCHOLOGICAL
STRAIN

TURNOVER
INTENTIONS

ROLE CONFLICT

Figure 2.1. Direct and Mediated Relationships of Role Variables and Uncertainty with
Psychological Strain and Turnover Intentions
SOURCE: Adapted from O'Driscoll and Beehr (1994).

and uncertainty on psychological strain and turnover intentions. That is,
role ambiguity and uncertainty were related to job satisfaction, which in
turn was associated with (reduced) psychological strain and turnover
intentions (see Figure 2.1), although there was also some direct relationship between ambiguity and strain. Interestingly, O'Driscoll and Beehr
found only a direct relationship between role conflict and strain, rather
than one mediated by job satisfaction, as was the case for ambiguity and
E → P and P → O uncertainty.

Before turning to the next organizational factor, we would note that
almost all research on role variables has been based upon self-reports of
the amount of ambiguity, conflict, and overload that workers experience. From the transactional perspective, this is entirely appropriate
because it focuses on individuals' perceptions of their environment as
the critical determinant of psychological strain. However, it would also
be valuable to map these perceptions onto more objectively defined
work conditions.

Responsibility

Responsibility has been identified as a potential stressor associated
with workers' roles in their organization. A distinction is made

between responsibility for things (such as budgets or equipment) and responsibility for people (e.g., in a supervisory capacity). Though too much responsibility (exceeding a person's perceived capacity to cope) is clearly a source of strain, lack of responsibility may also be stressful if the individual perceives this as work underload.

For some workers, responsibility for other people's lives and safety is a major source of psychological strain. For example, a crane driver is aware of the potentially serious consequences of making mistakes (Cooper & Kelly, 1984). Offshore drilling crews also recognize the consequences of mistakes, the need to work as a team, and the need to watch over new employees. A mistake by a petroleum engineer on a rig can result in a blowout or explosion, which could cause large-scale injury or death, including the total loss of the drilling rig itself (Sutherland & Cooper, 1986). Similarly, responsibility for people's safety may be a major factor in predicting risk of heart disease among air traffic controllers.

Further research needs to be undertaken to ascertain the relative effects of different forms (and levels) of responsibility and potential moderating factors. For instance, it seems clear that some individuals assume responsibility more readily than do others and cope better with the demands that responsibility carries, yet little is known about factors that enhance the positive outcomes of responsibility and alleviate potential negative outcomes. Two questions that demand further research attention are: Does responsibility for people (e.g., in a supervisory or managerial role) have more impact than responsibility for things (e.g., equipment) on individual strain, and what is the relationship between *perceived* (or felt) and *actual* levels of responsibility within organizations? To date, neither of these issues has been systematically investigated.

Work Relationships

Both the quality of interpersonal relationships and lack of social support (from others in the workplace) have been examined as potential sources of job-related strain. As we shall discuss in Chapter 5, there is some dispute over the role of social support as a moderator (or buffer) of the impact of stressors on individual strain and well-being. Nevertheless, it is clear that negative interpersonal relations and the absence of support from colleagues and superiors can be a major stressor for many workers (Motowidlo, Packard, & Manning, 1986; Narayanan et al., 1999). Conversely, having social support from others within the organization can directly alleviate psychological strain (Beehr & McGrath, 1992).

McLean (1979) suggested that social support in the form of group cohesion, interpersonal trust, and liking for a supervisor is associated with decreased levels of perceived job strain and better health. On the other hand, inconsiderate or nonsupportive behavior from a supervisor appears to contribute significantly to feelings of job pressure (Buck, 1972; McLean, 1979), and close supervision and rigid performance monitoring can also be stressful (O'Driscoll & Beehr, 1994). A critical issue for research on supervisor support is the optimal level of various kinds of support, including the provision of information and advice, guidance on how to perform the job, and feedback on job performance. Also of interest are differences between individuals in terms of the amount of supervision required. For instance, O'Driscoll and Beehr (2000) found that the extent to which subordinates had a need for clarity moderated the relationship between role stressors and psychological strain. It is evident that some individuals can tolerate uncertainties in the work environment more readily than do others and that their need for close guidance and supervision may therefore be lower. Further work is needed to tease out the complexity of relationships between social support and worker affective experiences, including strain (Cooper, 1998).

Abrasive Personalities

Some individuals may unwittingly cause distress to others because they ignore the feelings and sensibilities of others. Levinson (1978) labeled these individuals "abrasive personalities." Usually they are achievement oriented, hard-driving, and intelligent, but they function less well at an emotional level. The need for perfection, the preoccupation with self, and the condescending, critical style of the abrasive personality induce feelings of inadequacy among other workers. As Levinson has suggested, the abrasive personality who is a peer is both difficult and stressful to deal with; when the abrasive personality is a superior, the consequences are potentially very damaging to interpersonal relationships and highly stressful for subordinates in the organization.

Leadership Style

As already mentioned, leadership style is a potential source of strain at work for employees. Specifically, autocratic and authoritarian leadership styles have generally been observed to induce strain among subordinates (Ashour, 1982; Seltzer & Numerof, 1988). As far back as the 1930s, Lewin, Lippitt, and White (1939) documented the effects of exposure to an authoritarian style of leader. A lack of consideration of employee needs, attitudes, and motivations, which characterizes a task orientation at the expense of relationships, has also been shown to create strain for many employees (O'Driscoll & Beehr, 1994). Task-oriented leaders may be less likely to engage in a participatory form of leadership or appreciate that feedback on performance and recognition for effort are also beneficial to the superior-subordinate relationship.

Reactions to an authoritarian style of leadership 'ary between individuals. Although some people appreciate a clear ser.se of direction and may prefer not having to make decisions relating to their work, the majority of employees would appear to value having input into (relevant) decision-making processes and some degree of self-determination in their workplace. As illustrated later in our discussion of Karasek's demands-control model of job strain (see Chapter 5), lack of opportunity to exercise some judgmental discretion contributes significantly to psychological strain for most individuals. But the impact of different leadership styles in various work settings and on different occupational groups is certainly an area that requires further exploration.

Career Development

This category of potential stressors includes job insecurity (the threat of unemployment), perceived underpromotion or overpromotion within the organization, and a general sense of lack of achievement of one's goals or ambitions. Recent years have witnessed a significant shift in the concept of career, with a wider array of different forms of employment contracts being negotiated (in some cases) or enforced. For many employees, the linear career development path is no longer a feasible, or perhaps even desired, option. Nevertheless, compared with some of the other factors described above, the relationship between career issues and strain has been less studied empirically. There is a growing body of evidence that a perceived lack of promotion opportunities and lack of progress in one's career represent primary sources of job dissatisfaction (Rabinowitz, Falkenbach, Travers, Valentine, & Weener, 1983) and hence may function as major stressors for many people. There is also substantial evidence (Burke & McKeen, 1994) that, despite changes in societal attitudes concerning equal employment opportunities, women and minority groups still encounter organizational barriers to their career development, which inevitably will lead to higher levels of psychological strain for these groups of employees. Although many organizations are making efforts to enhance career development opportunities for women and minorities in particular, there is clearly a need for more significant progress in this area (Davidson & Cooper, 1994). Research on how best to foster these developments should be a priority for psychologists interested in career development issues.

Job Insecurity

One aspect of many people's careers in the current, and future, employment context is the prospect or threat of job loss due to redundancy. With the increasing incidence of mergers and downsizing in industries around the world and with attempts to reduce levels of management within organizations, many individuals, especially those occupying middle-level managerial positions, face the threat of losing their jobs (Kozlowski, Chao, Smith, & Hedlung, 1993). Employment statistics from several regions and countries, including the United States, Canada, and Europe, illustrate that the rate of involuntary unemployment increased considerably in the late 1980s (Latack, Kinicki, & Prussia, 1995) and that this trend has persisted through the 1990s (Hanisch, 1999). Though all industries are affected by the prospect of redundancies, manufacturing is one industry where jobs are disappearing rapidly, and the corresponding rise in the number of jobs in the service sector is more likely to provide part-time and contract employment than tenured positions. Along with these changes is the introduction of new technologies that in many cases entail automation and consequently a simplification of jobs and deskilling of the labor force (Johansson, 1989; Korunka et al., 1995). To put it bluntly, in the new millenium job insecurity may be one of the single most salient sources of strain for employees, and its effects will be experienced at all organizational levels.

For individual workers, redundancy not only affects current and future income but also challenges the person's general self-esteem, which is closely linked with job status and overall well-being (Burke & Cooper, 2000). As Latack et al. (1995) noted, "The impact of job loss is generally detrimental to individuals by virtually any criteria a researcher chooses to examine" (p. 312). In addition to its potential socioemotional effects on individuals, the threat of job loss has been linked to several serious health problems, including ulcers, colitis, and alopecia (Cobb & Kasl, 1977), as well as increased muscular complaints (Smith, Cohen, Stammerjohn, & Happ, 1981). Other negative outcomes of job loss and subsequent unemployment have been well documented in the literature (Hanisch, 1999). Brockner and his colleagues, for example (see Brockner et al., 1994; Brockner et al., 1997), have investigated the impact of redundancy (or the threat of redundancy) on three categories of people: victims (those who are displaced from their job), survivors (those who retain their job), and "lame ducks" (those who are next in line for retrenchment). In a series of investigations, Brockner and associates have found that the negative impact of redundancy can extend beyond those who are directly affected by it (the victims) to other organization members, both survivors and especially "lame ducks."

Interestingly, the ultimate consequences of job layoffs for organizational productivity and effectiveness are far from clear-cut. Although managers and decision makers tend to subscribe to the view that making the organization "lean and mean" is essential to maintain competitiveness in today's economic climate, evidence suggests that downsizing can have both positive and negative influences on the bottom line (Luthans & Sommer, 1999). For example, Cole (1993) noted that downsizing may result in a loss of organizational "memory" and sharing of knowledge across departments and organizational levels, disruption of routines that have built up over time and that ensure that the organization functions smoothly, and even a decline in personal relationships between employees and custom- ers. In a study of the automotive industry in the United States, Cameron, Freeman, and Mishra (1993) observed negative outcomes such as increased interpersonal conflict (perhaps due to conflict between coworkers to retain their jobs) and resistance to change among employees, along with reduced employee morale and organizational commitment, factors that may contribute (negatively) to job performance and ultimately organizational effectiveness. Luthans and Sommer (1999) went so far as to suggest that "research on downsizing has shown an array of negative results and minimal positive results for organizations" (p. 50). Their study confirmed a decline in job satisfaction and organizational commitment among survivors of downsizing in a large medical rehabilitation hospital, although they were unable to systematically determine whether the overall performance of the organization had been affected.

Due to uncertainties in the employment market, individuals may remain in jobs that are disliked and that contain no prospects for advancement simply because there are no (or limited) alternative positions available. One study of personnel working for an offshore oil/gas contractor in the North Sea showed that 41% of workers reported feeling trapped in offshore work because no suitable onshore work was available (Sutherland & Cooper, 1986). This perception of entrapment can lead to job dissatisfaction and reduced psychological well-being. Finally, the strain associated with the need to change and/or retrain is also likely to be manifested at a time of life when the person is most vulnerable. An individual under the strain of impending job loss realizes that in middle age (re)learning seems to take longer, energy is more scarce, opportunities are fewer, and employers may prefer to hire younger workers (Cartwright & Cooper, 1997).

In this new century, it is clear that the nature of employment and careers will be dramatically affected by such factors as globalization of the labor market, increasingly sophisticated technologies that will make many current jobs superfluous or even obsolete, and the need for firms and companies to seek new ways of enhancing their competitive edge and to maintain (if not increase) their market share. The days of near-full employment are long gone, and many countries (in both economically "developing" and "developed" countries) face the prospect of rising levels of unemployment. Research on job stress therefore needs to extend beyond the immediate workplace environment to consider employment as one of the elements that make up individuals' lives. Hence, rather than focusing solely on strain that is manifested on the job, researchers will need to develop more comprehensive perspectives on the dynamic interrelationship between employment, family, and other elements of people's lives. Such research must include consideration of broader economic and social issues surrounding employment and unemployment in an era when job security may become the exception rather than the norm. We will return to this issue in Chapter 9.

Promotion and Career Advancement

Even in situations where individuals may believe that their job is secure, issues related to advancement in one's career or promotion within the organization are frequently cited as major sources of dissatisfaction and psychological strain (Jewell, 1998). Typically, strain is caused by a *lack of* advancement (or underpromotion), but in some cases the reverse may apply: Individuals feel promoted beyond their capabilities. This may occur, for example, when a person is promoted to the role of supervisor from the "shop floor" or is given new responsibilities for which he or she has received inadequate preparation or training. Both under- and overpromotion can have serious detrimental effects on individual well-being and satisfaction levels.

Related to the above is the issue of career plateauing. Formulations of career development proposed in the 1970s (see, e.g., Osipow, 1973) suggested that career development occurred in stages, one of these being the plateau stage, when individuals experience a leveling off in their career and skill development and their career reaches a point of maintenance. Recent research suggests, however, that the earlier developmental models do not necessarily provide an accurate characterization of career choices and career change. Socioeconomic factors within society in the 1990s, along with changing values and interests, have resulted in careers that do not necessarily progress in stages (Hall, 1994), and indeed some employees may never experience a plateauing effect because (either voluntarily or involuntarily through redundancy) these individuals change careers before they reach a plateau. Hall and Moss (1998) have referred to this as the *protean career*. Nevertheless, even for individuals who remain in the same job or career, it is clear that continued development is preferred by the majority and that any plateau effect is likely to have negative consequences in terms of dissatisfaction and psychological strain.

Organizational Factors

Psychological strain that may be attributed to organizational factors is often due to the culture and management style adopted within an organization (Cooper & Cartwright, 1994). There are, of course, multiple organizational factors that impinge upon organizational members and may generate feelings of strain. Here all we can do is highlight some that have been observed in research investigating organizational-level stressors.

Hierarchical, bureaucratic organizational structures may permit little participation by employees in decisions affecting their work. Inadequate communication, especially between managerial and nonmanagerial personnel, can also contribute to employee strain. Studies of organizational climate (e.g., Guzley, 1992; O'Driscoll & Evans, 1988) have indicated that the content and nature of communication processes within organizations contribute to employee reactions to their job and the organization as a whole. Where communications focus on negative attributions about other personnel, cynicism regarding leadership and management of the organization, and attempts by employees to further their own interests at the expense of others, feelings of mistrust and lack of support are generated, in turn leading to increased strain (O'Driscoll & Cooper, 1996).

Lack of participation in the decision-making process, lack of effective consultation and communication, office politics, and no sense of belonging have all been identified as potential organizational stressors. Increased opportunity to participate, on the other hand, has been associated with greater overall job satisfaction, higher levels of affective commitment to the organization, and an increased sense of well-being, even though evidence for the effects of participation on job performance and productivity is less consistent (Leana & Florkowski, 1992; Sagie & Koslowsky, 1994; Wagner, 1994; Wagner, Leana, Locke, & Schweiger, 1997).

Research conducted on Karasek's demands-control model supports these suggestions. Karasek's (1979) original prospective study demonstrated that lack of decision latitude and freedom to choose one's work schedule were significant predictors of the risk for coronary heart disease. Similarly, lack of consultation and feelings of being unable to make changes in one's job are commonly reported stressors among blue-collar workers in the steel industry (Kelly & Cooper, 1981), as well as among offshore operators and drilling personnel on rigs and platforms in the U.K. and Dutch sectors of the North Sea (Sutherland & Cooper, 1986). In another study, poor organizational climate, job insecurity, and the employee's relationship with the organization were all significant predictors of low psychological well-being among executives (Cooper & Melhuish, 1980).

A further organizational factor that has been closely studied is the extent of formalization of work and decision-making procedures, although the effects of formalization have been inconsistent and seem to vary between occupational groups. Whereas Organ and Greene (1981) found that formalization reduced role ambiguity among scientists but increased role conflict, Podsakoff, Williams, and Todor (1986) observed negative relationships between formalization and both ambiguity and conflict. Overall, it is apparent that clearly outlined formal work procedures may have positive benefits for employees (O'Driscoll, 1987) but that overly formalized organizational processes may be detrimental, particularly among professional groups.

Finally in this category, organizational politics also have a substantial impact on employee strain. In a series of interrelated studies, Ferris and his colleagues (Ferris et al., 1996; Zhou & Ferris, 1995) have noted strong relationships between employees' perceptions of a negative political climate within their organization and their experience of psychological strain. Cropanzano, Howes, Grandey, and Toth (1997) also found a significant relationship between organizational politics and employees' levels of strain.

Given the large range of organizational factors that have the potential to induce strain in employees, it is hardly surprising that few generalizations are possible. Lack of participation (in decision making), inappropriate levels of formalization of work procedures, lack of adequate communication within the organization, and organizational politics are all potential sources of strain, yet none function universally as stressors. Research needs to focus on the conditions under which these factors create a stressful environment for organizational members, as well as considering differential impacts on various levels and groups of employees. As we have noted in other places in this volume, the impact of these variables depends on the meaning and importance attached to them by individuals; hence, it is critical to explore individual perceptions and values relating to organizational processes.

The Home-Work Interface

Managing the interface between one's job and various roles and responsibilities off the job is another potential source of strain (O'Driscoll, 1996). Sometimes referred to as *work/nonwork conflict,* this issue has received considerable attention from researchers in recent years (Cooper & Lewis, 1998). Changes in family structures, increased participation by women in the workforce, and technological changes (such as usage of portable computers and cellular phones) that enable job tasks to be performed in a variety of locations have blurred the boundaries between the job and life off the job for many workers and have created the potential for conflict to occur between job and off-job roles (Hill, Miller, Weiner, & Colihan, 1998). This inter-role conflict has consistently been linked with psychological strain (Frone, Russell, & Cooper, 1992; O'Driscoll, Ilgen, & Hildreth, 1992) and is especially prevalent among women, employed parents, and dual-career couples (Aryee & Luk, 1996; Brayfield, 1995; Greenhaus & Parasuraman, 1994; Williams & Alliger, 1994).

Greenhaus and Beutell (1985) outlined three fundamental forms of potential conflict between individuals' jobs (or careers) and their family lives. One prominent form of conflict arises because people have finite resources in terms of time and energy, and demands from different roles will tax those resources. Gutek, Searle, and Klepa (1991) have labeled this the *rational* view because it presumes that the extent of inter-role conflict is directly proportional to the amount of time (or energy) expended in each domain. It has also been referred to as the *utilitarian* approach (Lobel, 1991) because it focuses upon the rewards and costs of investing time and energy in specific roles. The utilitarian model depicts life as a struggle between competing roles that have differential reward-to-cost ratios. From this perspective, conflict between roles is inevitable—the more time and energy required to perform specific roles successfully, the greater the extent of inter-role conflict. As noted by Lambert (1990), individuals may have to engage in a process of accommodation, where they limit or modify their involvement in one sphere to accommodate the demands of the other. For instance, intensive demands from the job may require them to significantly reduce their input into family life.

In addition to time-based conflict, Greenhaus and Beutell (1985) highlighted two other sources of inter-role conflict. One that is mentioned less often in the literature is the potential for conflict between role norms and expectations. Greenhaus and Beutell referred to this as *behavior-based conflict*. As well as competing for one's time and physical energy, the attitudes, values, and behaviors required in one role may be incompatible with those needed in another. For example, in the work context an employee may be expected to be aggressive, ambitious, hard-driving, and task oriented. Successful job performance (and the rewards associated with such performance) may be contingent upon demonstration of these behavioral characteristics. In the home situation, however, being loving, supportive, accommodating, and relationship oriented may be considered essential to the development of a positive family life. Clearly, these opposing behavioral expectations may create tension within individuals as they make the transition from one environment to another.

A third form of potential conflict between roles is strain-based conflict that is induced by emotional interference from one domain to the other. In particular, job conditions (such as work overload, poor interpersonal relations, job insecurity, and lack of opportunity to exercise control and self-direction) can produce negative emotional consequences (reduced self-esteem, feelings of uncertainty, loss of a sense of competence) that impinge upon interactions within the family (Menaghan, 1991). These negative emotional reactions within the work environment can lead to expressions of irritability toward family members or withdrawal from family interaction to recuperate (Burley, 1995; Menaghan, 1991). Similarly, the strains of family life may carry over into the work context, although evidence of this is less conclusive (Higgins & Duxbury, 1992; Williams & Alliger, 1994).

Empirical work on the home-work interface illustrates that this is a significant source of strain for both women and men but that gender differences may exist. Two primary questions have been explored: (a) Are there gender differences in the amount or extent of job-family conflict experienced? and (b) Are the correlates of job-family conflict different for men versus women? For instance, Davidson and Cooper (1994) noted that, compared with their male counterparts, female managers are often confronted with additional pressures from both their home and job environments. Similar findings have been reported by Beatty (1996) and Wiersma and van den Berg (1991). However, research that differentiates between job → family conflict or interference and family → job interference has obtained less clear-cut evidence for gender differences in the *amount* of inter-role conflict experienced. For example, Frone et al. (1992) and Milkie and Peltola (1999) found no overall difference between men and women in job-family conflict, whereas Williams and Alliger (1994) reported higher levels of both forms of interference among women than among men.

In sum, recent studies do not uniformly confirm the existence of gender differences in the level and direction of inter-role conflict, and some in fact contradict the popular belief that family responsibilities are more likely to intrude upon women's careers and job satisfaction (O'Driscoll, 1996). Nevertheless, it is evident that men and women *do* have different experiences. In particular, despite considerable shifts in societal attitudes and values surrounding gender roles, research indicates that women still shoulder the major responsibility for family and household activities, especially those related to child rearing. As suggested recently by Milkie and Peltola (1999), however, women may have developed more adaptive strategies for coping with these burdens and may be better able to juggle multiple demands from the job and family domains.

In any event, it is evident that inter-role conflict (in particular between job and family demands) is a major stressor for an increasing number of individuals, especially as economic pressures require people to spend more and more time in paid employment. Recent interest in job-family conflict has focused not just on the sources of this form of strain but also on strategies for alleviating it, including the use of flextime, on-site child care centers, and other "family-supportive" organizational programs (Kirchmeyer, 1995; Kramar, 1997). We also need to examine generational differences, comparing (for example) experiences of the "baby-boomer" generation (typically defined as those born between 1945 and 1960) and later cohorts. Research illustrates that there has been a significant increase in the number of multigenerational families in society, at a time when midlife individuals need to make provision for the onset of retirement and may themselves have health, relationship, and financial issues to contend with (Franks & Stephens, 1992; Higgins, Duxbury, & Lee, 1994). One consequence of this trend is that some generational cohorts may be expected to shoulder responsibility for the care of both their (typically adolescent or young adult) children and their aging parents (and in some cases grandparents!).

Conclusion

In this chapter, we have summarized the effects of a variety of sources of work-related strain that have been studied in stress research. This review has not been exhaustive but has highlighted some of the most commonly reported, and most intense, stressors that are experienced by

Summary

workers. Some of these variables will be discussed further in Chapter 4, which examines factors that contribute to job-related burnout.

Two further issues need to be recognized when conducting research on potential stressors. First, as noted earlier, frequently stressors are not confronted in isolation from each other but rather occur in combination. For instance, a worker may simultaneously experience role ambiguity (perhaps due to lack of a clearly specified job description) and other stressors, such as interpersonal conflict with colleagues (over job boundaries) and pressures from a supervisor (concerned about lack of productivity). The combined impact of these stressors needs to be ascertained, not just their individual effects, and the whole (effect) may well be more than the sum of the parts!

Second, there is continuing debate in the job stress literature about whether stressors should be investigated "subjectively" or "objectively." In support of the subjectivity position, the transactional model of stress emphasizes that the *perception* of a stimulus or event as threatening is critical for the experience of strain. Put bluntly, no awareness—no strain! The majority of stress studies in the occupational literature use self-reports of stressors and hence are based, either explicitly or implicitly, upon the assumption that subjective perceptions are the key to understanding stressor-strain relationships. On the other hand, stress management interventions, particularly those at the organizational level (see Chapter 7), are typically built upon a belief that certain stressors may transcend individual cognitions and attributions and can therefore be regarded as "objective." Again, to put this view simply, stressors may be assessed in some objective manner that is independent of how particular individuals perceive them. Alternatively, researchers should focus attention on environmental features where there is some level of consensus among individuals that these events are stressors, rather than analyzing data solely at the individual level. Similarly, limitations associated with self-report data, particularly when measures of stressors and strains are all based upon self-reports, need to be taken into account. (This issue is discussed further in Chapter 8 of this book.)

A valuable debate on this topic is presented in a recent issue of the *Journal of Organizational Behavior* (1999, Vol. 20, No. 5), where arguments are presented for both the "subjective perception" view (Perrewe & Zellars, 1999) and the "objective environment" perspective (Frese & Zapf, 1999; Schaubroeck, 1999). We concur with comments made by Spector (1999) in his editorial introduction to this debate:

These experienced job stress researchers agree that the job stress process involves both subjective and objective aspects. The major disagreement is on where the major emphasis should be in future research.... Undoubtedly, progress will be made in this domain by paying attention to both objective and subjective factors, so that we can better understand how the environment affects people's health and well-being. (p. 737)

As the nature and forms of jobs are continually changing, it is imperative that job stress researchers explore new kinds of stressors that may result from new and different working conditions. For example, as discussed briefly here, teleworking is a relatively new form of work that an increasing number of employees are engaging in, as organizations seek to increase the flexibility and efficiency of the labor force. The types of stressors associated with teleworking are only just beginning to surface, and the possible longer-term effects of this form of work are as yet unknown. Longitudinal investigations are needed to determine the types of stressors and outcomes related to teleworking and other newly emerging working arrangements. Chapter 3 explores in more detail the potential outcomes, for both individual employees and organizations, of job stressors.

Bailey and Bhagat (1987) drew attention to an important distinction in research on the impact of stressful work environments. They noted that one problem with research in this area is that often no differentiation is made between stressors that are short-term or one-off events (episodic stressors) and those that are ongoing (chronic stressors). They suggested that most research has focused predominantly on episodic events that might create strain for individual employees, giving relatively little attention to "chronic or ongoing situations that might plague an individual employee day in and day out" (p. 211). One possible reason for this bias could be that episodic events (such as a computer malfunction) and their effects are easier to capture in cross-sectional research designs, which form the basis of much job stress research. Whatever the reason, it is clear that a complete understanding of the phenomena that induce psychological strain among workers requires investigation of the full range of potential stressors, both short and long term.

Similarly, further research is needed on how individuals adapt and adjust to various job-related stressors and what organizations can do to offset the negative effects of environmental and psychosocial stressors in the workplace. In Chapter 6, we examine theoretical perspectives and empirical findings concerning individual stress-coping strategies, and Chapter 7 discusses stress management interventions at the organizational level. In our view, it is important to emphasize that the responsibility for stress management lies with both individual workers and employers and to explore how work environments may be constructed to minimize stressful experiences, as well as to alleviate psychological strain when it does occur.

References

Aryee, S., & Luk, V. (1996). Balancing two major parts of adult life experience: Work and family identity among dual-career couples. *Human Relations, 49,* 465-487.

Ashour, A. (1982). A framework of a cognitive-behavior theory of leader influence and effectiveness. *Organizational Behavior and Human Performance, 30,* 407-430.

Bailey, J., & Bhagat, R. (1987). Meaning and measurement of stressors in the work environment: An evaluation. In S. V. Kasl & C. L. Cooper (Eds.), *Stress and health: Issues in research methodology* (pp. 207-229). New York: John Wiley.

Beatty, C. (1996). The stress of managerial and professional women. *Journal of Organizational Behavior, 17,* 233-252.

Beatty, C., & Lee, G. (1992). Leadership among middle managers: An exploration in the context of technological change. *Human Relations, 45,* 957-990.

Beehr, T. (1987). The themes of social-psychological stress in work organizations: From roles to goals. In A. W. Riley & S. J. Zaccaro (Eds.), *Occupational stress and organizational effectiveness* (pp. 71-101). New York: Praeger.

Beehr, T., & Bhagat, R. (1985). Introduction to human stress and cognition in organizations. In T. A. Beehr & R. S. Bhagat (Eds.), *Human stress and cognition in organizations: An integrated perspective* (pp. 3-19). New York: John Wiley.

Beehr, T., & McGrath, J. (1992). Social support, occupational stress and anxiety. *Anxiety, Stress and Coping, 5,* 7-20.

Bohemier, A. (1985, May 23). *Mar-Tech.* Montreal: Lloyds List. p. 1.

Brayfield, A. (1995). Juggling jobs and kids: The impact of employment schedules on fathers' caring for children. *Journal of Marriage and the Family, 57,* 321-332.

Brockner, J., Konovsky, M., Cooper-Schneider, R., Folger, R., Martin, C., & Bies, R. (1994). Interactive effects of procedural justice and outcome negativity on victims and survivors of job loss. *Academy of Management Journal, 37,* 397-409.

Brockner, J., Wiesenfeld, B., Stephan, J., Hurley, R., Grover, S., Reed, T., DeWitt, R., & Martin, C. (1997). The effects on layoff survivors of their fellow survivors' reactions. *Journal of Applied Social Psychology, 27,* 835-863.

Buck, V. (1972). *Working under pressure.* London: Staples.

Burke, R., & Cooper, C. (2000). *Organizations in crisis: Downsizing, restructuring and privatizations.* Oxford, UK: Blackwells.

Burke, R., & McKeen, C. (1994). Career development among managerial and professional women. In R. Burke & M. Davidson (Eds.), *Women in management: Current research issues* (pp. 65-80). London: Paul Chapman.

Burley, K. (1995). Family variables as mediators of the relationship between work-family conflict and marital adjustment among dual-career men and women. *Journal of Social Psychology, 135,* 483-497.

Cameron, K., Freeman, S., & Mishra, A. (1993). Downsizing and redesigning organizations. In G. Huber & W. Glick (Eds.), *Organizational change and redesign* (pp. 19-63). New York: Oxford University Press.

Cartwright, S., & Cooper, C. (1997). *Managing workplace stress.* Thousand Oaks, CA: Sage.

Cheliot, F. (1979). Rythme theta posterieur au cour de la veille active chez l'homme. *Revue EEC en Neuropsychologie, 9,* 52-57.

Cobb, S., & Kasl, S. (1977). *Termination: The consequences of job loss.* Cincinnati, OH: HEW.

Cole, R. (1993). Learning from learning theory: Implications for quality improvement of turnover, use of contingent workers, and job rotation policies. *Quality Management Journal, 1,* 9-25.

Cooper, C. (1987). The experience and management of stress: Job and organizational determinants. In A. W. Riley & S. J. Zaccaro (Eds.), *Occupational stress and organizational effectiveness* (pp. 53-69). New York: Praeger.

Cooper, C. L. (1998). *Theories of organizational stress.* New York: Oxford University Press.

Cooper, C., & Cartwright, S. (1994). Healthy mind, healthy organization: A proactive approach to occupational stress. *Human Relations, 47,* 455-471.

Cooper, C. L., & Kelly, M. (1984). Stress among crane operators. *Journal of Occupational Medicine, 26*(8), 575-578.

Cooper, C. L., & Lewis, S. (1998). *Balancing career, family and life.* London: Kogan Page.

Cooper, C. L., & Melhuish, A. (1980). Occupational stress and managers. *Journal of Occupational Medicine, 22,* 588-592.

Cooper, C., & Roden, J. (1985). Mental health and satisfaction among tax officers. *Social Science and Medicine, 21,* 747-751.

Cropanzano, R., Howes, J., Grandey, A., & Toth, P. (1997). The relationship of office politics and support to work behaviors, attitudes and stress. *Journal of Organizational Behavior, 18,* 159-180.

Davidson, M., & Cooper, C. (1994). *Shattering the glass ceiling.* London: Chapman Paul.

Davidson, M., & Veno, A. (1980). Stress and the policeman. In C. Cooper & J. Marshall (Eds.), *White collar and professional stress.* Newbury Park, CA: John Wiley.

Elliot, D. (1985). The offshore worker. *Practitioner, 229,* 565-571.

Ferris, G., Frink, D., Galang, M., Zhou, J., Kacmar, K., & Howard, J. (1996). Perceptions of organizational politics: Predicting stress-related implications and outcomes. *Human Relations, 49,* 233-266.

Fisher, S., & Cooper, C. L. (1990). *On the move: The psychology of change and transition.* New York: John Wiley.

Folkard, S. (1996). Body rhythms and shiftwork. In P. Warr (Ed.), *Psychology at work* (4th ed., pp. 39-72). New York: Penguin.

Franks, M., & Stephens, M. (1992). Multiple roles and multi-generation caregivers: Contextual effects and psychological mechanisms. *Journal of Gerontology: Social Sciences, 47,* 123-129.

Frese, M., & Zapf, D. (1999). On the importance of the objective environment in stress and attribution theory: Counterpoint to Perrewe and Zellars. *Journal of Organizational Behavior, 20,* 761-766.

Frone, M., Russell, M., & Cooper, M. (1992). Prevalence of work-family conflict: Are work and family boundaries asymmetrically permeable? *Journal of Organizational Behavior, 13,* 723-729.

Greenhaus, J., & Beutell, N. (1985). Sources of conflict between work and family roles. *Academy of Management Review, 10,* 76-88.

Greenhaus, J., & Parasuraman, S. (1994). Work-family conflict, social support and well-being. In M. Davidson & R. Burke (Eds.), *Women in management: Current research issues.* London: Paul Chapman.

Gutek, B., Searle, S., & Klepa, L. (1991). Rational versus gender role explanations for work-family conflict. *Journal of Applied Psychology, 76,* 560-568.

Guzley, R. (1992). Organizational climate and communication climate: Predictors of commitment to the organization. *Management Communication Quarterly, 5,* 379-402.

Hall, D. (1976). *Careers in organisations.* Santa Monica, CA: Goodyear.

Hall, D. (Ed.). (1994). *Career development.* Aldershot, UK: Brookfield.

Hall, D., & Moss, J. (1998, Winter). The new protean career contract: Helping organizations and employees adapt. *Organizational Dynamics, 26*(3), 22-36.

Hall, L., & Torrington, D. (1986). Why not use the computer? The use and lack of use of computers in personnel. *Personnel Review, 15*(1), 3-7.

Hanisch, K. (1999). Job loss and unemployment research from 1994 to 1998: A review and recommendations for research and intervention. *Journal of Vocational Behavior, 55,* 188-220.

Hellesoy, O. (1985). *Work environment.* Bergen, Norway: Statfjord Field.

Higgins, C., & Duxbury, L. (1992). Work-family conflict: A comparison of dual-career and traditional-career men. *Journal of Organizational Behavior, 13,* 389-411.

Higgins, C., Duxbury, L., & Lee, C. (1994). Impact of life-cycle change and gender on the ability to balance work and family responsibilities. *Family Relations, 43,* 144-150.

Hill, E., Miller, B., Weiner, S., & Colihan, J. (1998). Influences of the virtual office on aspects of work and work/life balance. *Personnel Psychology, 51,* 667-684.

International Labour Office. (1986). *Psychosocial factors at work: Recognition and control. Report of the Joint ILO/WHO Committee on Occupational Health. Ninth Session, 1984.* Geneva, Switzerland: Author.

Ivancevich, J., & Matteson, M. (1980). *Stress at work.* Glenview, IL: Scott, Foresman.

Jackson, S., & Schuler, R. (1985). A meta-analysis and conceptual critique of research on role ambiguity and role conflict in work settings. *Organizational Behavior and Human Decision Processes, 36,* 16-78.

Jamal, M., & Baba, V. (1992). Shiftwork and department-type related to job stress, work attitudes and behavioral intentions: A study of nurses. *Journal of Organizational Behavior, 13,* 449-464.

Jewell, L. (1998). *Contemporary industrial/organizational psychology* (3rd ed.). Pacific Grove, CA: Brooks/Cole.

Johansson, G. (1989). Stress, autonomy and the maintenance of skill in supervisory control of automated systems. *Applied Psychology: International Review, 38,* 45-56.

Jones, D. (1983). Noise. In R. Hockey (Ed.), *Stress and fatigue and human performance.* New York: John Wiley.

Kahn, R., & Byosiere, P. (1990). Stress in organizations. In M. Dunnette & L. Hough (Eds.), *Handbook of industrial and organizational psychology* (2nd ed., Vol. 3, pp. 571-650). Palo Alto, CA: Consulting Psychologists Press.

Kahn, R., Wolfe, D., Quinn, R., & Snoek, J. (1964). *Organizational stress: Studies in role conflict and ambiguity.* New York: John Wiley.

Kalimo, R. (1980). Stress at work: Conceptual analysis and a study on prison personnel. *Scandinavian Journal of Work Environment Health, 6*(3), 148.

Karasek, R. (1979). Job demands, job decision latitude, and mental strain: Implications for job redesign. *Administrative Science Quarterly, 24,* 285-308.

Kelly, M., & Cooper, C. (1981). Stress among blue collar workers: A case study of the steel industry. *Employee Relations, 3*(2), 6-9.

Kirchmeyer, C. (1995). Managing the work-nonwork boundary: An assessment of organizational responses. *Human Relations, 48,* 515-536.

Kornhauser, A. (1965). *The mental health of the industrial worker.* New York: John Wiley.

Korunka, C., Weiss, A., Huemer, K.-H., & Karetta, B. (1995). The effects of new technologies on job satisfaction and psychosomatic complaints. *Applied Psychology: International Review, 44,* 123-142.

Kozlowski, S., Chao, G., Smith, E., & Hedlung, J. (1993). Organizational downsizing: Strategies, interventions and research implications. *International Review of Industrial and Organizational Psychology, 8,* 263-332.

Kramar, R. (1997). Developing and implementing work and family policies. *Asia Pacific Journal of Human Resources, 35,* 1-18.

Kushmir, T., & Melamed, S. (1991). Workload, perceived control and psychological distress in Type A/B industrial workers. *Journal of Organizational Behavior, 12,* 155-168.

Lambert, S. (1990). Processes linking work and family: A critical review and research agenda. *Human Relations, 43,* 239-258.

Latack, J., Kinicki, A., & Prussia, G. (1995). An integrative process model of coping with job loss. *Academy of Management Review, 20,* 311-342.

Lazarus, R., & Folkman, S. (1984). *Stress, appraisal and coping.* New York: Springer.

Leana, C., & Florkowski, G. (1992). Participation, individual development and organizational change. *Research in Personnel and Human Resource Management, 10,* 233-270.

Levinson, H. (1978, May-June). The abrasive personality. *The Harvard Business Review, 56,* 86-94.

Lewin, K., Lippitt, R., & White, R. (1939). Patterns of aggressive behaviour in experimentally created social climates. *Journal of Social Psychology, 10,* 271-299.

Lobel, S. (1991). Allocation of investment in work and family roles: Alternative theories and implications for research. *Academy of Management Review, 16,* 507-521.

Luthans, F., & Sommer, S. (1999). The impact of downsizing on workplace attitudes: Differing reactions of managers and staff in a health care organization. *Group and Organization Management, 24,* 46-70.

Martin, R., & Wall, T. (1989). Attentional demand and cost responsibility as stressors in shopfloor jobs. *Academy of Management Journal, 32,* 69-86.

McLean, A. (1979). *Work stress.* New York: Addison-Wesley.

Melamed, S., Ben-Avi, I., Luz, J., & Green, M. (1995). Objective and subjective work monotony: Effects on job satisfaction, psychological distress and absenteeism in blue-collar workers. *Journal of Applied Psychology, 80,* 29-42.

Menaghan, E. (1991). Work experiences and family interaction processes: The long reach of the job. *Annual Review of Sociology, 17,* 419-444.

Milkie, M., & Peltola, P. (1999). Playing the roles: Gender and the work-family balancing act. *Journal of Marriage and the Family, 61,* 476-490.

Motowidlo, S., Packard, J., & Manning, M. (1986). Occupational stress: Its causes and consequences for job performance. *Journal of Applied Psychology, 71,* 618-629.

Munsterberg, H. (1913). *Psychology and industrial efficiency.* New York: Houghton-Mifflin.

Narayanan, L., Menon, S., & Spector, P. (1999). Stress in the workplace: A comparison of gender and occupations. *Journal of Organizational Behavior, 20,* 63-74.

O'Driscoll, M. (1987). Attitudes to the job and the organization among new recruits: Influence of perceived job characteristics and organizational structure. *Applied Psychology: An International Review, 36,* 133-145.

O'Driscoll, M. (1996). The interface between job and off-job roles: Enhancement and conflict. *International Review of Industrial and Organizational Psychology, 11,* 279-306.

O'Driscoll, M., & Beehr, T. (1994). Supervisor behaviors, role stressors and uncertainty as predictors of personal outcomes for subordinates. *Journal of Organizational Behavior, 15,* 141-155.

O'Driscoll, M., & Beehr, T. (2000). Moderating effects of perceived control and need for clarity on the relationship between role stressors and employee affective reactions. *Journal of Social Psychology, 140,* 151-159.

O'Driscoll, M., & Cooper, C. (1996). Sources and management of excessive job stress and burnout. In P. Warr (Ed.), *Psychology at work* (4th ed., pp. 188-223). New York: Penguin.

O'Driscoll, M., & Evans, R. (1988). Organizational factors and perceptions of climate in three psychiatric units. *Human Relations, 41,* 371-388.

O'Driscoll, M., Ilgen, D., & Hildreth, K. (1992). Time devoted to job and off-job activities, interrole conflict and affective experiences. *Journal of Applied Psychology, 77,* 272-279.

Organ, D., & Greene, C. (1981). The effects of formalization on professional involvement: A compensatory process approach. *Administrative Science Quarterly, 26,* 237-252.

Osipow, S. (1973). *Theories of career development.* New York: Appleton-Century-Crofts.

Pearce, J. (1981). Bringing some clarity to role ambiguity research. *Academy of Management Review, 6,* 665-674.

Perrewe, P., & Zellars, K. (1999). An examination of attributions and emotions in the transactional approach to the organizational stress process. *Journal of Organizational Behavior, 20,* 739-752.

Pierce, J., & Dunham, R. (1992). The 12-hour work day: A 48-hour, eight-day week. *Academy of Management Journal, 35,* 1086-1098.

Podsakoff, P., Williams, L., & Todor, W. (1986). Effects of organizational formalization on alienation among professionals and nonprofessionals. *Academy of Management Journal, 29,* 820-831.

Poulton, E. (1978). Blue collar stressors. In C. Cooper & R. Payne (Eds.), *Stress at work.* New York: John Wiley.

Quick, J., & Quick, J. (1984). *Organizational stress and prevention management.* New York: McGraw-Hill.

Rabinowitz, W., Falkenbach, K., Travers, J., Valentine, C., & Weener, P. (1983). Worker motivation: Unsolved problem or untapped resource? *California Management Review, 25*(2), 48-53.

Ramsey, J. (1983). Heat and cold. In R. Hockey (Ed.), *Stress and fatigue in human performance.* New York: John Wiley.

Roethlisberger, F., & Dickson, W. (1939). *Management and the worker.* Cambridge, MA: Harvard University Press.

Sagie, A., & Koslowsky, M. (1994). Organizational attitudes and behaviors as a function of participation in strategic and tactical change decisions. *Journal of Organizational Behavior, 15,* 37-47.

Schaubroeck, J. (1999). Should the subjective be the objective? On studying mental processes, coping behavior and actual exposures in organizational stress research. *Journal of Organizational Behavior, 20,* 753-760.

Schaubroeck, J., Cotton, J., & Jennings, K. (1989). Antecedents and consequences of role stress: A covariance structure analysis. *Journal of Organizational Behavior, 10,* 35-58.

Seltzer, J., & Numerof, R. (1988). Supervisory leadership and subordinate burnout. *Academy of Management Journal, 31,* 439-446.

Selye, H. (1976). *Stress in health and disease.* London: Butterworths.

Seymour, F., & Buscherhof, J. (1991). Sources and consequences of satisfaction and dissatisfaction in nursing: Findings from a national sample. *International Journal of Nursing Studies, 28,* 109-124.

Smith, M., Cohen, B., Stammerjohn, L., & Happ, A. (1981). An investigation of health complaints and job stress in video display operations. *Human Factors, 23,* 389-400.

Smith, M., Cohen, H., Cleveland, R., & Cohen, A. (1978). Characteristics of successful safety programs. *Journal of Safety Research, 10,* 5-15.

Sparks, K., Cooper, C., Fried, Y., & Shirom, A. (1997). The effects of work hours on health: A meta-analytic review. *Journal of Occupational and Organizational Psychology, 70,* 391-408.

Spector, P. (1999). Objective versus subjective approaches to the study of job stress. *Journal of Organizational Behavior, 20,* 737.

Surry, J. (1968). *Industrial accident research: A human engineering appraisal.* Ontario, Canada: Department of Labour.

Sutherland, V., & Cooper, C. (1986). *Man and accidents offshore: The costs of stress among workers on oil and gas rigs.* London: Lloyds List/Dietsmann (International).

Toterdell, P., Spelten, E., Smith, L., Barton, J., & Folkard, S. (1995). Recovery from work shifts: How long does it take? *Journal of Applied Psychology, 80,* 43-57.

Wagner, J. (1994). Participation's effect on performance and satisfaction: A reconsideration of research evidence. *Academy of Management Review, 19,* 312-330.

Wagner, J., Leana, C., Locke, E., & Schweiger, D. (1997). Cognitive and motivational frameworks in U.S. research on participation. *Journal of Organizational Behavior, 18,* 49-66.

Warr, P. (1994). A conceptual framework for the study of work and mental health. *Work and Stress, 8,* 84-97.

Westman, M., & Eden, D. (1992). Excessive role demand and subsequent performance. *Journal of Organizational Behavior, 13,* 519-529.

Wiersma, U., & van den Berg, P. (1991). Work-home role conflict, family climate, and domestic responsibilities among men and women in dual-earner families. *Journal of Applied Social Psychology, 21,* 1207-1217.

Williams, K., & Alliger, G. (1994). Role stressors, mood spillover, and perceptions of work-family conflict in employed parents. *Academy of Management Journal, 37,* 837-868.

Yerkes, R. M., & Dodson, J. D. (1908). The relation of strength of stimulus to rapidity of habit formation. *Journal of Comparative Neurology and Psychology, 18,* 459-482.

Zhou, J., & Ferris, G. (1995). The dimensions and consequences of organizational politics perceptions. *Journal of Applied Social Psychology, 25,* 1747-1764.

3 Assessing Job-Related Strains

In this chapter, we discuss the assessment of strain—that is, the individual's physical, psychological, and behavioral responses to stressors—and we review the large array of measures that have been used to capture workplace strains. As noted in Chapter 1, strain may be conceptualized as a dependent variable (a response to disturbing or threatening stimuli) and may cover a range of manifestations. The variety and scope of strain measures may stem from the fact that the common expression "being under stress" illustrates that at times virtually any response may be seen as reflecting strain. In addition, because individuals respond in many different ways, a variety of different responses have been treated by researchers as indicators of strain. The aim of this chapter is to examine these strain indicators and to consider the implications of such measures for job stress research.

Classifying Strain

It is possible to identify a generally accepted approach to classifying manifestations of strain. Most reviews of stress (see, e.g., Kahn & Byosiere, 1992) distinguish between three major categories of possible

stress responses or strains: *physiological, psychological,* and *behavioral.*
Each of the three categories will be discussed in turn. Our aim is to draw
attention to the range of measures used, to explore difficulties associated with each of the three categories, and to raise issues that may help
to clarify stressor-strain relationships. We begin with an overview of
physiological indicators.

Physiological Strain

Kahn and Byosiere (1992) suggested that the assessment of physiological strain in job stress research is relatively rare. To confirm this, we
conducted a literature search of the Psychological Abstracts and ABI
databases, entering the key words *physiological/psychosocial strain* and
work stress. This search revealed only 15 references, a number that
increased to just over 100 when the more general term *stress* was used.
Nevertheless, studies of job-related stress are moving increasingly from
total reliance on self-report measures of (psychological) strain toward
measures that include some form of psychophysiological assessment
(McLaren, 1997). The fact that work stress researchers have only
recently begun to explore the utility of physiological responses does not
mean that such measures have been regarded as unimportant. Rather,
most job stress research has been psychologically based; hence, there
has been an emphasis on the measurement of psychological, rather than
physiological, strains (Jex & Beehr, 1991).

Two reviews (Fried, Rowland, & Ferris, 1984; Jex & Beehr, 1991) provide
an overview of the types and nature of physiological measures used in
job stress research. From their review, Fried et al. (1984) concluded that,
in general, research has focused on three types of physiological indicators: cardiovascular symptoms, biochemical symptoms, and gastrointestinal symptoms. Their analysis of 47 studies revealed that the most
popular measures were heart rate and blood pressure. Taking into
account that 24 of these studies incorporated more than one physiological index, 60.2% measured cardiovascular symptoms (blood pressure,
cardiac activity, and cholesterol), 30.7% measured biochemical symptoms
(especially catecholamines, cortisol, and uric acid), and 9% measured
gastrointestinal symptoms (particularly peptic ulcers).

Jex and Beehr (1991) adopted a similar approach to categorization,
although they used headings such as "physiological measures believed
to be associated with disease" and "actual disease conditions." Their first

category of strains contained the three types of response mentioned above (cardiovascular, biochemical, and gastrointestinal), and their second category was concerned with conditions or behaviors that are closely related to disease conditions, including both direct relationships between work conditions and disease (e.g., cancer, stroke, diabetes) and indirect relationships (e.g., cigarette smoking). Because many of the findings are open to alternative interpretations, it is not possible to draw firm conclusions from this line of research. However, the interesting conclusion to emerge from Jex and Beehr's review was that the most common approach for collecting physiological data simply involved asking people about their health or health-related behaviors. This entailed either asking individuals to indicate what specific symptoms they had experienced at work and whether they had sought medical advice for these symptoms or getting them to complete a symptoms checklist. Evidence suggests that self-report measures of physical symptoms are related to a variety of work stressors, although the size of the relationship is not high (Jex & Beehr, 1991).

It is important to note at this stage the program of work carried out by Ganster and his colleagues (Fox, Dwyer, & Ganster, 1993; Schaubroeck & Ganster, 1993). This work is significant for a number of reasons, not the least of which is that the authors thoughtfully and carefully developed their approach to exploring the relationship between job demands and physiological outcomes, making use at times of both subjective and objective measures. Schaubroeck and Ganster (1993) concluded that "occupational demands, which have not previously been addressed in studies of degeneration of autonomic responsivity due to conditioning from chronic exposures, should be examined seriously in the literature" (p. 84). Fox et al. (1993) concluded that their study "provides perhaps the clearest evidence yet that some medically meaningful outcomes [blood pressure; cortisol scores] are best explained by the joint effects of job demands and individual control beliefs" (p. 307). Although the use of physiological measures is challenging enough for researchers, it offers, as these researchers point out, a causal pathway with profound explanatory potential.

Work stress researchers are seldom forced to choose between objective (physiological) and subjective (self-report) measures of strain. However, they are frequently led to believe that direct physiological measures, because they are independent of individual perceptions, are more "objective" and hence that they are superior to self-report measures and result in fewer confounding factors. Jex and Beehr (1991), however, commented that "one of the most pressing issues in this area is to find more reliable ways to measure these physiological indicators within the context of occupational stress research" (p. 337). Fried et al. (1984) argued that three factors may affect the reliability of physiological measures and hence need to be controlled:

1. *Stable or permanent factors* (e.g., differences between individuals in their vulnerability to certain physiological symptoms, including age, gender, diet, genetic tendency)
2. *Transitory factors* (e.g., time- and context-specific conditions, including such factors as temperature, time of day, physical exertion, and substance consumption)
3. *Procedural factors* (e.g., the number of times measures are taken and the amount of time elapsing between measures)

The conclusions that can be drawn from reviewing physiological responses to job-related stressors suggest that this field represents an intriguing area for future research. However, it is clear that researchers must give due consideration to the above factors so that the measurement of physiological indicators can become more standardized and consistent (Fried et al., 1984). Furthermore, longitudinal studies are needed to clarify directions of causality and to unravel complex interrelationships over time (Kahn & Byosiere, 1992). Finally, as noted later, different stressors may be quite specific in terms of the strain they produce. If that is the case, the reliability of research findings will be improved by paying more attention to the nature of the stressor. For instance, as Fried et al. (1984) suggested, the type of physiological strain produced by an acute (episodic) stressor may be quite different from that produced by stressors that are more ongoing (chronic).

Failure to distinguish between different types of stressors may lead to the conclusion that some stressors have nonsignificant effects when in reality they produce a highly specific type of strain that has not been measured because little attention has been given to the nature of the stressor-strain relationship being investigated. Also, some stressors may induce a physiological reaction at a future point in time rather than immediately. Rather than assessing certain types of strain simply because they fall into recognized categories or have been examined in previous studies of job stress, researchers should give as much thought to selection of an appropriate strain index as they have to identifying and exploring the nature and characteristics of the stressors themselves.

In short, there needs to be careful consideration of the particular reactions (strains) that would be anticipated in response to specific stressors.

Finally, measurement reliability may be improved by using both objective and subjective indexes of physical strain. This would enable a comparison of the results from different measures, as well as an opportunity to explore the relationship between the two and a more comprehensive account that would enhance the appropriateness of interventions (Kahn & Byosiere, 1992). Objective and subjective measures both play an important role in the assessment of strain, and researchers should "aim to design a 'test battery' approach to the study of stress so that a greater picture can be obtained and more powerful predictive relationships achieved" (Travers & Cooper, 1994, p. 145).

Psychological Strain

As noted earlier, psychological strains resulting from job stressors are the most commonly studied (Jex & Beehr, 1991; Kahn & Byosiere, 1992). This does not mean that these manifestations of strain are necessarily the primary or the most frequent reactions to work stressors. It more likely reflects the fact that most job stress researchers have a background in psychology and are perhaps more familiar with this type of measurement (Jex & Beehr, 1991). Furthermore, many measures of psychological strain have been used, but only a few have been used consistently (Kahn & Byosiere, 1992). Interestingly, the most frequently used measure has been job dissatisfaction. This raises questions about how best to measure job dissatisfaction and, more importantly, whether job satisfaction is important to the individual and hence whether feelings of dissatisfaction actually have a significant impact on that person's well-being (Brief & Atieh, 1987).

Research reviews have revealed that, however they are conceptualized and assessed, psychological strains are strong correlates of work-related stressors (Jackson & Schuler, 1985; Jex & Beehr, 1991; Kahn & Byosiere, 1992). Two issues are of interest here: (a) whether any patterns can be identified in the number and types of strain measures used in research and (b) the extent of conceptual overlap between these measures (Kahn & Byosiere, 1992). The reviews noted above clearly illustrate that the two most frequently used psychological measures are job dissatisfaction and tension/anxiety. However, numerous other psychological indicators have also been adopted in job-stress research. For example, of the 96 studies identified by Jackson and Schuler (1985) in their review of the effects of role ambiguity and role conflict, 14 different measures of strain were used, of which 11 could be classified as psychological strains (Jex & Beehr, 1991). The three other strain measures assessed behavioral and performance factors. Of the psychological strains, job dissatisfaction was reported in 43 studies (just under 50%) and tension/anxiety in 22 studies (about 25%). Jackson and Schuler further classified measures of job dissatisfaction into six subcategories: general dissatisfaction, and dissatisfaction with supervision, work, coworkers, pay, and promotion. Other variables included as indexes of strain in the studies reviewed by Jackson and Schuler were organizational commitment, job involvement, propensity to leave, and absence.

Similar findings emerged from the review by Kahn and Byosiere (1992), who identified 43 different measures of psychological strain in 100 studies, once more illustrating a considerable range of approaches toward the assessment of strain. (Dissatisfaction with the job, life, and workload were most frequently used, in 24.5% of the studies.) Given that Kahn and Byosiere argued that their review of empirical research in this field was not exhaustive, the amount of methodological variation between studies is even more remarkable. The types of strains that were assessed in the research they reviewed included the following:

- Health, whether general, mental or physical, or from the job, including somatic complaints, illness, vigor, health problems, and physical symptoms (used in 16.3% of the studies)
- Anxiety/tension (15.4%)
- Strain—either general, physical, psychological, emotional, or from the job (10.0%)
- Boredom, fatigue, tedium, depersonalization, emotional exhaustion, and overall burnout (9.0%)
- Emotions, including confusion, irritation, resentment, emotional arousal, and alienation (8.1%)
- Depression (8.1%)
- Others—self-confidence, self-esteem, sexual maladjustment, and turnover intent (13.3%)

It is clear from the range of measures used that it would be possible to further categorize them according to those that are acute or chronic, those that capture states of intense arousal, and those that focus on underarousal or understimulation. It is also possible to identify specific feelings as well as those that are nonspecific and more general. Finally, the above list contains responses that are indicative of some feeling or illness, of a purported intention or feeling, and even of a particular behavior or a consequence of behavior (Kahn & Byosiere, 1992). All have been measured by way of self-report.

Two observations are pertinent at this juncture. First, there seems to be a degree of flexibility and looseness in the way in which the term *psychological strain* has been applied in job stress research. As noted earlier, it would appear that virtually any (negative) reaction to stressors has been interpreted as an indicator of strain—a finding that highlights a lack of conceptual differentiation. To some extent, the conceptual overlap between measures has been accentuated by the predominant reliance solely on self-report techniques. Although these have an important function in the assessment of psychological strain, future research needs to more clearly define the roles of different strain indicators, rather than assuming their functional equivalence.

More importantly, however, the issue of measure appropriateness has rarely been addressed in research on job stress. Although Kahn and Byosiere (1992) concluded that "the psychological effects of work stress have been plausibly established" and that psychological strains are "real, painful and costly" (p. 608), greater attention needs to be given to the relevance of each variable for individual well-being. The above reviews illustrate that it has been all too easy for researchers to quite legitimately select any one of a range of variables simply because "being under stress" can be measured in so many different ways. For example, as discussed previously, dissatisfaction with the job (or aspects of the employment relationship) may have differential impact on individuals who vary in terms of work or job involvement. Job dissatisfaction would be predicted to be more salient for individual well-being when the job is central to a person's self-concept and self-esteem than when the job is peripheral (Frone, Russell, & Cooper, 1995). In sum, researchers should give more careful consideration to the nature of the stressor-strain relationships that they are seeking to explore and hence the type(s) of strain that may be induced by those relationships, as well as the subjective meaning and importance of various strain indicators to the individuals under investigation. To make an informed judgment when selecting strain measures, it is also important to consider the context in which the stressor-strain process unfolds. As well as taking into account the psychometric properties of different measures of psychological strain, researchers must conceptualize the types of strain that are anticipated to occur in the particular context and must select measures of strain that better match the type of work event under consideration.

Behavioral Strain

Behavioral responses to work stressors are the least studied of all forms of strain (Briner, 1995a; Jex & Beehr, 1991; Kahn & Byosiere, 1992). As Jex and Beehr (1991) pointed out, this is "ironic since, at least from an organizational point of view, these may be the most important" (p. 337). Furthermore, behavioral responses "impose substantial costs on work organizations," and "their effects are manifest both on the job and away from it" (Kahn & Byosiere, 1992, p. 610).

Behavioral strain has been examined in a number of different but not mutually exclusive ways. Jex and Beehr (1991), for example, reviewed 17 studies and divided behavioral responses into two broad categories. The first category included those of *significance to the organization* (responses that have a direct impact on organizational functioning, including such behaviors as job performance, turnover, and absenteeism). The second set covered those of *significance to the individual* (including use of alcohol, smoking, other substance use, and destructive behaviors). Of the 14 response measures described by Jackson and Schuler (1985), 4 could be classified as behavioral measures. These 4 were used in 22.1% of the studies reviewed and were divided into *objective measures* (e.g., absenteeism and financial data such as sales volume and profit levels) and *self-report measures* (e.g., self-ratings of performance and ratings by others).

Kahn and Byosiere's (1992) review identified 15 behavioral responses, which they classified into five groups. It would be possible to describe three of these groups as "work focused" or "organization focused." Kahn and Byosiere labeled these behaviors as *work role disruptions* (e.g., performance levels, mistakes, errors and accidents, and substance taking at work), *job flight* (e.g., turnover, absenteeism, early retirement, and strikes) and *aggressive behavior at work* (e.g., vandalism, stealing, rumor spreading, and counterproductive activities). The final two categories developed by Kahn and Byosiere covered individual-focused behaviors and included *disruptions to nonworking life* (e.g., marital, friendship, and community difficulties) and *self-damaging behaviors* (e.g., substance use and accidents).

Caution needs to be exercised in the interpretation of the above categories because simply identifying and assessing behavioral responses does not necessarily mean that they were caused by work-related stressors. They may, for instance, be the result of other factors operating in an individual's life, including off-the-job stressors and even dispositional tendencies (see Chapter 3). Second, research on behavioral indicators of strain has been described as being of "limited value" (Briner, 1995a, p. 4) because it is based largely on self-reports and cross-sectional designs and because it generally fails to capture the presumed complexity of the stressor-strain relationship. Again, it seems that the most common approach when collecting behavioral data simply involves asking people to describe their responses, rather than collecting other (perhaps more objective) behavioral observations.

There is considerable agreement among reviewers on the state of current research and what has to be done. For example, it is widely accepted that unreliable performance measures can only result in wrong conclusions and make it impossible to obtain supportive evidence of stressor-strain relationships (Jackson & Schuler, 1985). There is also recognition that individuals will resist reporting antisocial behaviors because of the consequences that may flow from admitting such behaviors (Kahn & Byosiere, 1992) and that such resistance has implications for using behavioral indicators of strain. Finally, the relationship between potentially stressful events (stressors) and behavior is complex; understanding this relationship entails unraveling the process through which different variables are linked (Jex & Beehr, 1991). At the very least, it is necessary to determine whether a direct relationship can be assumed (e.g., work overload causes absence from work) or whether the causal pathway between stressors and strains is always mediated by some affective state (e.g., workload causes anxiety, which in turn causes absence).

Clearly, there is much to be done to increase our knowledge of the behavioral manifestations of job-related strain. As with psychological indicators, research on behavioral strain has tended not to differentiate between behavioral responses toward various workplace stressors, and there has also been a proclivity to assume causal mechanisms without explicitly testing their validity. Nevertheless, as we shall see in later chapters, recent research has begun to explore the utility of behavioral measures of strain, along with the extreme manifestation of strain known as burnout (see Chapter 4), and to illustrate their relevance in the investigation of stress processes in organizations.

What About Emotions?

In their review of the role of emotions in work and achievement, Pekrun and Frese (1992) concluded that, at least in the organizational psychology literature, "there is little research that speaks directly to the issue of work and emotions" and that "industrial and organizational psychology *ought* to take the issue of emotions at work more seriously" (p. 153). Given that models of stress are essentially theories about emotional reactions (Lazarus, 1993) and that "stress constitutes an emotional subset referring largely to emotions that are distress related" (Lazarus, 1995, p. 183), the lack of explicit attention to emotions in job stress research is disconcerting. Earlier, we referred to emotions like confusion, anxiety, irritation, and resentment under the heading of psychological responses. However, despite the inclusion of these variables as potential indicators of psychological strain, there is a lack of systematic treatment of the general construct of emotion within the job stress framework and, more specifically, the role that emotions play in the stress-coping process.

Several reasons have been posited for the absence of an integrated model of emotions in job stress research (see, e.g., Briner, 1995b; Wright & Doherty, 1998). One is that there is frequently a confounding of emotions and attitudes. The confusion of these constructs is well illustrated by Wright and Doherty (1998), using job satisfaction as an example. Their argument is that, in a search for the happy and productive worker, happiness (an emotion) becomes synonymous with job satisfaction (an attitude). Although there is an affective component to job satisfaction, and evidence of a linkage between people's evaluations of their job and their overall happiness (Diener, Suh, Lucas, & Smith, 1999), researchers should nevertheless treat these as separate constructs that function at different levels of specificity, rather than regarding job satisfaction as a surrogate measure of emotional well-being.

Another reason why emotions have received less recognition in job stress research follows from the generally held belief that organizational behavior can best be explained primarily in rational-cognitive terms (Wright & Doherty, 1998). This "myth of rationality," based around the goal-directed nature of most organizational behavior theory, has "encouraged the view that emotions have little to do with, and even get in the way of, the proper legitimate, and highly successful business-like business of work" (Briner, 1995b, p. 3). Also, as Briner suggested, emotions may simply be more difficult to study than attitudes and other responses.

As we have discussed, however, emotional constructs are important, even critical, to investigate in research on job stress. Pekrun and Frese (1992) have argued that "emotions are among the primary determinants of behavior at work ... and profoundly influence both the social climate and the productivity of companies and organizations" (p. 154). Similarly, because paid employment occupies a significant portion of most people's lives, and because individuals experience a range of emotions within the employment context, efforts to understand and predict human behavior in organizational settings would be incomplete without attention to this domain. In addition, Hochschild's (1983) work on emotional labor in service organizations—that is, the expectation that individuals at work will display certain appropriate, organizationally desired emotions—further illustrates the importance of the emotional dimension. Organizational prescriptions give rise to what has been described (see Ashforth & Humphrey, 1993; Briner, 1995b; Rafaeli & Sutton, 1987) as *display rules* (emotions that are expected to be expressed) and *feeling rules* (what should be felt when confronted with different events). Put simply, in any work setting there may well be emotions that *ought to be expressed*, and these may be distinct from emotions that *are expressed*. Being required to display "appropriate" emotions, and therefore perhaps being constrained from expressing an emotion actually felt, may in itself generate psychological strain.

In sum, as Lazarus (1995) has made clear, emotions offer a rich and useful source of information about what is happening to a person. Exploring emotional processes in work settings would increase our knowledge and understanding of the transaction between the individual and the environment. At one level, this entails unraveling the emotional process so that we gain an understanding of the meaning behind the emotion (Lazarus, 1993), in much the same way as understanding why an event is stressful (primary appraisal) has enhanced conceptualizations of the coping process. At another level, it also involves exploring whether certain work events are more likely to be associated with specific emotions, and under what circumstances emotions are a moderating factor operating between stressors and strains (Briner, 1995a; see also Chapter 6 of this book).

An important step toward understanding how emotions function in work settings is to classify them into meaningful categories.

Lazarus (1995), for instance, suggested that it is possible to identify 15 different emotions that can be grouped together under three headings: *negative emotions* (anger, fright, anxiety, guilt, shame, sadness, envy, jealousy, disgust), *positive emotions* (happiness, pride, relief, love), and those that may best be described as *mixed* (hope, compassion, gratitude). Pekrun and Frese (1992) agreed that classifying emotions according to some common underlying dimensions has considerable merit. They also argued, however, that in a work situation this type of classification may not go far enough because it does not take account of the fact that particular aspects of the job may arouse specific emotions.

Pekrun and Frese developed a schema for classifying workplace emotions into discrete categories of emotion. Their approach begins by ordering emotions into those that are positive and those that are negative. These two categories are then divided into task-related and social emotions. Task-related emotions are further divided into *process* (doing the task), *prospective* (anticipating outcomes or consequences), and *retrospective* (evaluating accomplishments). Social emotions are those that reflect the social context within which the job is performed. Each of these different categories has both positive and negative emotions associated with it. For example, among prospective task-related emotions, hope would be positive and anxiety negative.

The approaches advocated by Lazarus and by Pekrun and Frese should not be seen as being in competition with each other. Both reflect efforts to provide structure to a field of study that has received limited attention from job stress researchers. Another approach (Rafaeli & Sutton, 1987) is to focus on those emotions displayed in satisfying role expectations and to classify these emotions according to whether they are positive or negative, and esteem enhancing or esteem degrading. Irrespective of how different schemas for classifying emotions are constructed, it is clear that the role of emotions in the stress-coping process and the management of job-related stress requires more systematic attention than it has received to date.

Conclusion

Despite the large number of physiological, psychological, and behavioral measures available, researchers have paid only moderate attention to delineating the strain side of stress transactions. A main reason for this is that "being under stress" has a wide variety of meanings, and to some extent almost any negative reaction could be considered as "strain." To advance our understanding of work-related stress, it is time to consider the context within which different measures are being used and whether what is assessed captures the essence of the encounter being experienced. These are issues to reflect upon in Chapter 4, where we discuss burnout, an extreme form of job-related strain, and in Chapter 5, where we examine moderators of stressor-strain relationships.

One major theme emerging from a review of empirical work in this field is that researchers must consider the appropriateness of the type(s) of strain being measured and should specify which strains might be anticipated in different contexts, rather than simply selecting a strain on the basis that it can be classified as one or another form of strain. Focusing more attention on the nature of the person-environment transaction and, in particular, the nature of events confronted by individuals in their work setting would enable researchers to develop more coherent (and comprehensive) theories concerning the linkages between encounters and anticipated strains. It is necessary to move, as Kahn and Byosiere (1992) have, from generic categories of strains to more detailed descriptions that identify whether, for example, strains are acute or chronic, whether they reflect over- or understimulation, and whether they reflect general or more specific feelings.

The issue of "fit" between stressors and strains also means that researchers must take into account the conceptual overlap between measures of stressors and strain, conducting research that probes the meaning of these measures (to respondents), along with their construct and discriminant validity. This type of research would generate a clearer understanding of the nature of, and distinctions between, stressor and strain variables, as well as providing a framework for determining the appropriateness of strain measures. As suggested by Travers and Cooper (1994), a test battery approach, including behavioral, physiological, and psychological indicators of strain, has considerable merit in the context of job stress investigations. Similarly, inclusion of multiple "outcomes" in job stress research would enable researchers to explore the range of effects that a particular stressor, or set of stressors, might induce, and it would go some way toward addressing the criticism that job stress research has often adopted too narrow a focus when it comes to measuring strains in the workplace (Newton, 1989).

It is not just a question of "fit" between stressors and strain. There is also the question of the relationship across different types of strain. Research exploring the relationship between different strains may well begin to push us toward considering them in terms of notions like risk factors and whether the experience of one strain may make individuals more vulnerable to other types of strain. For example, what are the long-term consequences of job dissatisfaction? Would having a clearer understanding of this help to clarify its impact on health and well-being and provide a context for considering its role as a likely risk factor, thus enabling researchers to reevaluate the significance of such a measure? As our understanding of the stressor-strain relationship improves, it may be time to consider the role of different strain measures and the utility of thinking of them more in terms of notions like risk, vulnerability, and health, in much the same way as we have applied terms like *chronic* and *episodic* to stressors. This type of research would certainly require a test battery approach involving the careful selection of measures, the use of both psychological and physiological measures, and the use of methods like structural equation modeling and longitudinal design.

A further issue to consider is the significance or importance to research participants themselves of some of the variables currently designated as strains in job stress investigations. For instance, earlier we referred to the frequent inclusion of job dissatisfaction as a strain variable without first determining whether the job occupies an important niche in the individual's self-concept and hence whether dissatisfaction in this domain has any significant bearing on the person's overall well-being (see Brief & George, 1991). Similarly, more research is needed on the conditions under which environmental events are perceived as positive challenges versus negative stressors and on when a challenge becomes a stressor. For example, one of the most frequently studied organizational stressors is role ambiguity, which has been found in numerous studies to be positively correlated with a variety of strain variables (see Chapter 3). Despite this pervasive finding, however, there are circumstances in which a certain degree of ambiguity might be valued by individuals, especially those whose tolerance for uncertainty is high (O'Driscoll & Beehr, 2000). This suggests that, rather than assuming that variables such as role ambiguity have uniformly negative impact on people, stress researchers should further investigate the situational and personal moderators of the ambiguity-strain relationship and spend more time exploring the process by which ambiguity and other stressors influence individual well-being, not just the magnitude of the correlation between stressors and strains.

As we have illustrated earlier, the role of emotions in workplace stress needs more systematic attention from researchers. Two conclusions clearly emerge from a review of the organizational behavior literature: (a) Emotions are fundamental to an understanding of stress, as well as other responses; and (b) our knowledge of their functioning in work settings is extremely limited (Wright & Doherty, 1998). From a research perspective, this means that it is imperative to "understand real-time feelings and emotions, rather than the abstract and non-specific ratings gathered in studies of stress and satisfaction" (Briner, 1995a, p. 12). Identifying the meaning of emotions to individuals, specifying the links between specific emotions and environmental events, and delineating the conditions under which particular emotions fu nction as moderators of stressor-strain relationships are high-priority issues for future investigations of job-related stress. As an extension to these suggestions, it would be valuable for researchers to explore the emotional costs associated with work, including what Fineman (1995) has referred to as the consequences of *explicit feeling rules*—"the impact on the individual when the tension between inner feelings and required emotions becomes too great" (p. 129)—and *implicit feeling rules*—adapting "required feelings" so that they are better managed, and having to deal with the emotional cost of that adaptation.

Finally, there is the issue of objective or subjective measurement. This is not simply an issue of replacing one set of measures by another. The consensus seems to be that more research is needed "in order to determine the quality of measures, regardless of whether they are self report or not" (Jex & Beehr, 1991, p. 352; see also Travers & Cooper, 1994). Strain measures need to be evaluated on their own merits. The empirical evidence presented by Jex and Beehr (1991, pp. 350-352) suggests that although common-method variance may be a problem with self-report measures of strain, that in itself is not a basis to dismiss all such measures or the relationships they produce. The message that we should take from the objective-subjective debate is that each method comes with its own set of difficulties and that consequently measurement should be taken seriously. Irrespective of the measurement approach, problems will always emerge from measures that are poorly developed or not well understood. Therefore, researchers are faced with two priorities. The first is to focus on issues of measurement exploring scale properties to establish their psychometric properties, what such scales are measuring, and the relationship between different measures. The second priority is to take the test battery idea discussed by Travers and Cooper (1994) and further explore the relationships between objective and subjective measures, their predictive abilities, and the utility of juxtaposing objective and subjective methodologies.

The issues raised in this chapter are no different from those presented in other chapters in this book. They all require that researchers give careful consideration to the context within which job stress encounters take place, particularly the processes that link different components. They also require new and innovative ways of thinking about what is being measured, whether measures capture the essence of the variable under investigation, and the meaning behind the measures. In this way, new directions can be identified, creative measurement strategies can be put in place, and research will make a constructive contribution to the creation and maintenance of healthy work environments.

References

Ashforth, B. E., & Humphrey, R. H. (1993). Emotional labor in service roles: The influence of identity. *Academy of Management Review, 18,* 88-115.

Brief, A. P., & Atieh, J. M. (1987). Studying job stress: Are we making mountains out of molehills? *Journal of Organizational Behavior, 8,* 115-126.

Brief, A. P., & George, J. M. (1991). Psychological stress and the workplace: A brief comment on Lazarus' outlook. *Journal of Social Behavior and Personality, 6,* 15-20.

Briner, R. B. (1995a, April). *Beyond stress and satisfaction: Understanding and managing emotions at work.* Paper presented at the 1995 EAWOP Conference, Györ, Hungary.

Briner, R. B. (1995b, April). *The experience and expression of emotion at work.* Paper presented at the 1995 British Psychological Society Occupational Psychology Conference, Warwick, UK.

Diener, E., Suh, E., Lucas, R., & Smith, H. (1999). Subjective well-being: Three decades of progress. *Psychological Bulletin, 125,* 276-302.

Fineman, S. (1995). Stress, emotions and intervention. In T. Newton (Ed.), *Managing stress: Emotion and power at work* (pp. 120-135). Thousand Oaks, CA: Sage.

Fox, M. L., Dwyer, D. J., & Ganster, D. C. (1993). Effects of stressful job demands and control on physiological and attitudinal outcomes in a hospital setting. *Academy of Management Journal, 36,* 289-318.

Fried, Y., Rowland, K. M., & Ferris, G. R. (1984). The physiological measurement of work stress: A critique. *Personnel Psychology, 37,* 583-615.

Frone, M., Russell, M., & Cooper, M. (1995). Job stressors, job involvement and employee health: A test of identity theory. *Journal of Occupational and Organizational Psychology, 68,* 1-11.

Hochschild, A. R. (1983). *The managed heart: Commercialization of human feeling.* Berkeley: University of California Press.

Jackson, S. E., & Schuler, R. S. (1985). A meta-analysis and conceptual critique of research on role ambiguity and role conflict in work settings. *Organizational Behavior and Human Decision Processes, 36,* 16-78.

Jex, S. M., & Beehr, T. A. (1991). Emerging theoretical and methodological issues in the study of work-related stress. *Research in Personnel and Human Resources Management, 9,* 311-365.

Kahn, R. L., & Byosiere, P. (1992). Stress in organizations. In M. D. Dunnette (Ed.), *Handbook of industrial and organizational psychology* (pp. 571-648). Chicago: Rand McNally.

Lazarus, R. S. (1993). From psychological stress to the emotions: A history of changing outlooks. *American Review of Psychology, 44,* 1-21.

Lazarus, R. S. (1995). Vexing research problems inherent in cognitive-mediational theories of emotion—and some solutions. *Psychological Inquiry, 6,* 183-196.

McLaren, S. (1997). Heart rate and blood pressure in male police officers and clerical workers on workday and non-workdays. *Work and Stress, 11,* 160-174.

Newton, T. J. (1989). Occupational stress and coping with stress. *Human Relations, 38,* 107-126.

O'Driscoll, M., & Beehr, T. (2000). Moderating effects of perceived control and need for clarity on the relationship between role stressors and employee affective reactions. *Journal of Social Psychology, 140,* 151-159.

Pekrun, R., & Frese, M. (1992). Emotions in work and achievement. *International Review of Industrial and Organizational Psychology, 7,* 153-200.

Rafaeli, A., & Sutton, R. I. (1987). Expressions of emotions as part of the work role. *Academy of Management Review, 12,* 23-37.

Schaubroeck, J., & Ganster, D. C. (1993) Chronic demand and responsivity to challenge. *Journal of Applied Psychology, 78,* 73-85.

Travers, C. J., & Cooper, C. L. (1994). Psychophysiological responses to teacher's stress: A move towards more objective methodologies. *European Review of Applied Psychology, 44,* 137-146.

Wright, T. A., & Doherty, E. M. (1998). Organizational behavior "rediscovers" the role of emotional well-being. *Journal of Organizational Behavior, 19,* 481-485.

4 A Special Form of Strain

JOB-RELATED BURNOUT

The phenomenon of burnout was first identified by Bradley (1969) in a paper on probation officers and was further elaborated upon by Freudenberger (1974) from his observations of the extreme psychological strain often experienced by workers in the human service professions, such as nurses, police officers, social workers, and schoolteachers. Since that time, there have been numerous studies of this extreme and specific manifestation of job-related strain. For instance, Schulz, Greenley, and Brown (1995) estimated that 2,500 papers had been published on job burnout over a 20-year period, primarily among human service professionals but increasingly in other areas of employment also. Given the widespread attention given to burnout in recent years in both academic and applied publications and the popular media, along with the very severe consequences of burnout for individuals and their organizations, we believe that this issue warrants separate consideration from other forms of job-related strain.

Our discussion of this construct is couched within the overall framework of the transactional model described in Chapter 1 because burnout, like other manifestations of strain, is a product of the inter-action between environmental factors (demands) and individual percep-tions and behaviors (such as coping). As we have outlined earlier in this volume, stress does not reside solely within the environment or within the individual but results from the dynamic transactions that occur between these elements. The same overarching framework needs to be applied when considering the unique variety of strain known as burnout.

In this chapter, therefore, we will examine the concept of burnout, alternative theoretical models of burnout development, various methods for measuring levels of job-related burnout, and some of the major antecedents and consequences of this unique form of job strain. Finally, we will discuss the generality of burnout beyond human service occu-pations and consider its cross-cultural relevance. Chapters 6 and 7 explore strategies for combating strain, including burnout.

Maslach (1993), a foremost contributor to the study of burnout, noted that it "is now recognized as an important social and individual problem" (p. 19). Similarly, Cordes and Dougherty (1993) suggested that there is substantial empirical evidence that job-related burnout carries significant costs for individual well-being and organizational functioning, including personal ill health, absenteeism, turnover, and reduced productivity. Hobfoll and Shirom (1993) have also highlighted some of the health-related consequences of excessive strain and burnout, especially cardiovascular and coronary heart disease, drug and alcohol abuse, and accidents (see also Chapter 3 of this book). We will examine some of the specific outcomes of burnout a little later in this chapter. Suffice it to say that, as with strain generally, there is considerable concern over the negative impact that burnout can have on individual employees and organizations.

As previously mentioned, early research on this topic concentrated on employees in the helping occupations, especially health care profession-als, and attempted to identify the extent and pervasiveness of burnout in these occupational groups, as well as some of the possible causes of burnout. This line of research has continued, but in recent years atten-tion has also been given to nonservice occupations, including managers and supervisors, the military, and various other employee groups. Toward the end of this chapter, we consider the generalizability of the burnout construct beyond the helping professions.

Definition

One difficulty in studying burnout is the wide variety of definitions of this concept. In their review of burnout research, Cordes and Dougherty (1993) summarized various conceptualizations of the term, including

> (a) to fail, wear out, become exhausted; (b) a loss of creativity; (c) a loss of commitment for work; (d) an estrangement from clients, co-workers, job, and agency; (e) a response to the chronic stress of making it to the top; and finally (f) a syndrome of inappropriate attitudes toward clients and toward self, often associated with uncomfortable physical and emotional symptoms. (p. 623)

These definitions have common threads, but they also carry some differing connotations.

Burke and Richardsen (1993) have provided a valuable summary of four distinct definitions. The first definition is that offered by Freudenberger and Richelson (1980), who described burnout in terms of chronic fatigue, depression, and frustration, typically engendered by commitment to undertakings that did not realize the person's ambitions and expected rewards. Although this conceptualization incorporates some of the key elements of the burnout phenomenon, it is problematical because it confounds burnout with variables that are normally considered as distinct from, although related to, burnout—especially depression and chronic fatigue. Depression should be differentiated from burnout, in that the former refers to a particular psychological condition that should be regarded as a potential outcome of burnout rather than as part of the burnout syndrome itself.

Similarly, it is important to differentiate burnout from fatigue. Though some authors (e.g., Shirom, 1989) include physical fatigue as part of the burnout syndrome, the latter clearly encompasses much more than fatigue. Individuals may experience physical (and even cognitive) weariness as a result of being overloaded in their jobs, but in our view this is not equivalent to burnout. As outlined by Hobfoll and Shirom (1993), the medical condition known as chronic fatigue syndrome (CFS) refers to long-term physical exhaustion associated with an imbalance between demands from the environment and a person's ability to cope with those demands and is characterized by tiredness or lethargy, impairment of one's activities and performance, and a general depletion of energy resources. These features are shared with, and may be precursors of, burnout as it is operationalized in the stress literature. However, burnout encompasses emotional (as well as physical and cognitive) exhaustion, especially that emanating from dealing with "people problems," whereas CFS may arise simply from work overload. Furthermore, the medical literature on CFS tends to ascribe this condition to dispositional factors within the person, whereas research findings over the last 20 years have illustrated few significant personality or dispositional correlates of burnout (Burke & Richardsen, 1993). (As a possible exception to this conclusion, later we will consider arguments put forward by Garden [1989, 1991], who has suggested that certain personality types are more prone to the experience of burnout.)

The second definition of burnout presented by Burke and Richardsen (1993) is that of Cherniss (1980), who described it as a process of disengagement in response to job-related stressors. Imbalance between job demands and available resources leads to an emotional response characterized by anxiety, tension, fatigue, and strain (or exhaustion). This response in turn produces changes in the individual's attitudes and behavior, including defensive coping (preoccupation with gratifying one's own needs) and depersonalization (a cynical detachment from clients and their problems).

A third definition of burnout is that proposed by Pines and her colleagues (Pines & Aronson, 1988; Pines, Aronson, & Kafry, 1981), who describe it as "a state of physical, emotional and mental exhaustion caused by long-term involvement in situations that are emotionally demanding" (Pines & Aronson, 1988, p. 9). Initially, Pines and her colleagues referred to the above as "burnout" when applied to human service workers and as "tedium" when applied to nonservice occupations (Shirom, 1989). However, this distinction does not seem entirely appropriate, and it is arguable whether the above offers an accurate characterization of tedium. In their more recent writings, Pines and Aronson did not distinguish between tedium and burnout.

In the late 1970s and early 1980s, systematic investigations of burnout led to greater communality in definitions. At that time, Christina Maslach and her colleagues (Maslach, 1982; Maslach & Jackson, 1981) conceptualized burnout as having three core components: emotional exhaustion, depersonalization, and (lack of) personal accomplishment.

Maslach's model of burnout characterizes emotional exhaustion as a depletion of emotional energy and a feeling that one's emotional resources are inadequate to deal with the situation. This emotional exhaustion may also be linked with physical fatigue and cognitive "weariness."

The second component of burnout, according to Maslach, is a tendency toward *depersonalization* of other individuals in the work setting (e.g., clients, patients, or even coworkers)—that is, treatment of them as objects rather than people. Although this may help to reduce intense emotional arousal, which can interfere with functioning in crisis situations, excessive detachment from others can produce a callous and cynical approach to their welfare (Jackson, Schwab, & Schuler, 1986). Finally, the third component of burnout in Maslach's formulation is diminished *personal accomplishment,* characterized by a tendency to evaluate one's behavior and performance negatively. As a result, the person experiences feelings of incompetence on the job and an inability to achieve performance goals.

The above three-component conceptualization is the most widely accepted model of burnout (O'Driscoll & Cooper, 1996), partly at least because Maslach and her associates constructed an easy-to-use questionnaire (the Maslach Burnout Inventory [MBI]) to measure the three dimensions of burnout (see the section "Measurement of Burnout" later in this chapter). More recently, Maslach and her colleagues (Maslach, Jackson, & Leiter, 1996) have developed a definition and measure of burnout that is intended to generalize beyond human service occupations. This new formulation retains the original emotional exhaustion dimension, although it extends the sources of exhaustion beyond problems with people (especially clients). However, the new characterization substitutes *cynicism* for *depersonalization* and *professional efficacy* for *personal accomplishment.* Whereas *depersonalization* refers specifically to relationships with other people, cynicism represents indifference or a "distant" attitude toward work generally, which may (or may not) include people encountered in the context of the job. "Cynicism represents dysfunctional coping ... in that [it] reduces the energy available for performing work and for developing creative solutions to the problems work presents" (Leiter & Schaufeli, 1996, p. 231). Like depersonalization, cynicism is expected to correlate positively with emotional exhaustion. Finally, professional efficacy is a similar construct to personal accomplishment but has "a broader focus, encompassing both social and nonsocial aspects of occupational accomplishments ... and explicitly assesses an individual's expectations of continued effectiveness at work" (Leiter & Schaufeli, 1996, p. 232).

As we shall see later, there is some controversy over the inclusion of depersonalization (or cynicism) and reduced personal accomplishment (or professional efficacy) as core components of burnout, with some investigators (e.g., Evans & Fischer, 1993; Koeske & Koeske, 1989, 1993; Lee & Ashforth, 1993a) suggesting that they may be separate, albeit related, variables. This distinction is important because (at least initially) Maslach argued that the term *burnout* should be reserved for human service occupations, where depersonalization in particular may be a prevalent response to excessive demands from clients or patients, whereas more recently she and other researchers have proposed that burnout may generalize to nonservice occupations and hence that emotional exhaustion is the key construct. We return to this debate later.

A further issue of relevance here is the temporal development of burnout. Golembiewski and Munzenrider (1988) distinguished between acute and chronic onset of burnout. In their view, acute onset occurs with a sudden momentous negative event, such as job loss or demotion. Golembiewski and Munzenrider suggested that this might catapult the individual into a traumatized condition. Hobfoll and Shirom (1993) referred to this as *episodic* strain because these stressors appear from time to time but are not ongoing. Chronic burnout, on the other hand, results from progressively worsening conditions at work, such as might be experienced with an increasingly heavy client caseload or having to deal with incessant and unremitting client problems. Most conceptualizations of the construct refer to burnout as a reaction to chronic or ongoing demands from the job (Hobfoll & Shirom, 1993; Westman & Eden, 1997; Zohar, 1997), involving the progressive development of emotional exhaustion (and perhaps other responses) as a result of ongoing, and seemingly insurmountable, job-related problems or demands.

To summarize, the term *burnout* refers to an extreme state of psychological strain and depletion of energy resources arising from prolonged exposure to stressors that exceed the person's resources to cope, particularly stressors associated with human resource professions, although it may also develop in other occupational groups. According to the prevailing viewpoint (e.g., Evans & Fischer, 1993; Koeske & Koeske, 1993; Lee & Ashforth, 1996), the major component of burnout is emotional exhaustion, and there has been considerable dispute over the role of Maslach's two additional dimensions, depersonalization (or cynicism) and reduced personal accomplishment (or professional efficacy). Later in this chapter, we will reflect further on the adequacy of current conceptualizations of burnout. Finally, whereas psychological strain may result from both episodic and chronic stressors, burnout probably develops over an extended time period and, accordingly, tends to be more difficult to eliminate than other forms of job-related strain.

The Development of Burnout

Along with the variety of definitions, several theories of the development of burnout have been proposed. In the main, these theories build upon the three-dimensional model of burnout proposed by Maslach and her colleagues, although there is considerable debate about the centrality of each component and the chain of events in burnout development. Four major developmental models will be discussed here, along with a more overarching theory of burnout proposed by Hobfoll and Freedy (1993).

Cherniss's Model of Burnout

One of the earliest theories about how burnout develops was advanced in 1980 by Cherniss, from research conducted among novice professionals in the fields of mental health, poverty, law, public health nursing, and teaching. His process model is illustrated in Figure 4.1 (adapted from Burke & Richardsen, 1993).

Cherniss suggested that aspects of the work environment and characteristics of the individual can both function as sources of strain: for example, by creating doubts in the person's mind about his or her competence, bureaucratic interference with task completion or goal achievement, and lack of collegial coworker relationships. Individuals endeavor to cope with these stressors in a variety of ways, some of which may entail negative attitude changes, including reducing work goals, taking less responsibility for work outcomes, becoming less idealistic in one's approach to the job, and becoming detached from clients or the job itself. Together, these negative attitude changes constitute Cherniss's definition of the burnout phenomenon. A number of studies have explored

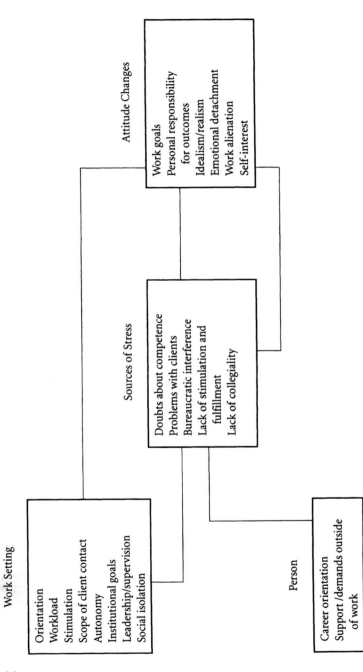

Figure 4.1. Cherniss's Process Model of Burnout

SOURCE: Reprinted from "Psychological Burnout in Organizations" (p. 269), by R. Burke & A. Richardsen, in *Handbook of Organizational Behavior*, edited by R. Golembiewski, 1993, New York: Marcel Dekker, by courtesy of Marcel Dekker Inc.

Cherniss's view of burnout and have provided some support for this conceptualization. In particular, Burke and Greenglass (1995) found that work setting characteristics such as inadequate induction, lack of autonomy, work overload, poor leadership and supervision, and unclear goals contributed to negative attitude changes among a sample of teachers, school department heads, and principals.

A potential limitation of Cherniss's theory, however, is its overinclusiveness. By equating burnout with "negative attitude changes," it incorporates a wide range of potential variables under the heading of burnout. This may make burnout indistinguishable from job strain more generally and certainly does not identify the principal characteristics or uniqueness of burnout. Hence, although Burke and others have argued the merits of this model of burnout development, we believe that Cherniss's definition of the concept itself is perhaps too broad to identify burnout as a separate construct.

Golembiewski's Phase Model

A more widely known theory of how burnout develops is the phase model proposed by Golembiewski and colleagues (Golembiewski & Munzenrider, 1984, 1988; Golembiewski, Munzenrider, & Stevenson, 1986). Golembiewski and his colleagues adopted the Maslach three-component model of burnout but claimed that the second component in that model, depersonalization, is the aspect that is first experienced in the sequence. They contended that a certain amount of professional detachment is functional when dealing with clients or patients in a professional manner and that this detachment is reinforced by the ethics and norms of the profession. However, when role demands and pressures reach a certain level, this detachment can be transformed into depersonalization as the individual strives to deal with demands that go beyond his or her coping capacity.

In Golembiewski's view, depersonalization is therefore the first manifestation of burnout and has the effect of impairing performance, especially because the person recognizes an inconsistency between his or her treatment of clients and the precepts and ethics of the profession (e.g., caring for people's problems). As a result, the individual's sense of personal achievement on the job is jeopardized. According to Golembiewski's theory, reduced personal accomplishment is the second phase in the development of burnout.

Finally, increasing depersonalization and the diminished sense of accomplishment in turn lead to the development of emotional exhaustion, as the strain associated with the first two elements surpasses the person's coping ability. Emotional exhaustion, therefore, has the most potency and represents the end stage of burnout development in the Golembiewski model.

Consistent with the above formulation of how burnout emerges, Golembiewski and his associates constructed a phase model of burnout that illustrates various stages in the development of this form of stress among individuals. This phase model is depicted in Table 4.1, which shows eight phases of burnout. A person may be categorized as high or low on each of the three dimensions of burnout and can then be assigned to one of the eight levels. Phase I represents a low level of burnout in that depersonalization and emotional exhaustion are barely present and the individual has a high sense of personal accomplishment on the job. Phases II and III reflect first the appearance of depersonalization, then a reduction in feelings of personal accomplishment. Phase IV includes both of these symptoms of burnout. Emotional exhaustion, on the other hand, does not appear until Phase V but is present in all phases thereafter. The progression of burnout is strongly associated with the development of emotional exhaustion. In essence, the phase model assumes that burnout becomes more virulent as the individual progresses through depersonalization to reduced personal accomplishment to emotional exhaustion and that individuals in more advanced phases will experience more serious consequences than those in earlier phases (Golembiewski, Scherb, & Boudreau, 1993).

Although the phases are developmental, Golembiewski et al. (1993) indicated that their model does not imply that a particular person will necessarily proceed through all eight phases. For instance, it does not appear likely that a person would move from Phase II to Phase III when the former includes high levels of depersonalization whereas the latter does not. In these cases, it is more likely that the person would skip a phase in the process of burnout development.

Herein lies some inconsistency in the notion of phases in burnout development. Although the chain of events from depersonalization → (reduced) personal accomplishment → emotional exhaustion has intuitive appeal, and although the argument can be tested empirically, the phase levels depicted in Table 4.1 are not totally consistent with the

Table 4.1   Golembiewski Phase Model of Burnout

Phase	Depersonalization	Personal Accomplishment (reversed)	Emotional Exhaustion
I	Low	Low	Low
II	High	Low	Low
III	Low	High	Low
IV	High	High	Low
V	Low	Low	High
VI	High	Low	High
VII	Low	High	High
VIII	High	High	High

SOURCE: Reproduced with permission from Leiter, M. (1993). Burnout as a developmental process: Consideration of models. In W. Schaufeli, C. Maslach, and T. Marek (Eds.) *Professional burnout: Recent developments in theory and research*, page 241. Washington, DC: Taylor & Francis.

development process suggested by Golembiewski. For example, in Phase VII emotional exhaustion is high even though depersonalization is low. Similarly, Phase VI shows high emotional exhaustion despite elevated levels of personal accomplishment, which supposedly is a precursor of emotional exhaustion.

The Golembiewski phase approach has also been queried by Leiter (1993), who noted that although the eight phases of the model simplify the process of categorizing individuals as high or low in burnout, in effect this perspective reduces the role of depersonalization and personal accomplishment because the critical element is emotional exhaustion. Leiter also questioned whether the eight phases would adequately capture the complexity of the burnout phenomenon. A similar query has been voiced by Burke (1989), who reported studies using three or four phases rather than the full eight proposed by Golembiewski and associates. These studies collapsed some of the phases together: for example, I to III, IV and V, and VI to VIII. Burke suggested that use of fewer phases may provide a way of resolving questions about where individuals can enter the burnout process and transition from one phase to another. This recommendation does not, however, address the issue raised by Leiter (1993).

Empirically, the Golembiewski phase model has received mixed support. Golembiewski et al. (1993) reported that there is considerable evidence in favor of this perspective. Despite some reservations about the utility of the full eight-phase model, Burke and colleagues (Burke, 1989; Burke & Richardsen, 1993) have also cited evidence in support of the phase model. In contrast, Lee and Ashforth (1993b) conducted a longitudinal investigation that illustrated greater support for an alternative perspective, the Leiter and Maslach (1988) model (which is outlined below). From a meta-analysis of the correlates of burnout, Lee and Ashforth (1996) also obtained results that are more consistent with Leiter's (1993) proposal that personal accomplishment develops relatively independently of emotional exhaustion and depersonalization, rather than being a consequence of the latter variable.

In summary, the Golembiewski phase model offers an insightful portrayal of the process of burnout development and contains an inherent logic about the relationship between the three major components of burnout, plus a relatively simple procedure for categorizing individuals along the burnout continuum. However, the conceptual difficulties noted above and evidence from empirical research do not entirely confirm the validity of this perspective.

Leiter and Maslach's Model of Burnout Development

An alternative to Golembiewski's conceptualization of burnout development is the perspective initially proposed by Leiter and Maslach (1988) and later modified by Leiter (1991, 1993). Leiter and Maslach argued, as did Golembiewski, that emotional exhaustion is the critical component in the burnout process. However, in contrast to Golembiewski, these authors contended that emotional exhaustion develops first in that process rather than as the final stage of burnout.

The original Leiter and Maslach (1988) model is displayed in Figure 4.2. Stressors from jobs that have high interpersonal contact with clients or other individuals with significant problems lead to emotional exhaustion on the part of the human service worker. This emotional exhaustion then induces depersonalization as workers attempt to cope or deal with their feelings of exhaustion. Depersonalization is essentially a coping response that is called upon when other forms of coping (e.g., changing the demands from the job) have not succeeded in alleviating the amount of strain experienced. However, as depersonalization occurs, the individual begins to lose a sense of accomplishment on the job because the very act of depersonalizing clients undermines his or

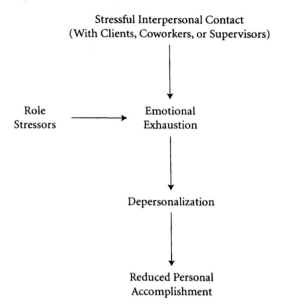

Stressful Interpersonal Contact
(With Clients, Coworkers, or Supervisors)

Role Stressors ⟶ Emotional Exhaustion

Depersonalization

Reduced Personal Accomplishment

Figure 4.2. Leiter and Maslach's (1988) Model of the Burnout Process

SOURCE: From "Burnout as a Developmental Process: Consideration of Models" (pp. 241, 245), by M. Leiter, in *Professional Burnout: Recent Developments in Theory and Research*, by W. Schaufeli, C. Maslach, and T. Marek, (Eds.), 1993, Washington, DC: Taylor & Francis. Copyright 1993 by Taylor & Francis. Reprinted with permission.

her professional values and goals. Put another way, depersonalization mediates the relationship between emotional exhaustion and reduced personal accomplishment.

As already noted, Leiter (1991, 1993) has generated a modified version of the above model based upon structural equations modeling of the burnout process. For example, Lee and Ashforth (1993a, 1993b) observed that emotional exhaustion and depersonalization shared several correlates (e.g., role stressors) but that these correlates were only marginally linked with reduced personal accomplishment. Similarly, there appears to be a stronger association between exhaustion and depersonalization than between these two variables and personal accomplishment (Lee & Ashforth, 1993a). It seems that the relationship of personal accomplishment with the two other burnout dimensions may be explained better by their shared relationship with other variables, particularly the extent of resources available to the person in the work environment, such as the amount of social support and skill utilization (Leiter, 1991).

Reflecting on these findings, Leiter (1993) reformulated the relationship between personal accomplishment and the two other factors. He depicted depersonalization as a direct function of emotional exhaustion but suggested that personal accomplishment may develop independently of both emotional exhaustion and depersonalization:

> In general, the model proposes that demanding aspects of the environment (e.g., workload, personal conflict, hassles) aggravate exhaustion, which in turn contributes to increased depersonalization, while the presence of resources (social support, opportunities for skill enhancement) influences personal accomplishment. For the most part, these two aspects of burnout have distinct predictors, although some conditions, such as coping styles, appear to contribute to both exhaustion and diminished accomplishment. (Leiter, 1993, p. 245)

In short, (reduced) personal accomplishment develops in parallel with emotional exhaustion, rather than sequentially via depersonalization.

Evidence supporting Leiter's revised model has been reported by Lee and Ashforth (1996) in a meta-analysis of the correlates of burnout, in which they examined demands and resources in relation to each of the three burnout components. Using the conservation-of-resources theory of job stress developed by Hobfoll and colleagues (Hobfoll, 1989; Hobfoll & Freedy, 1993), which is outlined next, Lee and Ashforth (1996) found that emotional exhaustion and depersonalization were strongly correlated with organizational commitment and turnover intentions, whereas these variables were only weakly related to personal accomplishment. On the other hand, control coping (which is parallel to Lazarus and Folkman's [1984] notion of problem-focused coping; see Chapter 6 of this book) was more closely linked with personal accomplishment than with either exhaustion or depersonalization.

To summarize, empirical support for the Leiter and Maslach (1988) model of burnout development, particularly Leiter's (1993) reformulation of that model, has been obtained in recent research, and it seems plausible that emotional exhaustion should be considered as the initial outcome of excessive and chronic job demands and pressures. Depersonalization (or cynicism) would appear to be a response adopted by workers as they endeavor to cope with this exhaustion. Finally, (reduced) personal accomplishment (or professional efficacy) may be regarded as a separate element in the process that can be influenced by emotional exhaustion but is also dependent upon other factors in the work environment, as well as the person's use of coping strategies (especially control coping).

Conservation of Resources Theory

Hobfoll and his colleagues (Hobfoll, 1989; Hobfoll & Freedy, 1993; Hobfoll & Shirom, 1993) have constructed a general perspective on stress that has particular relevance to burnout in work organizations, is very compatible with Lazarus and Folkman's (1984) transactional model of stress coping, and has been used as a framework for recent empirical research in the field of burnout. Their conservation of resources (COR) theory postulates that individuals have access to four major categories of resources: objects (e.g., a house, a car), conditions (e.g., a steady job), personal characteristics (e.g., self-esteem), and various forms of energy (e.g., money, favors owed by other persons).

The basic tenet of COR theory is that stress occurs when individuals are threatened with a loss of resources, actually lose those resources, or fail to (re)gain resources after they have been invested. Hence, events such as the loss of one's job, impaired health, and breakdown in a personal relationship are serious forms of resource loss. Although these traumatic events sometimes may be compensated by a resource gain (such as finding a better job), in many cases there is a net loss of resources, which produces strain for the individual.

In essence, COR theory proposes that burnout can occur when valued resources are lost, are inadequate to meet the demands confronted by the person, or do not generate expected returns on investment (Lee & Ashforth, 1996), producing a downward spiral in energy loss for the individual. In a work situation, some of the major resources available to workers are social support (from their colleagues, supervisors, and others), personal control over their job, involvement in important decision-making processes, and appropriate reward systems (Burke & Richardsen, 1993). Major demands that might bring about resource loss include role ambiguity and conflict, role overload, inadequate resources to perform the job, and unremitting demands from clients or other people in the work environment. Chronic strain or burnout can arise when there is a significant and ongoing draining of one's resources, particularly as individuals strive to meet the above or other demands on their energy. According to Hobfoll and Shirom (1993), burnout results from "a process of wearing out and wearing down of a person's energy . . . or the combination of physical fatigue, emotional exhaustion and cognitive wearout that develops gradually over time" (p. 50). At the advanced stages of burnout, the person develops a sense of helplessness (to address the situation), hopelessness (for any improvement), and depression.

COR theory is pitched at a more general (and abstract) level than the other models outlined here and, as mentioned above, accords well with the transactional approach. Rather than providing a specific model of burnout itself, it focuses on the general conditions under which job-related strain and burnout arise. Nevertheless, it offers a conceptual framework of principles that can underpin other approaches, such as the Leiter and Maslach model. COR theory also highlights the environmental factors that may contribute to burnout development. Before addressing the antecedents and potential consequences of burnout, however, we will examine methods used to assess and measure the extent of burnout experienced by individuals in their workplaces.

Measurement of Burnout

As with all other constructs, measurement is a critical issue in the study of burnout. Early work in this field was based primarily on observations of human service workers (Freudenberger, 1974), but in the late 1970s efforts were directed toward the development of questionnaires to assess self-reported levels of burnout. Two questionnaire measures have figured prominently in the research literature: the Maslach Burnout Inventory (MBI; Maslach & Jackson, 1981, 1986; Maslach, Jackson, & Leiter, 1996) and the Burnout Index (BI; Pines, Aronson, & Kafry, 1981).

Maslach Burnout Inventory

By far the most widely employed measure of burnout is the Maslach Burnout Inventory (MBI; Maslach & Jackson, 1981, 1986), which was initially developed to gauge levels of burnout specifically among human service professionals but in 1996 was modified for use with other occupations. The original MBI is a self-report questionnaire containing 22 items, divided into the three subscales described earlier: emotional exhaustion (9 items), depersonalization (5 items), and (reduced) personal accomplishment (8 items). In the 1981 version of the questionnaire, respondents were asked to report both frequency (*never* to *every day*) and intensity (*very mild* to *very strong*) for each item. However, though some researchers (e.g., Brookings, Bolton, Brown, & McEvoy, 1985; O'Driscoll & Schubert, 1988) have investigated both frequency and intensity of burnout, typically a high correlation between these indices has been obtained, and most studies have assessed the frequency dimension only. The 1986 modification of the MBI excluded the intensity dimension.

Exploratory factor analyses of the three MBI scales have tended to support the construct validity of the instrument, as well as its convergent and discriminant validity (Burke & Richardsen, 1993; Cordes & Dougherty, 1993), although Walkey and Green (1992) observed that emotional exhaustion and depersonalization may merge into a single factor. Confirmatory factor analyses have questioned the factor structure of the MBI and the reliability of particular items in the questionnaire. For example, although Lee and Ashforth (1990) obtained a three-factor structure in their CFA investigation of burnout among human service supervisors and managers, Evans and Fischer (1993) found three clear factors in a sample of teachers, but "depersonalization indicators did not form a coherent or meaningful factor for the sample of computer company employees" (p. 35). Byrne (1991) and Yadama and Drake (1995) also failed to support the original three-factor model of the MBI and explored respecifications of the instrument to obtain a better fit. These respecifications entailed removal of some items and correlation of error terms for other items.

Schaufeli and van Dierondonck (1993) compared the construct validity of the MBI and the BI. As noted above, their data did not illustrate a single dimension for the BI, although they did obtain some support for a three-dimensional MBI. Like Byrne (1991) and Yadama and Drake (1995), however, Schaufeli and van Dierondonck noted specification errors in their model, with some factors loading onto common items, suggesting lack of factor independence.

More recently, Kalliath, Gillespie, O'Driscoll, and Bluedorn (2000) also conducted a confirmatory factor analysis of the MBI. These authors observed that personal accomplishment did not form a coherent factor; hence, it was eliminated from the respecified model. Emotional exhaustion was clearly the most robust of the three MBI factors. As with the above studies, there were also indications that several emotional exhaustion and depersonalization items did not contribute to factor reliability, so these were removed from the measure. The resulting two-factor instrument showed good reliability and predictive validity, indicated by significant negative correlations with variables such as job satisfaction, organizational commitment, and significant positive correlations with turnover intentions.

One implication of the above confirmatory analyses is that the originally developed MBI may not always provide a valid measure of burnout among different occupational groups. In particular, following arguments presented by Leiter (1993), it would appear that (reduced) personal accomplishment may not be a "core component" of burnout (Walkey & Green, 1992) but may be better considered as an outcome of burnout. Similarly, although there is strong evidence for the role of emotional exhaustion, it is not totally clear whether depersonalization represents a major component of burnout in all samples. Additional analyses are required to confirm the status of depersonalization as a key burnout variable for various occupational groups.

The Modified MBI

In 1996, Maslach and her colleagues published a version of the MBI modified for use with nonservice occupations (Maslach et al., 1996). The new MBI-GS (General Survey) contains 24 items, although Schaufeli, Leiter, Maslach, and Jackson (1996) recommended retention of 16 of these items: 5 assessing emotional exhaustion, 5 cynicism, and 6 professional efficacy. Leiter and Schaufeli (1996) tested and then replicated the three-dimensional structure of the MBI-GS in several samples of hospital workers and proposed that "burnout, as measured by the MBI-GS, pertains to any occupation in which people are psychologically engaged in the job" (p. 240). Although Maslach and her colleagues still consider emotional exhaustion to be the fundamental dimension of burnout, they have also suggested that the cynicism dimension may in fact be more critical to burnout than is depersonalization.

In summary, the MBI has been the measure of choice for most research on burnout and has exhibited reasonable psychometric properties and predictive validity. Nevertheless, the applicability of the instrument (particularly the original 1981 and 1986 versions) to all occupational samples has been questioned, and confirmatory analyses have not always generated three coherent factors. Initial findings on the more recent (Maslach et al., 1996) version of the MBI are promising, but further research is needed to confirm its utility in various occupations and settings.

Burnout Index

As an alternative to the MBI, Pines et al. (1981) constructed a 21-item instrument to tap into burnout, or what they initially labeled as "tedium." This measure uses a 7-point frequency rating scale, with end points of *never* and *always*, and an overall burnout score is derived by computing the person's mean score across the 21 items. These items focus predominantly on cognitive and emotional elements, such as feeling worthless, depressed, and rejected. As noted earlier, Pines et al. (1981) contended that burnout and tedium are identical constructs but that whereas tedium may apply to workers in a wide range of situations, burnout results from working with people in situations that are emotionally demanding (Burke & Richardsen, 1993). In contrast to the earlier versions of the Maslach Burnout Inventory, the BI was developed for usage with both human service and nonservice occupations.

Schaufeli and van Dierondonck (1993) reported that the Burnout Index is the "second most widely employed burnout self-report questionnaire" (p. 633) and reflects the core dimension of exhaustion. Although the authors of the instrument distinguished conceptually between three kinds of exhaustion (physical, mental, and emotional), in practice a single index of burnout is obtained; hence, the BI can be thought of as a unidimensional measure. Factorial studies of the BI have typically obtained just a single dimension (Schaufeli & van Dierondonck, 1993). However, to date there would appear to have been little attempt to apply confirmatory factor analysis (e.g., via LISREL) to the Burnout Index. Schaufeli and van Dierondonck (1993) reported confirmatory factor analysis data that indicated better fit for a three-dimensional model of the BI than for a one-dimensional structure.

Compared with the MBI, the BI has been used by relatively few studies as an index of burnout levels. Perhaps this is a reflection of the predominant focus on human service occupations, to which the original version of the MBI is eminently suited, but doubts about the BI's factor structure may also have contributed to its lack of usage. However, in a recent study based upon the COR theory, Westman and Eden (1997) used the BI to study longitudinally the effects of vacation relief on burnout among clerical employees in an electronics firm in Israel. Using an interrupted time-series design that entailed administering the BI at five time periods, Westman and Eden found that burnout levels declined significantly during a 2-week vacation period but rose to pre-vacation levels within 3 weeks of returning to work. Although this study confirmed the utility of the BI, further exploration of the construct and predictive validity of this instrument is definitely warranted as a possible alternative to the more popular MBI.

Other Burnout Measures

Burke and Richardsen (1993) and Schaufeli, Enzmann, and Girault (1993) have summarized other self-report questionnaire measures of burnout, which are similar in content to the BI and MBI, and some of which are occupation specific. However, none of these has received much attention in the research literature. Friedman (1995) developed a self-report questionnaire, based upon Cherniss's (1980) conceptualization of burnout, to assess four components of burnout among school principals: exhaustion, aloofness, self-dissatisfaction, and deprecation. In Friedman's view, the first two of these elements represent internal (exhaustion) and external (aloofness) weariness, whereas the remaining two reflect internal (self-dissatisfaction) and external (deprecation) discontent. These experiences are quite similar to those contained in the Maslach Burnout Inventory. Whether the Friedman instrument is more suited than the MBI to nonservice samples has yet to be determined.

As is evident from the above discussion, almost all measures of burnout that have been used in empirical research have focused on individuals' own reports of their level of burnout. There has been little effort to develop alternative indexes of burnout, such as reports from other people (e.g., coworkers or supervisors) or observational measures of burnout. Given the oft-cited problem of common-method variance in research based solely on self-report measures, it is perhaps surprising that more attention has not been devoted to the development of corroborative measures. In particular, although burnout may be a subjective individual experience, this experience is associated with certain behavioral manifestations, such as depersonalization (cynicism) or aloofness (in Friedman's terms). We would anticipate, therefore, that these signs of burnout would be observable within the organizational setting and could be reported upon by other organizational members or clients.

An investigation by Lawson and O'Brien (1994) provided a starting point in this direction. Along with administering the MBI to individual staff members in facilities serving developmentally disabled adults, they used three trained observers to record staff behaviors that the authors argued were burnout related, such as positive and negative interactions with clients, avoiding clients, and spending time off task. There were several significant relationships between the behavioral activities, but few statistically significant correlations were obtained between self-reports of burnout (via the MBI) and the behavioral observations. Lawson and O'Brien argued that "direct measures of behavior may provide the best evidence of burnout" (p. 52). Unfortunately, however, there was no independent evidence that the behaviors observed in their study were indeed burnout criteria.

Correlates of Burnout

Cordes and Dougherty (1993) grouped correlates of burnout into three major categories: individual (or personal), job, and organizational. Many of the stressors that fall in these categories are comparable to those linked with job strain in general (see Chapter 2), although some would appear to be more explicitly associated with burnout. Furthermore, although some investigators have differentiated between antecedents and consequences of burnout, given the cross-sectional design of most research in this field it is not always feasible to classify variables clearly as causes or outcomes. For this reason, we refer to these variables as correlates, rather than differentiating between predictors (or causes) and outcomes of burnout. We will, however, note where researchers have made this distinction.

Individual-Level Correlates

Demographic variables (such as age and gender) represent examples of variables studied at the individual level. Gender, in particular, has been frequently investigated as a correlate of burnout, although findings for this variable are very mixed. Early results suggested that females may exhibit higher levels of burnout than males, but this may be confounded by the gender composition of the samples investigated (e.g., nurses, social workers). Pines et al. (1981) suggested that women experience higher levels of burnout due to greater overload and inter-role conflict, such as between job and family. More recent research, however, does not support this argument (Burke & Richardsen, 1993; Leiter & Harvie, 1996; Pretty, McCarthy, & Catano, 1992). Interestingly, there is some evidence that males report higher scores on the depersonalization subscale of the MBI (Schaufeli & Buunk, 1996), perhaps suggesting that they are more likely than their female counterparts to respond to emotional strain by psychologically separating themselves from their clients. In another study, Burke, Greenglass, and Schwarzer (1996) found that male teachers and school administrators were significantly higher on both emotional exhaustion and depersonalization. Further research exploring whether men and women cope in different ways with emotional exhaustion, and other symptoms of burnout, would contribute significantly to our under-standing of potential gender differences.

Few studies have observed a consistent link between age and burnout (Leiter & Harvie, 1996). Younger human service professionals may be more prone to burnout than older ones (Schaufeli & Buunk, 1996), but as with gender the results need to be interpreted cautiously because older workers who have become burned out may have quit their job for something less strain inducing. Nevertheless, age differences are of interest, as they may highlight potential mechanisms for preventing or alleviating burnout, as well as pointing to effective coping strategies.

Personality variables have also been explored in relation to burnout. Again, many of these variables (e.g., hardiness) have been incorporated into the more general stress literature. An interesting proposition has been advanced by Garden (1989). Using the Myers-Briggs Indicator, she contended that individuals denoted as "feeling types," characterized by a high need for affiliation and nurturance, are more likely to experience burnout than "thinking types," and she has argued that the former are more likely to be found in the human service professions. In her view, burnout is a function more of personality type than of occupational classification.

Despite the obvious relevance of personality issues, relatively little attention has been given to these variables in empirical research, and evidence for their association with burnout is inconclusive. More attention has been given, however, to attitudinal variables, such as job involvement, job satisfaction, and commitment to the organization. Lee and Ashforth (1996) reviewed studies that explored the relationship between Maslach's burnout dimensions and these three work attitudes. Their meta-analysis revealed negative relationships between emotional exhaustion and organizational commitment, and between depersonalization and both satisfaction and commitment. Job involvement, on the other hand, was not significantly linked with any of the three burnout components.

Several studies have reported a substantial relationship between burnout and job satisfaction (Cordes & Dougherty, 1993), with the inference that high levels of burnout lead to reduced satisfaction with one's job. This inference may not always be warranted, as there is evidence that satisfaction can be a predictor, rather than an outcome, of psychological strain (O'Driscoll, Ilgen, & Hildreth, 1992). In their meta-analysis, Lee and Ashforth (1996) found that satisfaction was significantly correlated only with the depersonalization component of burnout.

Linkages between organizational commitment and other organizationally relevant variables, such as absenteeism and turnover intentions, have been consistently demonstrated (Mathieu & Zajac, 1990; Shore, Barksdale, & Shore, 1995); hence, the relationship between commitment and burnout is of considerable interest. However, in their meta-analysis of research conducted between 1982 and 1994, Lee and Ashforth (1996) located just seven empirical studies of this relationship. As previously noted, emotional exhaustion and depersonalization both displayed significant negative correlations with commitment. Typically, it has been assumed that burnout is the predictor variable in this relationship. Leiter and Maslach (1988), for example, observed that emotional exhaustion exerted both a direct effect and an indirect effect (via depersonalization) on commitment, although in their study there was no direct contribution of depersonalization to commitment.

Although it seems intuitive that burnout can lead to a deterioration of employee commitment to the organization, the possibility that causality may also operate in the opposite direction does not appear to have been given much consideration. Kalliath, O'Driscoll, and Gillespie (1998) argued that high levels of commitment may in fact shield an individual from the impact of stressful working environments, hence leading to a reduction in burnout. Their structural equations analysis demonstrated that this chain of events is a plausible alternative to the burnout → commitment hypothesis.

A third category of individual differences that has been explored in burnout research is coping strategies. We will be discussing stress-related coping in more detail in Chapter 6, so we will comment only briefly here on this issue. Of particular relevance is research conducted by Leiter (1990, 1991, 1992) on the relationship between coping patterns and burnout levels. In keeping with the COR perspective (Hobfoll & Freedy, 1993) discussed earlier in this chapter, Leiter conceptualized coping as a resource available to the individual. Specifically, he distinguished between control coping, which equates with Lazarus and Folkman's (1984) problem-focused coping and is reflected by proactive efforts aimed at removing the source(s) of burnout, and escapist coping, which is reflected in avoidance of dealing with these burnout source(s). As predicted, control coping was found to be negatively related to burnout, whereas escapist coping showed a positive association with burnout levels.

Further investigation of the effectiveness of these and other coping strategies is clearly needed. In particular, it would be valuable to explore the conditions under which control-oriented coping is more and less effective. For example, would this strategy produce less positive outcomes when demands and pressures are outside the individual's control? Are there limits to the effectiveness of control and other forms of problem-focused coping? These and related issues will be explored in Chapter 6.

Finally, under the heading of personal correlates, consideration needs to be given to burnout's relationship with performance. Although much has been written about the potential deleterious effects of burnout on individuals' job performance and ultimately organizational productivity, empirical research on this relationship is relatively sparse. Nevertheless, some studies have demonstrated a negative correlation between these variables (Burke & Richardsen, 1993). Using the MBI, Wright and Bonett (1997) conducted a longitudinal investigation of burnout among professionals in a public sector human services department. Hierarchical regressions of job performance, controlling for age, gender, and prior performance, demonstrated that emotional exhaustion contributed significantly to decrements in subsequent performance, as evaluated by a superior. However, neither depersonalization nor reduced personal accomplishment was found to influence later performance. As well as providing further support for the centrality of emotional exhaustion in the burnout construct, this study also highlights the need to examine differential effects of the three MBI components.

Garden (1991) noted that it is important to distinguish between perceived and actual job performance when assessing the impact of burnout on employees' behavior. She found significant linkages between scores on her Energy Depletion Index, which parallels the emotional exhaustion dimension of the MBI, and MBA students' reports of their performance, but not their actual performance as determined by their examination results. Her explanation for this was that individuals suffering from burnout experience decreased self-esteem, which in turn leads them to believe that their performance has declined even when their actual performance may not have altered dramatically. She further speculated that employees may even exert additional effort to maintain their level of performance, despite being burned out. This is worthy of further exploration, along with the differentiation of perceived versus actual performance.

Finally, although there has been some research on physiological correlates of strain generally (see Chapter 3 of this volume), very little attention has been given to the relationship between burnout and physiological responses. This reflects a significant gap in our understanding of the burnout phenomenon and its manifestations. Though some preliminary research by Melamed, Shirom, and their colleagues (Melamed, Kushnir, & Shirom, 1992; Melamed et al., 1999; Shirom, Westman, & Carel, 1997) has illustrated connections between burnout levels and white blood cell aggregations, cholesterol levels, and salivary cortisol levels, further systematic investigations of physiological mechanisms are needed to enhance our knowledge of the biological pathways associated with burnout.

Despite researchers' interest in personality, attitudinal, and behavioral (e.g., performance) correlates of burnout, the predominant research focus has been on job-related and organizational factors, particularly because their relationship with burnout may be more directly assessed and because of the more obvious implications for interventions to reduce burnout levels.

Job-Related Correlates

Like the more general literature on work stressors (see Chapter 2), research on job characteristics related to burnout has focused particularly on role demands, including role ambiguity, role conflict, and role overload. Numerous studies have demonstrated positive links between each of these variables and burnout, especially emotional exhaustion and depersonalization (Burke & Richardsen, 1993; Schaufeli & Buunk, 1996). Role conflict in particular would appear to be very salient in the development of emotional exhaustion.

Zohar (1997) used hierarchical regression to examine the relative contribution of these three role demands after controlling for age, tenure, negative affectivity, and social support. A significant incremental contribution for the role variables was obtained. In addition, however, Zohar demonstrated that recently encountered hassles on the job also contributed to burnout, even after the role demand variables had been taken into account. This suggests that recurring demands (hassles) may be as important in the etiology of burnout as the (more general) role demands that are typically investigated in job stress research.

Also of considerable relevance to burnout among helping professionals is client caseload, which can be divided into quantitative and qualitative dimensions (Jackson et al., 1986). Both would appear to be related to burnout, although perhaps for different reasons. The quantitative aspect of caseload is equivalent to role overload in the general stress literature and has been observed by several researchers to induce burnout (e.g., Jackson, Turner, & Brief, 1987; Koeske & Koeske, 1989; Lawson & O'Brien, 1994; Reilly, 1994). The effects of qualitative overload may be more complex, however. Leiter and Maslach (1988) referred to interpersonal contact as a potential source of burnout, especially when that contact entails dealing with people's problems. As noted earlier, the strain associated with this form of contact may lead to emotional exhaustion, and then depersonalization, as the helping professional endeavors (unsuccessfully) to resolve these seemingly intractable problems.

There has also been consideration of the nature of client difficulties and how these might differentially contribute to burnout. Maslach (1978) suggested that the type of client problem (e.g., seriousness of an illness), the personal relevance of the client's problem to the helping professional (e.g., the professional's possible overidentification with the client), and the approach taken by the client (e.g., passive dependency, aggressive hostility) can have a large impact on the human service professional's burnout level. Burke and Richardsen (1993) have summarized other client factors that may impinge upon workers in other occupations, including teachers, school principals, and administrators.

Overall, it is evident that characteristics of the client and of the interaction between the professional and the client have a significant bearing on the extent of burnout experienced.

A further issue that warrants attention in relation to burnout is the degree of autonomy available to the person in his or her job. The ability to determine one's work methods, work schedules, and even issues such as breaks and vacations would be expected to have an ameliorating impact on burnout. Not many studies have explored this variable. Jackson et al. (1987) included it as one element of job conditions but did not describe the specific relationship between autonomy and burnout dimensions. Landsbergis (1988) observed a negative correlation between autonomy and burnout, but Lee and Ashforth (1993b) obtained no direct effect of autonomy on emotional exhaustion and depersonalization, although they did observe an indirect influence via role ambiguity and role conflict.

As with other areas of stress research, it is important to move beyond simple bivariate correlations of specific job factors with burnout. From a transactional perspective, of greater interest are the interactive effects of these factors and other variables, including personality and attitudinal variables, as well as coping strategies. To date, with a few notable exceptions (e.g., the work of Leiter), there has been little systematic exploration of these interactive effects. This type of investigation is needed to tease out the complex relationships between aspects of the job and individuals' feelings of being burned out. In addition, further work is needed on variables that may induce burnout in nonservice occupations.

Another issue needing more systematic attention in research on burnout (as well as other forms of job-related strain) is the perennial problem of common-method variance. Typically, this research uses self-report questionnaires that ask respondents for their perceptions of their work environment, including job factors, and at the same time gather self-ratings of burnout levels. Such methodology introduces a potential confounding due to response bias. Research using multimethod approaches to data collection would be valuable to ascertain objective relationships between environmental factors on the job and worker burnout levels and (as discussed earlier with respect to behavioral indicators of burnout) to establish the ecological validity of the burnout construct.

Organizational Correlates

The influence of organizational factors in the development of burnout has also received considerable attention from researchers. For instance, Schulz et al. (1995) suggested that management processes play a vital role in either creating or alleviating burnout among employees. Where individuals are involved in decision making related to their job and can determine important work processes, burnout may be less likely to occur. On the other hand, inflexible and rigid organizational rules and policies may exacerbate burnout levels (Gaines & Jermier, 1983).

Research in the area of organizational climate has also illustrated the relationship of organizational variables and employee burnout. O'Driscoll and Schubert (1988) found that lack of communication between organizational levels and influence processes used by managers were strongly related to burnout among social workers, whereas participation in decision making was associated with reduced levels of burnout. Schulz et al. (1995) observed that in organizations possessing a "clan" culture, characterized by teamwork, participation, and autonomy, employees displayed less burnout because they functioned in favorable work conditions. Similarly, transactional and transformational leadership processes enhanced the development of positive work attitudes by contributing to employee-organization goal congruence, job clarity, and work satisfaction, all of which were linked with reduced burnout.

One organizational variable that has consistently been linked with burnout reduction is social support. In Chapter 5, we will examine some of the potential moderating (buffering) effects of this variable; hence, our comments here will be brief. Schaufeli and Buunk (1996) noted the importance of the social environment of the workplace for the development (and alleviation) of burnout. This environment includes not just the recipients of services (e.g., clients) but also coworkers, supervisors, and subordinates. Several studies have obtained evidence for a negative relationship between social support (from colleagues and supervisors in particular) and levels of burnout among employees. For example, Eastburg, Williamson, Gorsuch, and Ridley (1994) found that both support from supervisors and peer cohesion contributed to decreased emotional exhaustion in a nursing sample; Jackson et al. (1986) obtained significant effects of support from the principal on teachers' feelings of personal accomplishment (although interestingly not on the two other MBI dimensions); and Pretty et al. (1992) observed that a sense of community in the work setting was linked with lower levels of exhaustion and depersonalization. Finally, Greenglass, Burke, and Konarski (1998) found that support from coworkers led to reduced emotional exhaustion among female teachers and that both supervisor and coworker support increased personal accomplishment in their male colleagues.

In their meta-analysis of 61 burnout studies reported in the research literature until 1994, Lee and Ashforth (1996) obtained significant negative correlations of social support (from various sources) with the frequency of emotional exhaustion and of supervisory support with emotional exhaustion and depersonalization. However, no significant relationships were obtained between support and personal accomplishment. As will be seen in the next chapter, the impact of support on employees is by no means certain. Some studies indica e a stress-buffering influence, but others suggest a direct correlation beween support and employee affective reactions, with little or no buffering effect. Hobfoll and Freedy's (1993) COR theory suggests that support is a resource that can energize individuals and enable them to deal with stressors in their work environment. However, the extent of influence of support may depend on a variety of other factors, including the individual's willingness (and ability) to harness this resource, as well as the nature of support available. Many studies have simply examined the overall amount of support, with little or no consideration of the nature and quality of support provided. This may partly explain the inconsistent results obtained for this variable.

Overall, there are clear indications that organizational variables, along with personal and job-related factors, can make a difference in burnout levels experienced by individuals. Employees functioning in organizational cultures and climates that foster collaboration and cohesion, that enable employee participation in decision making, and that acknowledge individuals' efforts (via appropriate reward systems) are less prone to burnout and other stress-related symptoms. It would be simplistic, however, to assume that provision of an environment that enhances these features would totally offset the negative impact of excessive role demands and the emotionally draining effects of continually having to respond to challenging client problems or difficulties with colleagues.

Finally, a brief comment on levels of analysis is warranted here. Burnout research typically focuses upon measurement at the individual level. That is, researchers interested in burnout and its correlates gather individuals' perceptions of their environment, along with data on burnout levels in individual workers. It cannot be assumed that these data are necessarily reflective of processes occurring at the organizational level. For instance, aggregating individuals' perceptions of the climate in which they work does not ipso facto provide an index of work group or "organizational" climate. For inferences about the latter to be viable, it is important to demonstrate a relatively high degree of consensus among individuals' perceptions of the environment in which they operate. (For a more extensive discussion of this issue, refer to James, Joyce, & Slocum, 1988.)

Generalization of Burnout

A major assumption in most of the burnout literature is that burnout emerges predominantly in caregiving and/or people-oriented roles, such as nursing, social work, teaching, and policing. The pervasive use of the MBI to measure burnout reinforces this view of the construct, for the three dimensions and their items were originally designed with these professions in mind, and a very large proportion of studies in this field have focused on human service samples. A few studies (e.g., Westman & Eden, 1997) have investigated burnout in other occupational groups with alternative measures, such as the BI, which focuses solely on the exhaustion dimension of burnout.

In recent years, however, there has been some debate about the generality of burnout to nonservice professions. Curiously, although this issue would seem to be quite important for theoretical conceptualizations as well as practical interventions, of three recent major overviews of the burnout literature (Burke & Richardsen, 1993; Cordes & Dougherty, 1993; Schaufeli & Buunk, 1996), only Burke and Richardsen even mention this topic, and then only briefly. Golembiewski and his associates (e.g., Golembiewski, Munzenrider, & Carter, 1983) have contended that burnout is applicable to a wide range of occupational groups, including those that do not have direct contact with clients. Hobfoll and Shirom (1993) share this view, suggesting that although current measures of burnout do seem more applicable to human service occupations, other samples may also experience this phenomenon, albeit with perhaps different manifestations.

Garden (1989) noted that the limited application of the construct to human service samples is due to the depersonalization component, which cannot readily be applied in other settings. Evans and Fischer (1993) conducted a confirmatory factor analysis of the MBI among samples of teachers and computer company employees and found that the depersonalization dimension of the MBI did not form a coherent and meaningful factor in the latter group, even though it was a stable factor among teachers. From these results, Evans and Fischer argued that if depersonalization (of clients) is considered to be a necessary component of burnout, this precludes the use of the burnout construct in nonservice samples. These occupations may experience exhaustion and other negative effects of stressful work environment, but should this be referred to as burnout?

It is possible, of course, that some nonservice roles (e.g., human resource managers, sales personnel) entail interpersonal relationships that parallel those encountered in human service professions. These individuals may experience burnout in the full sense of the original definition (Evans & Fischer, 1993; Lee & Ashforth, 1993b). Furthermore, as noted earlier, the new version of the MBI (Maslach et al., 1996) has replaced "depersonalization" with "cynicism" and (reduced) "personal accomplishment" with (diminished) "professional efficacy." These changes reflect a substantial shift of thinking about the exact nature of burnout dimensions and the occurrence of burnout in other than human service occupations. Whereas Maslach (1993) questioned the generalization of burnout beyond human service contexts, the development of the new MBI indicates that she and her colleagues now believe that burnout is a more pervasive phenomenon and may indeed be found in a variety of occupational groups (Cordes, Dougherty, & Blum, 1997), not just those associated with providing services to clients.

A related issue to the above is the transportability of the burnout construct across national or cultural boundaries. In other words, to what extent is burnout a "Western" phenomenon versus one that may be observed in a variety of national contexts? Very little research has been conducted on this issue, despite its importance in the stress literature. An overview of findings from cross-national research in this field has been presented by Golembiewski and colleagues (1993), who discussed several generalizations. From their review of research, Golembiewski et al. concluded that burnout and its effects are spreading across the globe. Although its incidence may be lower in some countries (those with a more "relaxed" lifestyle), there would appear to be evidence of burnout in both "developed" and "developing" countries. The emergence of strain-related and burnout-related symptoms would appear to be prominent in several developing countries, although the incidence of these symptoms in Western countries (and Japan!) is also increasing. Though it is clear that more extensive and systematic cross-national research is needed, there would appear to be sufficient evidence to conclude that burnout is not limited to one particular cultural group.

Nevertheless, although burnout may be a global phenomenon, further comparative research needs to be undertaken to assess similarities and differences in the symptoms or manifestations of burnout in different countries. Golembiewski and his colleagues cited findings suggesting differences between American, Japanese, and Indian managers, but simple comparisons of this kind do not shed much light on (a) how burnout is actually experienced in different countries and (b) whether the correlates of burnout differ substantially between countries. In sum, more systematic exploration of cultural factors relating to the experience of burnout is urgently needed, as well as investigation of the conse-quences of burnout in different societies.

Conclusion

In this chapter, we have explored the phenomenon of burnout as a unique and intense form of job-related strain. Research in this field has mushroomed in the past 20 years, and the topic itself is of immense interest to researchers and practitioners and receives wide media cover-age. In one sense, popular interest in burnout is a disadvantage in that lay conceptions of the term abound, sometimes confounding the quest for clear conceptualization and operationalization of burnout in work environments. Nevertheless, sufficient evidence has accrued to enable some conclusions about the nature and occurrence of burnout and its correlates.

However, as should be clear from our discussion in this chapter, there is still no universally accepted definition of burnout, which suggests that further work is needed to reveal the exact nature of this complex phenomenon, and it is possible that other (as yet unexplored) dimen-sions of burnout may be uncovered. The current emphasis in burnout research on "emotional" exhaustion may overlook some of the less tangible resources that contribute to an individual's overall well-being, including the spiritual dimension of human life, which is very salient and important for many people. A broader perspective on burnout may be needed to recognize that it is a depletion of a person's total resources, including his or her spiritual resources.[1]

Another issue that clearly warrants more systematic investigation is the question of whether burnout is "contagious." That is, can the experience of burnout spread throughout a work group or even an organization, ultimately resulting in organization-level burnout? To date, despite evidence indicating that certain work environment factors are conducive to burnout (see our earlier discussion), there has been no research exploring the possibility that burnout may exist in entire work groups or even the organization as a whole. Before embarking upon such enquiries, it will be necessary to develop a methodology for determining how burnout might be measured at these levels. As became evident many years ago in research on organizational climate (see Schneider, 1990), aggregation of individual levels of burnout (gathered from self-report questionnaires) may not be sufficient in itself to draw conclusions about the pervasiveness of burnout within groups or entire organizations. This issue represents an important challenge for future burnout research.

Finally, there is a need for greater investigation of strategies and interventions to prevent burnout development or to alleviate symptoms of burnout when it does occur. In Chapters 6 and 7, we will discuss various strategies for stress reduction, some of which may be salient to burnout. Two distinguishing features of this syndrome are that it has a long gestation period and that it is resistant to most forms of intervention that are based solely on individual coping efforts. For effective and long-term alleviation of burnout, fundamental changes in job conditions and organizational environments may be required to reduce the exhaustion encountered by individuals and to promote an expectancy that their efforts and performance will be successful and rewarded.

Note

1. We are indebted to Tom Kalliath for this suggestion.

References

Bradley, H. (1969). Community-based treatment for young adult offenders. *Crime and Delinquency, 15*, 359-370.

Brookings, J., Bolton, B., Brown, C., & McEvoy, A. (1985). Self-reported job burnout among female human service professionals. *Journal of Occupational Behaviour, 6*, 143-150.

Burke, R. (1989). Toward a phase model of burnout. *Group and Organization Studies, 14*, 23-32.

Burke, R., & Greenglass, E. (1995). A longitudinal examination of the Cherniss model of psychological burnout. *Social Science and Medicine, 40*, 1357-1363.

Burke, R., Greenglass, E., & Schwarzer, R. (1996). Predicting teacher burnout over time: Effects of work stress, social support, and self-doubts on burnout and its consequences. *Anxiety, Stress and Coping, 9*, 261-275.

Burke, R., & Richardsen, A. (1993). Psychological burnout in organizations. In R. Golembiewski (Ed.), *Handbook of organizational behavior* (pp. 263-298). New York: Marcel Dekker.

Byrne, B. (1991). The Maslach Burnout Inventory: Validating factorial structure and invariance across intermediate, secondary and university educators. *Multivariate Behavioral Research, 26*, 583-605.

Cherniss, C. (1980). *Professional burnout in human service organizations*. New York: Praeger.

Cordes, C., & Dougherty, T. (1993). A review and integration of research on job burnout. *Academy of Management Review, 18*, 621-656.

Cordes, C., Dougherty, T., & Blum, M. (1997). Patterns of burnout among managers and professionals: A comparison of models. *Journal of Organizational Behavior, 18*, 703-708.

Eastburg, M., Williamson, M., Gorsuch, R., & Ridley, C. (1994). Social support, personality and burnout in nurses. *Journal of Applied Social Psychology, 24*, 1233-1250.

Evans, B., & Fischer, D. (1993). The nature of burnout: A study of the three-factor model of burnout in human service and non-human service samples. *Journal of Occupational and Organizational Psychology, 66*, 29-38.

Freudenberger, H. (1974). Staff burnout. *Journal of Social Issues, 30*, 159-164.

Freudenberger, H., & Richelson, G. (1980). *Burn-out: The high cost of achievement*. New York: Anchor Press.

Friedman, I. (1995). School principal burnout: The concept and its components. *Journal of Organizational Behavior, 16*, 191-198.

Gaines, J., & Jermier, J. (1983). Emotional exhaustion in a high stress organization. *Academy of Management Journal, 26*, 567-586.

Garden, A.-M. (1989). Burnout: The effect of psychological type on research findings. *Journal of Occupational Psychology, 62*, 223-234.

Garden, A.-M. (1991). Relationship between burnout and performance. *Psychological Reports, 68*, 963-977.

Golembiewski, R., & Munzenrider, R. (1984). Active and passive reactions to psychological burnout: Toward greater specificity in a phase model. *Journal of Health and Human Resources Administration, 7*, 264-268.

Golembiewski, R., & Munzenrider, R. (1988). *Phases of burnout: Developments in concepts and applications*. New York: Praeger.

Golembiewski, R., Munzenrider, R., & Carter, D. (1983). Phases of progressive burnout and their work site covariates. *Journal of Applied Behavioral Science, 19*, 461-481.

Golembiewski, R., Munzenrider, R., & Stevenson, J. (1986). *Stress in organizations: Toward a phase model of burnout*. New York: Praeger.

Golembiewski, R., Scherb, K., & Boudreau, R. (1993). Burnout in cross-national settings: Generic and model-specific perspectives. In W. Schaufeli, C. Maslach, & T. Marek (Eds.), *Professional burnout: Recent developments in theory and research* (pp. 217-236). Washington, DC: Taylor & Francis.

Greenglass, E., Burke, R., & Konarski, R. (1998). Components of burnout, resources and gender-related differences. *Journal of Applied Social Psychology, 28,* 1088-1106.

Hobfoll, S. (1989). Conservation of resources: A new attempt at conceptualizing stress. *American Psychologist, 44,* 513-524.

Hobfoll, S., & Freedy, J. (1993). Conservation of resources: A general stress theory applied to burnout. In W. Schaufeli, C. Maslach, & T. Marek (Eds.), *Professional burnout: Recent developments in theory and research* (pp. 115-129). Washington, DC: Taylor & Francis.

Hobfoll, S., & Shirom, A. (1993). Stress and burnout in the workplace. In R. Golembiewski (Ed.), *Handbook of organizational behavior* (pp. 41-60). New York: Marcel Dekker.

Jackson, S., Schwab, R., & Schuler, R. (1986). Toward an understanding of the burnout phenomenon. *Journal of Applied Psychology, 71,* 630-640.

Jackson, S., Turner, J., & Brief, A. (1987). Correlates of burnout among public service lawyers. *Journal of Occupational Behaviour, 8,* 339-349.

James, L., Joyce, W., & Slocum, J. (1988). Comment: Organizations do not cognize. *Academy of Management Review, 13,* 129-132.

Kalliath, T., Gillespie, D., O'Driscoll, M., & Bluedorn, A. (2000). A test of the Maslach Burnout Inventory in three samples of healthcare professionals. *Work and Stress, 14,* 35-50.

Kalliath, T., O'Driscoll, M., & Gillespie, D. (1998). The relationship between burnout and organizational commitment in two samples of health professionals. *Work and Stress, 12,* 179-185.

Koeske, G., & Koeske, R. (1989). Work load and burnout: Can social support and perceived accomplishment help? *Social Work, 34,* 243-248.

Koeske, G., & Koeske, R. (1993). A preliminary test of a stress-strain-outcome model for reconceptualizing the burnout phenomenon. *Journal of Social Service Research, 17,* 107-135.

Landsbergis, P. (1988). Occupational stress among health care workers: A test of the job demands-control model. *Journal of Organizational Behavior, 9,* 217-239.

Lawson, D., & O'Brien, R. (1994). Behavioral and self-report measures of staff burnout in developmental disabilities. *Journal of Organizational Behavior Management, 14,* 37-54.

Lazarus, R., & Folkman, S. (1984). *Stress, appraisal and coping.* New York: Springer.

Lee, R., & Ashforth, B. (1990). On the meaning of Maslach's three dimensions of burnout. *Journal of Applied Psychology, 75,* 743-747.

Lee, R., & Ashforth, B. (1993a). A further examination of managerial burnout: Toward an integrated model. *Journal of Organizational Behavior, 14,* 3-20.

Lee, R., & Ashforth, B. (1993b). A longitudinal study of burnout among supervisors and managers: Comparisons between the Leiter and Maslach (1988) and Golembiewski et al. (1986) models. *Organizational Behavior and Human Decision Processes, 54,* 369-398.

Lee, R., & Ashforth, B. (1996). A meta-analytic examination of the correlates of the three dimensions of job burnout. *Journal of Applied Psychology, 81,* 123-133.

Leiter, M. (1990). The impact of family resources, control coping and skill utilization on the development of burnout: A longitudinal study. *Human Relations, 43,* 1067-1083.

Leiter, M. (1991). Coping patterns as predictors of burnout: The function of control and escapist coping patterns. *Journal of Organizational Behavior, 12,* 123-144.

Leiter, M. (1992). Burnout as a crisis in professional role structures: Measurement and conceptual issues. *Anxiety, Stress and Coping, 5,* 79-93.

Leiter, M. (1993). Burnout as a developmental process: Consideration of models. In W. Schaufeli, C. Maslach, & T. Marek (Eds.), *Professional burnout: Recent developments in theory and research* (pp. 237-250). Washington, DC: Taylor & Francis.

Leiter, M., & Harvie, P. (1996). Burnout among mental health workers: A review and research agenda. *International Journal of Social Psychiatry, 42,* 90-101.

Leiter, M., & Maslach, C. (1988). The impact of interpersonal environment on burnout and organizational commitment. *Journal of Organizational Behavior, 9,* 297-308.

Leiter, M., & Schaufeli, W. (1996). Consistency of the burnout construct across occupations. *Anxiety, Stress and Coping, 9*, 229-243.

Maslach, C. (1978). The client role in staff burnout. *Journal of Social Issues, 34*, 111-124.

Maslach, C. (1982). *Burnout: The cost of caring.* Englewood Cliffs, NJ: Prentice Hall.

Maslach, C. (1993). Burnout: A multidimensional perspective. In B. Schaufeli, C. Maslach, & T. Marek (Eds.), *Professional burnout: Recent developments in theory and research* (pp. 19-32). Washington, DC: Taylor & Francis.

Maslach, C., & Jackson, S. (1981). *MBI: Maslach Burnout Inventory.* Palo Alto, CA: Consulting Psychologists Press.

Maslach, C., & Jackson, S. (1986). *MBI: Maslach Burnout Inventory* (2nd ed.). Palo Alto, CA: Consulting Psychologists Press.

Maslach, C., Jackson, S., & Leiter, M. (1996). *Maslach Burnout Inventory Manual* (3rd ed.). Palo Alto, CA: Consulting Psychologists Press.

Mathieu, J., & Zajac, D. (1990). A review and meta-analysis of the antecedents, correlates and consequences of organizational commitment. *Psychological Bulletin, 108*, 171-194.

Melamed, S., Kushnir, T., & Shirom, A. (1992). Burnout and risk factors for cardiovascular disease. *Behavioral Medicine, 18*, 53-61.

Melamed, S., Ugarten, U., Shirom, A., Kahana, L., Lerman, Y., & Froom, P. (1999). Chronic burnout, somatic arousal and elevated salivary cortisol levels. *Journal of Psychsomatic Research, 46*, 591-598.

O'Driscoll, M., & Cooper, C. (1996). Sources and management of excessive job stress and burnout. In P. Warr (Ed.), *Psychology at work* (4th ed., pp. 188-223). New York: Penguin.

O'Driscoll, M., Ilgen, D., & Hildreth, K. (1992). Time devoted to job and off-job activities, interrole conflict and affective experiences. *Journal of Applied Psychology, 77*, 272-279.

O'Driscoll, M., & Schubert, T. (1988). Organizational climate and burnout in a New Zealand social service agency. *Work and Stress, 2*, 199-204.

Pines, A., & Aronson, E. (1988). *Career burnout: Causes and cures* (2nd ed.). New York: Free Press.

Pines, A., Aronson, E., & Kafry, D. (1981). *Burnout: From tedium to personal growth.* New York: Free Press.

Pretty, G., McCarthy, M., & Catano, V. (1992). Psychological environments and burnout: Gender considerations within the corporation. *Journal of Organizational Behavior, 13*, 701-711.

Reilly, N. (1994). Exploring a paradox: Commitment as a moderator of the stressor-burnout relationship. *Journal of Applied Social Psychology, 24*, 397-414.

Schaufeli, W., & Buunk, B. (1996). Professional burnout. In M. Schabracq, J. Winnubst, & C. Cooper (Eds.), *Handbook of work and health psychology* (pp. 311-346). New York: John Wiley.

Schaufeli, W., Enzmann, D., & Girault, N. (1993). The measurement of burnout: A review. In W. Schaufeli, C. Maslach, & T. Marek (Eds.), *Professional burnout: Recent developments in theory and research* (pp. 199-215). Washington, DC: Taylor & Francis.

Schaufeli, W., Leiter, M., Maslach, C., & Jackson, S. (1996). The Maslach Burnout Inventory—General Survey. In C. Maslach, S. Jackson, & M. Leiter (Eds.), *Maslach Burnout Inventory Manual* (3rd ed.). Palo Alto, CA: Consulting Psychologists Press.

Schaufeli, W., & van Dierondonck, D. (1993). The construct validity of two burnout measures. *Journal of Organizational Behavior, 14*, 631-647.

Schneider, B. (Ed.). (1990). *Organizational climate and culture.* San Francisco: Jossey-Bass.

Schulz, R., Greenley, J., & Brown, R. (1995). Organization, management and client effects on staff burnout. *Journal of Health and Social Behavior, 36*, 333-345.

Shirom, A. (1989). Burnout in work organizations. *International Review of Industrial and Organizational Psychology, 4*, 25-48.

Shirom, A., Westman, M., & Carel, R. (1997). Effects of work overload and burnout on cholesterol and triglycerides levels: The moderating effects of emotional reactivity among male and female employees. *Journal of Occupational Health Psychology, 2,* 275-288.

Shore, L., Barksdale, K., & Shore, T. (1995). Managerial perceptions of employee commitment to the organization. *Academy of Management Journal, 38,* 1593-1615.

Walkey, F., & Green, D. (1992). An exhaustive examination of the replicable factor structure of the Maslach Burnout Inventory. *Educational and Psychological Measurement, 52,* 309-323.

Westman, M., & Eden, D. (1997). Effects of a respite from work on burnout: Vacation relief and fade-out. *Journal of Applied Psychology, 82,* 516-527.

Wright, T., & Bonett, D. (1997). The contribution of burnout to work performance. *Journal of Organizational Behavior, 18,* 491-499.

Yadama, G., & Drake, B. (1995). Confirmatory factor analysis of the Maslach Burnout Inventory. *Social Work Research, 19,* 184-192.

Zohar, D. (1997). Predicting burnout with a hassle-based measure of role demands. *Journal of Organizational Behavior, 18,* 101-115.

5 Moderators of Stressor-Strain
Relationships

In previous chapters, we have outlined the basic processes involved in
the development of job-related strain and burnout and have discussed
some of the major sources and outcomes of these affective experiences.
So far, however, we have examined only the direct association between
stressors and their potential outcomes and have not discussed other
factors that may affect this relationship. In this chapter, we address
these potential influences by considering variables that may function as
moderators of the stressor-strain relationship.

A moderator is defined as a variable that "affects the direction and/or
strength of the relation between an independent or predictor variable
and a dependent or criterion variable" (Baron & Kenny, 1986, p. 1174).
A moderator is, therefore, some third factor that exerts an influence
on the zero-order correlation between two variables (see Figure 5.1).
Moderator effects are typically assessed by the interaction between the
predictor variable and the moderator in a hierarchical regression, where
the predictor and moderator are entered first into the regression equation, followed by entry of the interaction term (predictor × moderator).

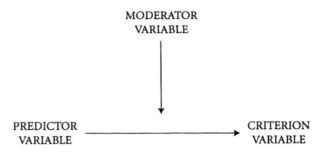

Figure 5.1. The Moderator Effect

This enables determination of the incremental contribution of the moderator effect once the main effects have been taken into account.

As we noted earlier (see Chapter 1), various kinds of moderator variables have been identified in research on stress processes. For clarity and simplicity, we will group these variables into three categories of factors: (a) personality or dispositional, (b) situational, and (c) social. The following discussion reviews the relevance of these three categories of moderator variables.

Personality/Dispositional Moderators

Dispositional or personality characteristics have been of considerable interest to researchers investigating relationships between job-related stressors (e.g., excessive job demands, role conflict, role ambiguity) and indexes of strain (e.g., psychological strain, job dissatisfaction, and physiological symptoms). Based on the person-environment fit model of strain (Edwards, 1996), discussions of the influence of dispositional variables have typically concluded that there are two basic mechanisms by which personality might influence stressor-strain relationships. These mechanisms have been outlined by Cohen and Edwards (1989) and more recently by Bolger and Zuckerman (1995). Bolger and Zuckerman suggested that personality may play an important role in the stress process by influencing individuals' exposure to stressful events, by affecting their reactivity to these events, or by both of these processes. (They also discussed how dispositional factors may influence people's choices of coping mechanisms and the effectiveness of coping strategies. Coping strategies and behaviors are reviewed in Chapter 6 and hence will not be covered here.)

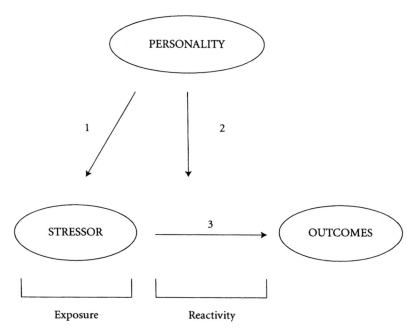

Figure 5.2. The Differential Exposure and Reactivity Hypotheses

SOURCE: From "A Framework for Studying Personality in the Stress Process" by N. Bolger and A. Zuckerman, 1995, *Journal of Personality and Social Psychology, 69,* p. 891. Copyright 1995 by the American Psychological Association. Reprinted with permission.

Figure 5.2, from Bolger and Zuckerman (1995), illustrates mediating and moderating linkages between personality variables and outcomes, such as strain. (In contrast to moderator variables, a *mediating* variable is one that "accounts for the relation between the predictor and the criterion" (Baron & Kenny, 1986, p. 1176): That is, it provides a link between one variable and another.) According to the *differential exposure* perspective, personality factors may determine the extent to which individuals are exposed to certain kinds of stressful events or circumstances (Pathway 1 in Figure 5.2), which may then lead to strain (Pathway 3). For example, individuals who are high on the Type A behavior pattern may actively position themselves in situations that require ambition, drivenness, and competitive behavior; these situations, in turn, may induce greater psychological strain. Although this hypothesis is certainly plausible and worthy of investigation, there has been little effort to examine it in studies of job stress. It should also be noted that this model positions stressors, not personality factors, as the mediating variables.

An alternative, and more commonly held, view is the *differential reactivity* perspective, which suggests that certain dispositional variables may moderate the impact of job stressors on individuals' affective outcomes. In Figure 5.2, this perspective is reflected in the diagonal arrow (Pathway 2) intersecting the horizontal linkages between stressors and outcomes (Pathway 3). Put simply, this means that the effects of stressors will vary depending on whether an individual is high or low on a specific personality or dispositional attribute. A large variety of personality variables have been studied in the context of the differential reactivity perspective, and these potential moderating effects are discussed in more detail below.

Before turning to specific variables, however, it is important to note that there are several mechanisms by which personality may act as a moderator variable. Prominent among these is the effect that personality has on individuals' appraisals of situations (Cohen & Edwards, 1989). As will be noted in our discussion of coping in Chapter 6, the appraisal of a situation as threatening is a major component of the transactional model of the stress-coping process. Individuals who perceive an event or circumstance as threatening to their physical or psychological well-being are more likely to experience negative outcomes. It follows that any factor that influences the appraisal process is also likely to contribute to stressor outcomes.

Drawing on these general perspectives on the role of personality in stressor-strain relationships, stress researchers have investigated the moderating effects of specific dispositional characteristics. Our intention here is not to discuss all possible dispositions that have been identified empirically but to highlight major findings from this research and to direct attention to their implications for our understanding of stress transactions in work environments.

Type A Behavior Pattern

In the job stress literature, considerable attention has been focused on the Type A behavior pattern (TABP) as a predictor of strain (and strain-related outcomes). This cluster of characteristics was first identified as a potential contributor to strain-related outcomes by cardiologists Friedman and Rosenman in the 1950s (Rosenman et al., 1964) and since that time has been examined both as a direct predictor of strain and as a moderator in the chain of events between stressors and strain. Type A individuals are characterized as displaying very high levels of concentration and alertness, achievement striving (ambitiousness), competitiveness, time urgency, and aggressiveness. Further potential characteristics of this disposition include irritability (when things do not go according to plan), along with hostility and anger toward others who are perceived by the Type A individual as impeding his or her goal achievement (Lee, Ashford, & Jamieson, 1993). Individuals with a propensity toward TABP also exhibit a strong desire for personal control over their environment, and any perceived lack of control will be a source of intense frustration (Davidson & Cooper, 1980; Lee, Ashford, & Bobko, 1990).

TABP is one of the most interesting dispositional characteristics in stress research in that it may lead to both positive and negative outcomes for the individual. In a positive sense, the strong achievement motivation and desire for control may drive the individual toward very high levels of performance in the work setting, as well as producing rewards from goal achievement. Such individuals may be highly sought after by organizations and rewarded for their accomplishments. On the downside, however, there are suggestions that these achievements may come at some personal cost to the individual in terms of higher levels of psychological strain, possibly longer-term somatic complaints, and neglect of other (non-performance-related) areas of life. Similarly, the competitiveness and aggressiveness of Type A individuals may create incompatible relationships with other people in their work context. In sum, possession of Type A characteristics is a veritable double-edged sword.

Turning to the moderator hypothesis, unfortunately research findings to date have been inconsistent in demonstrating that TABP functions as a moderator of stressor-strain relationships. Theoretically, it is predicted that individuals who adopt a more "relaxed" approach to their work will experience less psychological (and perhaps physical) strain than those exhibiting Type A characteristics. Some research has confirmed this (Moyle & Parkes, 1999; Payne, 1988), but other studies have uncovered little support for a moderator effect of this variable (Burke, 1988; Edwards, Baglioni, & Cooper, 1990; Jamal, 1999). As suggested by George (1992) and by Ganster, Schaubroeck, Sime, and Mayes (1991), future investigations should examine more closely the specific components of TABP, especially the anger/hostility dimension. As indicated by Ganster et al. (1991), "Because persons scoring high on the hostility component tended to both hyperreact to a challenging stimulus and recover less quickly" (p. 165), individuals who display anger/hostility toward other people may be more prone to the adverse consequences of stressful work conditions than Type A persons who score relatively low on this dimension. Similarly, although by itself TABP does not necessarily exhibit strong moderator effects, it may interact with other variables, especially perceptions of control over the work environment (Kushnir & Melamed, 1991), to predict the degree of strain experienced in response to job stressors. These combined interactions will be examined later.

Empirical research on TABP has been plagued by controversy, particularly surrounding the measurement of this behavioral disposition. In a comprehensive review and discussion of the validity of this construct, Ganster et al. (1991) summarized some of the more serious methodological concerns about extant research on TABP. They noted that the Structured Interview (SI), the instrument developed by Friedman, Rosenman, and their colleagues (Rosenman et al., 1964) to assess Type A tendencies, is regarded as the prototype assessment device due to its relative success in predicting coronary heart disease and coronary artery disease in epidemiological studies. The SI consists of a series of behaviorally based questions that are responded to in an interview situation, where the interviewer rates interviewees on Type A dimensions. These ratings are based on the form of interviewees' verbal responses, as well as the content of their responses. For instance, the interviewer deliberately asks (some) questions slowly and with pauses, which provides the respondent with an opportunity to interrupt before the interviewer has finished the question, thereby exhibiting one characteristic of the Type A disposition, namely verbal competition. Other behaviors that the interviewee might display during the interview, such as hostility, are also recorded. Interviews are typically audiotaped or videotaped for later review. After rating respondents on each dimension, the interviewer categorizes each respondent as fitting the broad Type A or Type B classification. In some studies, degrees of Type A or Type B disposition have been coded, rather than simply whether the person fits one or the other classification. Two or three coders (including the original interviewer) rate each respondent independently, then discuss their classifications to resolve any coding discrepancies.

Despite its widespread usage, "Inconsistent research results have led researchers to question the viability of studying global TABP as a strategy for identifying coronary-prone persons" (Ganster et al., 1991, pp. 144-145). In particular, several studies have achieved nonsignificant correlations between global TABP, as assessed by the SI, and cardiovascular health outcomes. In their research, Ganster and his colleagues identified three distinct components within the SI but found that only one of these elements—hostility toward others—was significantly associated with physiological outcomes. These findings support arguments that specific dimensions of TABP may be responsible for negative outcomes rather than the behavior pattern as a whole (George, 1992).

Similar results were obtained by Lee et al. (1993), using a different assessment device, a revised version of the Jenkins Activity Survey (JAS; Jenkins, Zyzanski, & Rosenman, 1971), which is a self-report questionnaire. Although Lee et al. focused particularly on two of the TABP elements mentioned above, achievement striving and impatience/irritability, they noted that the anger/hostility dimension of the TABP may be more strongly associated with physical illness than other components. George (1992) stated that the SI is the preferred method of assessing TABP but suggested that there is a relatively low correlation between TABP scores derived from this instrument and those obtained by other means, such as the JAS. Edwards et al. (1990) reached the same conclusion. Consequently, it is difficult to compare the results of studies that have used the SI and those using other indexes of TABP. Furthermore, TABP itself is multidimensional, and some dimensions (such as anger/hostility) may make a greater contribution than others to individuals' affective reactions. More research is needed to ascertain the relative contributions of specific components of the Type A construct.

Perhaps even more importantly, however, there is a need for clearer conceptualization of the role of Type A behavior in the stress process. As noted above, researchers need to clarify the conditions under which positive and negative consequences occur for Type A individuals and whether these consequences apply to all Type A persons or only to certain subgroups, such as those scoring high on anger and hostility. In addition, George (1992) noted that although TABP was not associated with psychological strain or distress, Type A persons do appear to be at risk in terms of physical health problems. This suggests that TABP does not necessarily have across-the-board negative consequences and that further teasing out of its effects on a range of psychological and physiological reactions is needed.

Negative Affectivity

In an overview of dispositional factors, work-related strain, and health, Semmer (1996) discussed the concept of vulnerable versus resilient personality, noting that several personality variables may function as vulnerability or resilience factors. One variable that may be viewed as a component of vulnerability is negative affectivity (NA), a construct that overlaps to some extent with neuroticism (Bolger & Zuckerman, 1995; George, 1992) and that reflects a relatively stable predisposition to experience low self-esteem and negative emotional states (Watson & Clark, 1984). According to Semmer, persons who are high on NA are more inclined to experience psychological strain and other negative outcomes in their work setting. NA may therefore increase individuals' susceptibility to the effects of stress-inducing environments (Parkes, 1990).

Spielberger, Gorsuch, and Lushene (1970) were perhaps the first to suggest that NA may operate as a moderator of stressor-strain linkages. From their perspective, NA serves to attenuate correlations between stressors and psychological strain, such that individuals high on NA will exhibit a stronger relationship between stressors and outcomes than their counterparts with low NA. Watson and his associates, however, have argued that NA is generally unrelated to reactivity to stressors and that high-NA individuals uniformly report greater strain (distress) over a range of both stressful and nonstressful situations (Watson & Clark, 1984; Watson & Pennebaker, 1989). Over the past 15 years or so, there has been considerable debate, therefore, about whether the effects of NA on strain are direct or indirect, and it would seem that the role of NA in the stress-coping process is complex.

Recent papers by Spector and his colleagues have further elucidated the ways in which NA might influence stressor-strain relationships. Spector, Zapf, Chen, and Frese (2000), for instance, have outlined six possible mechanisms for these effects:

1. The *symptom perception* hypothesis, an explanation favored by Watson and Pennebaker (1989), is that individuals high on NA tend to have a negative "view of the world." In a job situation, they tend to perceive (and hence report) the environment as containing a high level of stressors. In other words, according to this view, NA directly influences (the perception of) stressors, rather than the relationship between stressors and strains.
2. An alternative to the above is that high-NA individuals may exhibit a heightened response to stressors because they are more sensitive to the impact of stressors. Given the same environmental conditions, these people will show more strain

than their low-NA counterparts. As with the symptom perception hypothesis, the *hyper-responsivity* mechanism suggests that the effect of NA is direct (rather than moderating) but is on strain rather than on stressors themselves.

3. The *differential selection* perspective is that high-NA individuals are more likely to be located in jobs that are "stressful." There is some supportive evidence for this hypothesis (e.g., Spector, Fox, & van Katwyk, 1999), but an explanation for the selection mechanism is not entirely clear. It may be that high-NA people choose work that is low in autonomy and job scope (Spector, Jex, & Chen, 1995), conditions that research has demonstrated are conducive to strain. Alternatively, Kohn and Schooler (1983) proposed that individuals displaying high NA are less attractive as applicants for better jobs that are more complex and hence that they are less likely to be selected for these positions, but to date there has been no systematic investigation of this proposition.

4. Another possible explanation is that by their behavior high-NA individuals actually create stressors. Spector et al. (2000) have labeled this the *stress creation* mechanism. For instance, negative feelings about life in general may spill over into a person's verbal and nonverbal behaviors, hence inducing negative reactions from colleagues and leading to a conflictual social environment. This explanation may be especially relevant, therefore, to the effects of social stressors in the workplace. The end result would be similar to that predicted by the symptom perception hypothesis, even though these two predictions posit different mechanisms.

5. *Transitory mood,* which is affected by job conditions, may also have a substantial influence on individuals' reactions to stressors and their experience of strain. This suggests that high levels of stressors cause workers to feel anxious, upset, or frustrated, and that these fluctuations in mood result in their reporting higher strain, as well as elevated levels of NA. From this perspective, NA is an outcome of mood rather than a potential cause of strain.

6. Finally, consistent exposure to stressors may itself induce high levels of negativity or exacerbate existing levels of this disposition. This *causality* hypothesis suggests that although NA is typically conceived as a stable trait, job conditions can have an influence on dispositions, including NA.

Spector et al. (2000) discussed empirical evidence that lends some support for each of the above perspectives, thereby illustrating that the role of NA in the stress process is by no means simple and that observed relationships of NA with stressors and strains may be explained by various mechanisms. In sum, no single explanation for the effects of NA is likely to encapsulate the full influence of this variable. As noted by Spector et al., further investigations of its potential moderating influence should use multiple measures of stressors and strains and longitudinal and quasi-experimental research designs that enable more explicit differentiation between possible mechanisms.

Further complicating this debate is the issue of common-method variance. Because stressors, psychological strain, and NA are frequently all assessed via self-report questionnaires, it is possible that NA serves as a confounding variable in the relationship between stressors and strain (Chen & Spector, 1991). This possibility was explored in research by Brief, Burke, George, Robinson, and Webster (1988), Parkes (1990), and Schaubroeck, Ganster, and Fox (1992). Brief et al. (1988) found that observed relationships between a composite index of stressors and various strain indicators were inflated by NA, suggesting that this variable may be a "nuisance factor" in studies of job stress. Some support for this argument was obtained by Parkes (1990), who noted that the variance in strain explained by work environment factors was reduced after controlling for NA, although the stressor-strain relationship remained statistically significant. In contrast, Chen and Spector (1991) and Jex and Spector (1996) reported that NA accounted for little variance in the association between stressors and affective (psychological) strain.

Using confirmatory factor analysis, Schaubroeck et al. (1992) concluded that although NA may significantly attenuate the effects of job stressors, there is no reliable evidence that it measures a factor in common with indexes of strain or work stressors. These authors suggested that Watson and Pennebaker's (1989) symptom perception hypothesis (that high-NA individuals are more prone to report symptoms of strain) provides a better explanation than the confounding-variable hypothesis for observed relationships between NA and strain. They also noted that although their findings suggest that NA does not necessarily predispose individuals to physical health problems, more systematic investigation is needed of the etiological role of this variable in stress research. In addition, it is important to determine which specific strain variables are influenced by NA, as it is apparent that not all stress-related outcome criteria are affected by this dispositional factor (Chen & Spector, 1991).

Hardiness

The construct labeled as *hardiness* in the 1970s by Kobosa (1979) is a further variable falling under the rubric of vulnerability/resilience factors that has been hypothesized to moderate the effects of environmental stressors on individuals' experience of strain and ill health. Kobosa characterized the "hardy personality" as one that encompasses high levels of *commitment* or involvement in day-to-day activities, the perception that one has *control* over life events, and a tendency to view unexpected change as a *challenge* rather than a threat to well-being. Gentry and Kobosa (1984) argued that hardiness "mitigates the potentially unhealthy effects of stress and prevents the organismic strain that often leads to illness" (p. 99).

Although this construct would appear to be highly salient to strain reactions, there has been relatively little investigation of its role in job stress. Kobosa and her colleagues' research on the impact of hardiness on strain in general found that hardy persons tended to report fewer illnesses and higher levels of general well-being (e.g., Kobosa, 1982), although some other studies have failed to replicate this finding (see Allred & Smith, 1989). It has been suggested that the positive link between hardiness and health arises because hardy individuals have more adaptive cognitions concerning stressors than do their less hardy counterparts and that these cognitions are reflected in lower levels of physiological arousal under conditions that might be stressful (Allred & Smith, 1989).

Direct investigations of the relationship between hardiness and indicators of strain, including physiological measures, have not consistently confirmed a stress-buffering effect of hardiness (Benishek & Lopez, 1997). For instance, Allred and Smith (1989) assessed both cognitive and physiological responses of high- and low-hardiness individuals in a challenging situation that presented either high or low threat to their self-concept. There was some evidence that hardy persons experienced less psychological strain than their nonhardy counterparts, but no moderating effect of hardiness was obtained with respect to physiological outcomes, a finding that calls into question the presumed linkage between hardiness and physical health.

Roth, Wiebe, Fillingham, and Shay (1989) obtained self-ratings of health symptoms from their respondents but also failed to demonstrate that hardiness either was directly associated with self-reported health or moderated the impact of stressful life experiences on illness ratings. These authors suggested that hardiness may affect health indirectly, in perhaps two ways: "Hardy individuals may simply experience fewer negative life events, or [they] may possess a cognitive style such that troubling life events are interpreted less negatively" (p. 140). However, neither of these propositions explains *why* hardiness might exert such effects.

More recently, Benishek and Lopez (1997) examined gender differences in frequency and severity of "life stress" scores and examined the moderating influence of hardiness on the relationship between life stressors and self-reported health in men and women. This study identified a hardiness buffering effect only in male respondents. The researchers suggested that men may be more likely to use hardiness-related problem-focused coping strategies that override the deleterious impact of stressors in their lives, whereas women (who reported higher levels of neuroticism in this study) may be more likely to use emotion-focused coping that addresses the consequences rather than the stressors themselves. Further work is needed to confirm this speculation.

Measurement issues may partially explain the lack of consistent evidence for a buffering effect of hardiness. Hull, van Treuren, and Virnelli (1987) commented that "there now exist nearly as many ways to measure hardiness and its subcomponents as there are people conducting research on the topic" (p. 521). In her original research, Kobosa (1979) used several instruments to assess the three components of hardiness (commitment, control, and challenge), including measures of alienation from self and work, external locus of control, powerlessness, and a scale assessing a sense of security. An abridged 20-item measure developed by Kobosa was used in some later studies, and others (including Benishek & Lopez, 1997) have used a 36-item scale also developed by Kobosa. Rhodewalt and Zone (1989), for example, used the 20-item version to assess the role of hardiness in the linkage between life changes, depression, and physical health among female college students in the United States. These authors drew several conclusions from their findings, but two of particular interest in the present context were that (a) hardiness is closely associated with NA and (b) the appraisal of life changes, rather than hardiness per se, moderates the impact of stressful life changes on levels of depression and health. Framed in terms of the transactional model of stress coping, these findings suggest that hardy and nonhardy individuals engage in different appraisal processes when they encounter potentially stressful life events.

In summary, although the concept of hardiness and its proposed impact on the experience of strain has intuitive appeal, to date evidence to support its effects has been somewhat disappointing, partly perhaps because of the different measurement approaches adopted in research. Also, as noted by Allred and Smith (1989), a possible (negative) overlap between hardiness and neuroticism (and perhaps NA) may confound empirical findings. Furthermore, there have been suggestions that the hardiness construct is too global and that further research should examine the three specific components more closely (Hull et al., 1987; Roth et al., 1989), especially the commitment component. At this point, there is a lack of substantive evidence that hardiness per se demonstrates a consistent moderating effect on either psychological well-being or physical health. Its influence may in fact be due to other mechanisms, especially the forms of appraisal undertaken by individuals confronting stressors. A tighter specification of the theoretical construct and a more systematic approach to its measurement are needed to enhance our understanding of this interesting concept.

Self-Esteem and Self-Efficacy

In their 1989 review of moderator effects, Cohen and Edwards concluded that data on the buffering effect of self-esteem were inconclusive. However, several studies since then have suggested that self-esteem or self-efficacy may play a significant role in the stress process. Although self-esteem and self-efficacy are not identical constructs, in their most generalized expressions they are virtually indistinguishable (Semmer, 1996), and the explanation for their effects is the same. For the present purpose, therefore, we have integrated the discussion of these two variables.

Ganster and Schaubroeck (1995) noted that the growing evidence that certain dispositional variables may protect individuals from the adverse consequences of stressors can be explained by Brockner's (1988) behavioral plasticity hypothesis. *Behavioral plasticity* refers to the degree to which a person is affected by external factors. Brockner argued that persons with high self-esteem are less susceptible to environmental events than their low-self-esteem counterparts. Conversely, low-self-esteem persons are more reactive to adverse conditions (such as role stressors) because they react more to external cues. There are three major reasons for this. First, low-self-esteem individuals are more likely to experience uncertainty about the correctness of their thoughts and emotional reactions and hence to rely more upon social cues. Second, they seek social approval by conforming (attitudinally and behaviorally) with others' expectations. Third, they tend to be more self-critical and permit negative feedback on one area of their behavior to generalize to other dimensions of their self-concept.

Support for the plasticity hypothesis has come from studies conducted by Mossholder, Bedeian, and Armenakis (1981) and Pierce, Gardner,

Dunham, and Cummings (1993). Mossholder et al. (1981) found that self-reports of role stressors (ambiguity and conflict) were negatively related to job satisfaction (for ambiguity) and supervisor ratings of performance (for conflict) among low-self-esteem nurses but not among high-self-esteem nurses in a hospital setting. Pierce et al. (1993) investigated the moderator effects of organization-based self-esteem and again observed that relationships between role stressors and employee responses (satisfaction and performance) were more pronounced among low-self-esteem employees.

However, neither of these studies explicitly focused on physical health or psychological strain. As noted by Ganster and Schaubroeck (1995), the Mossholder et al. (1981) and Pierce et al. (1993) findings support the plasticity hypothesis but do not actually explain its relevance to health outcomes. Ganster and Schaubroeck suggested that self-esteem might influence individuals' choice of coping strategies and that low-self-esteem persons are apt to be more passive copers due to a lack of confidence in their ability to influence their environment. In their study of the buffering effect of self-esteem on the relationship of role conflict and ambiguity with somatic complaints among fire officers, Ganster and Schaubroeck found an interaction between role conflict and self-esteem, with low-self-esteem employees displaying a significant relationship between perceptions of role conflict and somatic complaints. Self-esteem did not moderate the impact of role ambiguity, which Ganster and Schaubroeck suggested may have been less salient for this occupation.

Three studies that have examined self-efficacy, rather than self-esteem, were reported by Jex and Gudanowski (1992), Schaubroeck and Merritt (1997), and Zellars, Perrewe, and Hochwarter (1999). For instance, Schaubroeck and Merritt (1997) obtained data indicating that job self-efficacy may play an important role in reducing the cardiovascular consequences of job-related strain. Their research extended Karasek's (1979) job demands-control model of job-related strain (see page 135) by examining two-way interactions between job demands and self-efficacy, along with three-way interactions of demands × control × efficacy. Both these interaction terms significantly predicted systolic and diastolic blood pressure, and the demands × efficacy two-way interaction also predicted diastolic (but not systolic) pressure. Schaubroeck and Merritt concluded that self-efficacy influences the interaction effect of job demands and control on blood pressure, such that "when people are confident in their abilities, having control mitigates the stress consequences of demanding jobs" (p. 750). They also suggested that "high control combined with high job demands had negative health consequences among those reporting lower self-efficacy" (p. 750).

Jex and Gudanowski (1992) distinguished between "individual" self-efficacy, the person's beliefs about whether he or she is capable of performing, and "collective" self-efficacy, the individual's assessment of his or her group's collective ability to perform relevant tasks. Interestingly, they found that individual self-efficacy displayed no mediating or moderating effects in stressor-strain relationships, whereas collective self-efficacy moderated the effects of one stressor (number of work hours) on job satisfaction, anxiety, and turnover intentions, although the percentage of variance accounted for by moderator effects was relatively small in each case (3%-4%).

More recently, Zellars et al. (1999) also obtained evidence that collective self-efficacy—that is, perceptions that the group or team has the capacity to meet challenges confronting it—reduced burnout among nurses, especially in respondents who were high in NA. These researchers found that, for high-NA nurses, working in an efficacious group appeared to mitigate the effects of situational stressors (role ambiguity, conflict, and overload) on emotional exhaustion. From their findings, Zellars et al. concluded that "steps to improve group cohesion may benefit high-NA individuals through decreased burnout levels" (p. 2264). They also noted that confidence in the group's ability to coordinate its activities may lead to greater persistence in the face of challenging situations and hence higher performance levels.

In summary, the above evidence would appear to contrast with Cohen and Edwards's (1989) conclusion about the role of self-esteem or generalized self-efficacy in the stress process. Clearly, additional research is needed to confirm these initial findings, but there would appear to be a sound case for the plasticity hypothesis that beliefs about the self and one's abilities may function as effective buffers against the adverse effects of stressful job conditions, particularly role stressors. The mechanisms by which this buffering occurs require further delineation. As noted by Ganster and Schaubroeck (1995), self-esteem or self-efficacy may influence the coping strategies used to combat stressors, with low-self-esteem individuals selecting less effective coping behaviors. This hypothesis has yet to be tested directly in empirical research.

Other Dispositional Variables

In addition to the variables outlined above, several other dispositional factors have been implicated as potential moderators of the relationship between job stressors and psychological strain. The buffering effects of two of these variables will be reviewed briefly.

Optimism

Despite their generally cautious appraisal of the stress-moderating effects of personality variables, Cohen and Edwards (1989) indicated that optimism, along with feelings of personal control and self-esteem or self-efficacy, might function as a "superordinate" moderator: that is, one that reflects the essence of other dispositional factors. *Optimism* refers to a "conviction that the future holds desirable outcomes, irrespective of one's personal ability to control those outcomes" (Marshall & Lang, 1990, p. 132). An optimistic orientation to life may derive from various sources (including luck), but it can be distinguished from mastery or control over specific circumstances or outcomes (e.g., control over one's work environment) in that it constitutes a global expectation that there is a high probability of desirable outcomes occurring, irrespective of one's own actions.

Dispositional optimism has been found to exert a positive effect on personal adjustment, life satisfaction, and overall well-being (see Scheier & Carver, 1992, for a review of this literature). As with the other variables summarized above, one likely mechanism for this effect is via the selection of coping strategies, which we review in Chapter 6. Several studies have illustrated, for example, that optimists have more positive appraisals of stressors and engage different strategies for coping with stressful situations (Chang, 1998).

Given the suggestion raised by Cohen and Edwards over 10 years ago that optimism may represent a superordinate moderator, it is surprising that there has not been more systematic exploration of the optimism construct in studies of job-related strain. Recent investigations of this construct have tended to sample student populations (e.g., Chang, 1998; Lee et al., 1993) rather than employees in work settings. One of the few studies of occupational groups (Marshall & Lang, 1990) failed to find evidence of an independent direct effect of optimism on depression

among women professionals; a possible moderating effect on depression
was not explored in this study.

Locus of Control

Locus of control (LOC) is another dispositional factor that may play
a role in the stress-coping process, although again there has not been a
great deal of empirical research recently on the potential moderating
influence of this variable on stressor-strain relations. LOC differs from
perceived control (over the work environment) in that the former refers
to a generalized expectancy of having control over life events and hence
is a dispositional construct, whereas the latter reflects a person's perception of control in specific circumstances and can vary across situations.
Due to these differences in nature and function, our view is that,
although the two variables clearly may be interrelated, perceived control
should be classified as a situational variable rather than as a personality
disposition. (We discuss perceived control in the next section of this
chapter.)

From their review of research carried out in the 1970s and 1980s,
Cohen and Edwards (1989) concluded that there is "tentative support
for locus of control (as measured by the Rotter scale) as a buffer of the
relationship between life events stress and psychological strain" (p. 259).
An example of research conducted along these lines is a study reported
by Perrewe (1987), who found that individuals with high external LOC
experienced less anxiety and strain as a result of low perceived control
over their work environment than did those with high internal LOC.

Payne (1988) also reviewed research on the buffering role of LOC,
noting that evidence for moderator effects was mixed. As with optimism,
most studies of LOC have been conducted outside occupational settings
and have focused on strain from life events. Payne suggested, however,
that moderator effects found in these studies frequently can be explained
by the overlap between LOC and other constructs, such as NA and
neuroticism. More recently, Semmer (1996) has noted that research on
LOC in organizational contexts has also generated inconclusive findings.
Methodological problems in the measurement of LOC, including lack
of convergence between various measures of this construct (see Cohen &
Edwards, 1989), coupled with conceptual overlap between LOC and
other dispositional constructs, have seriously undermined researchers'

efforts to demonstrate consistent relationships between this factor and indicators of strain.

To conclude this discussion of personality moderators of the stressor-strain relationship, although there is some evidence that certain dispositional variables may buffer the impact of stressors on individuals' experience of strain (either psychological or physical), the conclusion drawn by Cohen and Edwards (1989) that this evidence is by no means persuasive would still seem to apply. A few dispositional factors, such as self-esteem or self-efficacy and possibly optimism, have shown promise in this regard, but further organizationally based studies are needed to confirm the effects of these variables. As mentioned above, one serious issue, both conceptually and methodologically, is the extent of overlap between various personality constructs. Several authors have commented on the possible confounding of effects due to lack of conceptual differentiation and measurement redundancy between variables such as optimism, self-esteem, NA, and neuroticism. Unless we can demonstrate that these constructs exert distinct influences on strain, the search for unique moderator effects will continue to produce ambiguous findings.

At another level, one might question whether the examination of moderator variables using cross-sectional research designs has deflected attention away from more central issues in job stress research, particularly exploration of the dynamic transactional stress-coping process. In brief, cross-sectional designs may not capture the dynamic interplay between dispositional variables and stress-coping behaviors. Hence, although variables such as those referred to above may have an important buffering effect, their exact role may not be clearly identified in studies that measure stressors and strain at a single time point.

Situational Moderators: Perceived Control Over the Environment

Among the situational variables that may buffer the impact of stressors (such as work demands, role ambiguity, and role conflict) on the extent of psychological strain experienced by workers, one that has received considerable attention is the degree of autonomy or control that individuals can exert over their work environment.

As explained earlier, we discuss perceived control as a "situational" factor because it reflects individuals' perceptions of their specific (work)

	Low Job Demands	High Job Demands
Low Control	Passive Job	High-Strain Job
High Control	Low-Strain Job	Active Job

Figure 5.3. Karasek's Job Demands-Control Model

SOURCE: Reprinted with permission of Academy of Management, P.O. Box 3020, Briarcliff Manor, NY 10510-8020. Effects of Stressful Job Demands and Control of Physiological and Attitudinal Outcomes in a Hospital Setting (Figure 1), Fox, Dwyer and Ganster, Academy of Management Journal 1993, 36(2), p. 291. Reproduced by permission of the publisher via Copyright Clearance Center, Inc.

environments rather than cross-situational dispositional beliefs. In other words, perceived autonomy or control has more to do with environmental characteristics (i.e., whether the situation permits individual control) than with beliefs about control in general (e.g., generalized LOC). Nevertheless, the interplay between specific control perceptions and global control beliefs should not be overlooked.

Most research in the last 20 years on the possible stress-moderating effects of control has been based upon Karasek's (1979) *job demands-control* model, also known as the *demands-discretion* model or simply the *decision latitude* model (Fox, Dwyer & Ganster, 1993). This framework has been comprehensively described and critiqued in several recent publications (see, e.g., Fox et al., 1993; Jones & Fletcher, 1996; Schaubroeck & Merritt, 1997) and hence will be outlined only briefly here.

Figure 5.3 demonstrates the basic elements of the Karasek model. His fundamental proposition is that although excessive work demands may clearly be associated with higher levels of psychological strain and even physiological health outcomes (such as cardiovascular disease; Kristensen, 1996), the impact of these demands may be offset by the perception that one has control over important aspects of the work environment. Indeed, highly challenging or demanding work combined with high control is considered by Karasek to indicate an "active" job that has beneficial outcomes for individuals. At the other extreme, jobs that have low demands and low levels of control (e.g., repetitive assembly line work) create strain and are referred to by Karasek as "passive" jobs.

The logic underlying the demands-control model is clearly described by Fox et al. (1993). The reason that high work demands are stressful is that they create anxiety about job performance and the personal consequences of not completing work in a specified time frame. In Karasek's theory, this anxiety can be ameliorated if workers (a) have the power to make decisions on the job (decision authority) and (b) can use a variety of skills in their work (skill discretion). Typically, researchers have combined these two factors into one construct, variously referred to as *decision latitude* or *control*. (We would note in passing that decision authority and skill discretion have much in common with elements of the job characteristics model of job design proposed by Hackman & Oldham, 1976, which underlies the bulk of research conducted on the impact of work restructuring or redesign on employees' attitudes and behaviors.)

It might be thought that actual control is essential for Karasek's argument, and much of his early epidemiological research was based on the assumed degree of control held by various occupational groups. One criticism of this line of research, however, is that it contains no direct measurement of the amount of control that different occupations may actually exert in their jobs. Recently, more attention has been given to workers' perceptions of control, on the assumption that, irrespective of objective levels of control, the extent to which individuals believe they have control is a major determinant of their affective responses, such as job satisfaction and strain (Schaubroeck & Merritt, 1997; Spector, 1986; Yoon, Han, & Seo, 1996).

Other theoretical accounts of the role of control in the stress process mirror the basic tenets of Karasek's model. For instance, Fletcher's (1991) catastrophe model suggests that "strain results when there is a lack of balance in the demands and constraints placed on a person in relation to the supports available to that person" (Jones & Fletcher, 1996, p. 34). Having a high level of autonomy or control in one's work is considered to be a "support" that may reduce the impact of job demands. Similarly, control is a significant element in Warr's (1987) vitamin model of stress in that it enables the person to make adjustments in his or her environment that can offset the aversive consequences of work stressors. Interestingly, however, Warr's vitamin model implies a curvilinear relationship between the extent of control and well-being: Too much control can be damaging for the person, just as too little control is harmful. Increased control may imply additional responsibility for outcomes, and for some individuals this added responsibility may be a burden rather than a challenge (Spector, 1998).

There is growing consensus among researchers that appropriate levels of control over the environment are important for workers' well-being and even their physical health (Fox et al., 1993; Kristensen, 1996; Sutton & Kahn, 1987), and considerable evidence has accumulated to indicate that control (or perceived control) is significantly associated with these outcomes (Jones & Fletcher, 1996). However, the critical issue for the present discussion is whether control functions as a moderator of the relationship between job demands (stressors) and individuals' affective and physiological outcomes (strains). Unfortunately, evidence relating to this question is not clear-cut. From their own research, Karasek and his colleagues argued that job demands and control have interactive effects on worker well-being. As noted above, however, some of this epidemiological research did not measure extent of control directly but rather inferred levels of control from occupational classification. It is not possible to gauge whether these inferences always accurately reflected the amount of control that workers actually possessed.

In addition, some studies did not analyze interaction effects statistically, and "critics have concluded that the epidemiological evidence mostly seems to support an additive model of demands and control rather than an interactive one" (Fox et al., 1993, p. 292). Whereas Fox and her colleagues obtained significant interactions between workload (measured both subjectively and objectively) and perceived control on both job satisfaction and blood cortisol levels, other studies have not demonstrated a moderator effect for control (e.g., Melamed, Kushnir, & Meir, 1991; O'Driscoll & Beehr, 2000; Schreurs & Taris, 1998), and still others have obtained mixed results. For instance, Tetrick and LaRocco (1987) found an interactive effect on job satisfaction but not psychological well-being; Perrewe and Ganster (1989) observed interactive effects on anxiety but not job satisfaction or physiological arousal; and Parkes, Mendham, and von Rabenau (1994) obtained demand × discretion interactions on job satisfaction but not somatic symptoms. Overall, therefore, research has not generated definitive conclusions about the moderating influence of the control variable.

Two fairly recent studies indicate that clearer specification of the control variable may be needed to obtain the expected interaction with job demands. Wall, Jackson, Mullarkey, and Parker (1996) noted that measurement of decision latitude is frequently based on Karasek's (1979) original conceptualization of this variable, "which represents a much broader construct than that of job control" (p. 157). In particular, it includes issues such as the opportunity to learn new things, show creativity, and experience variety, all of which seem to be more related to job scope than to control per se. Failure to confirm the demands-control model may therefore be attributed, at least partially, to inappropriate assessment of one of the critical elements of the model. Wall et al. (1996) developed a more focused measure of perceived job control, explicitly tailored to the job demands experienced by respondents in their study. From their investigation, Wall and his colleagues concluded that "where a more clearly descriptive measure of demands is used in conjunction with a more focused measure of control" (p. 162), the likelihood of demonstrating the expected interaction effect is increased, although they did caution that the amount of variance accounted for by this interaction was relatively small (around 1%), which is not atypical in field research of this kind.

Sargent and Terry (1998) have also argued that use of a global index of control may mask the impact of some forms of control. They suggested that control over some areas (such as the pace and organization of work, and scheduling) may be more central than control over other areas (e.g., resource allocation, organizational decisions). Following Cohen and Wills (1985) and Wall et al. (1996), Sargent and Terry proposed that there must be a match between the specific demands and the type of buffer for a stress-buffering effect to be observed. Their results revealed some support for this prediction, suggesting that the effects of job demands were moderated by high levels of task control but not by the other (more peripheral) aspects of control.

From these studies, it is clear that more precise specification of job demands and control variables is needed and that global measures of autonomy or control that combine a variety of different areas of control may not display the buffering effects predicted by the demands-control model. Other investigations also suggest that additional variables may themselves moderate the moderator effect. For example, Westman (1992) found that the moderating effect of decision latitude on the job stressor-strain relationship was itself moderated by the individual's position within a banking organization. A three-way interaction of role conflict × decision latitude × level significantly predicted psychological strain (although not job dissatisfaction). Specifically, employees at lower levels of the organizational hierarchy were more affected by lack of decision latitude. Westman suggested that this might be because employees at higher levels (i.e., managers) had greater resources to cope with role conflict. Interestingly, however, level within the organization showed no significant moderator effect in relation to role ambiguity, which may indicate that role conflict better represents the "demand" component of Karasek's model.

At the job level, the amount of information that employees are provided about job procedures and events (e.g., changes) within their organization may attenuate the moderating effects of control. Jimmieson and Terry (1998) hypothesized that the stress-buffering influence of (behavioral) control on employee adjustment would be more evident at high than at low levels of information access. In their study, there was no evidence of a moderating effect for behavioral control, but contextual information served as a buffer for employees who perceived that they did not have behavioral control. In other words, the negative effects of having low behavioral control over the work environment could be compensated for by access to job-related information, such as information about job procedures and changes occurring within the organization.

Dispositional variables may also be relevant in the context of the demand-control model. Schaubroeck and Merritt (1997), for example, identified self-efficacy as a moderator variable that may determine whether job control has a positive or negative influence on the relationship between job demands and strain. Their data on employee self-reports of blood pressure indicated that the combination of high job demands and high control had negative health consequences among employees who reported low self-efficacy, which suggests that increasing the level of control may be effective only when individuals experience high levels of mastery on the job. Schaubroeck and Merritt concluded from their findings that interventions to enhance job self-efficacy "may be as important to reducing the cardiovascular consequences of job stress as efforts to enhance control" (p. 738).

Finally, it is important to examine the relevance of cultural factors for the effects of control on job-related strain. Most research on the demands-control model has implicitly assumed that individual control over one's job is an important issue for workers and has not directly assessed the amount of control *desired* (as opposed to *possessed*). There may well be individual differences in the relevance and meaningfulness of autonomy and the extent of control that is desired (Schwalbe, 1985; Spector, 1998). Furthermore, almost all studies of the demands-control model have been conducted in the United States or European countries, which are characterized as having an individualistic culture (Hofstede, 1980). It is likely that personal control over the environment is more salient in such societies than in countries whose cultures are more collectivistic.

In a study that directly examined this proposition, Xie (1996) explored the cross-cultural generalizability of Karasek's demands-control model to the People's Republic of China, comparing results obtained from this collectivistic culture with findings reported in the literature. Data from her Chinese respondents showed significant interaction effects between demands and decision latitude on anxiety and health problems, although not on depression and job satisfaction. These findings parallel those obtained in Western cultures and are broadly consistent with predictions from the demands-control model, suggesting that this model may be applicable across cultural boundaries. It would be of interest, however, to investigate whether a sense of collective (or group/team) control over the work environment is more salient than individual autonomy in some circumstances, especially for people in collectivistic societies. If so, researchers should delineate the conditions under which group control is more important than individual control (see our earlier discussion of Jex and Gudanowski's 1992 findings on self-efficacy).

Although many other situational variables may function as moderators of the impact of job stressors on psychological strain and physical health, because of the substantial interest in and research conducted on Karasek's (1979) demands-control model we have focused attention here entirely on perceived control. Evidence to date shows some support for the Karasek model, particularly when salient job demands and areas of control are clearly identified and are matched with each other. Given inconsistencies across research findings, however, there is clearly a need for further investigations that include individual, organizational, and perhaps societal factors that may influence the moderating effects of perceived autonomy or control. There is also a need to examine the effects of control in combination with other factors, such as the amount of social support provided by other people within the individual's environment.

Effects of Social Support on Stressor-Strain Relationships

The literature on stress in general, including job stress, is replete with studies of the effects that support from others has on an individual's

Figure 5.4. Direct Relationship Between Social Support and Strain

level of well-being and psychological strain. However, although this research has indicated that social support may be an important influence on affective experiences, there is considerable debate (and dispute) over just how this influence is exerted. In the following discussion, we will examine the various mechanisms by which social support may operate, summarize evidence on the impact of support, and consider potential explanations for research findings.

Several definitions and models of social support have been proposed by social scientists, but in the organizational field a frequently used conceptualization of support is that advanced by House (1981), who differentiated between four kinds of support:

1. Instrumental support (giving direct help, often of a practical nature)
2. Emotional support (showing interest in, understanding of, caring for, and sympathy with a person's difficulties)
3. Informational support (giving the person information that may help him or her deal with problems)
4. Appraisal support (providing feedback about the person's functioning that may enhance his or her self-esteem)

These types of support, especially the first two, have formed the basis for much of the research on the impact of social support on stressor-strain relationships.

Social support may exert an influence on stressor-strain relationships in three distinct ways. First, there may be a *main* effect, whereby increases in support are directly associated with reduced strain, irrespective of the number or intensity of stressors that the individual encounters. This relationship between support and strain, shown in Figure 5.4, is expressed by a significant zero-order correlation between these variables. One explanation for this effect is that support increases individuals' self-esteem, making them less susceptible to the impact of stressors in their environment (Cohen & Wills, 1985; Fenlason & Beehr, 1994). In this context, self-esteem serves as a mediator between support and strain.

Social support may also function as a mediating variable in the stressor-strain relationship (see Figure 5.5). In this model, stressors (such as role

Figure 5.5. Social Support as a Mediating Variable

Figure 5.6. Alternative Mediation Mechanism

ambiguity, conflict, and overload) may spur individuals to mobilize their support resources, which in turn help to reduce the amount of strain experienced, either practically or in one of the other ways listed above. A variant of the mediating model, depicted in Figure 5.6, occurs when social support affects the experience of the stressor, rather than having a direct effect on strain itself. For instance, support from others may lead individuals to reappraise the intensity of a potential stressor (e.g., the level of insecurity in the job) or the significance of the stressor for their well-being. Scheck, Kinicki, and Davy (1997) found that both instrumental and emotional support were associated with employees' appraisals of negative life events (stressors), albeit in different directions. In this case, the stressor, rather than social support, is the mediating variable.

Finally, as illustrated in Figure 5.7, social support may act as a moderator of the relationship between stressors and affective outcomes. In this scenario, having support from others is hypothesized to attenuate the correlation between stressors and strain, primarily because support may help individuals to cope with their job demands and problems.

The model of events shown in Figure 5.7 reflects what is typically referred to as the *stress-buffering hypothesis,* which proposes that the relationship between stressors and strains will differ depending on the level of support a person utilizes. In other words, individuals who receive social support will experience less strain than their counterparts who do not receive support from others because support shields or protects individuals from the potentially harmful consequences of aversive events or circumstances. This may occur instrumentally, by helping them attend to a problem, or emotionally, by modifying their perception that the stressor is damaging to their well-being.

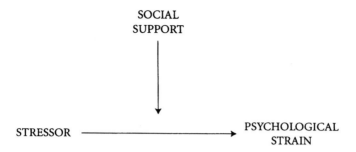

Figure 5.7. Social Support as a Moderating Variable

In summary, the model shown in Figure 5.5 depicts a direct effect of social support on perceptions of stressors, whereas Figure 5.7 suggests that support influences the impact of stressors on the individual, rather than having a direct influence on either stressors (Figure 5.6) or the resultant strain (Figure 5.4). In a statistical sense, only Figure 5.7 illustrates a moderating effect for social support. Research on strain has predominantly investigated predictions based upon this stress-buffering argument (Fenlason & Beehr, 1994; Winnubst & Schabracq, 1996).

Sources of Support

Almost invariably, research on social support has obtained individuals' self-reports of (a) the *amount* of support available to them and/or (b) their *utilization* of various sources of support. The potential confounding of these issues is discussed later. For now, our focus is on findings and conclusions derived from studies of the effects of support on job-related strain. We will not review all the studies that have been conducted on this topic but rather will summarize findings that reflect predominant themes in this area.

Ganster, Fusilier, and Mayes (1986) examined employees' perceptions of the amount of social support received from three sources (supervisors, colleagues, and family/friends), via the commonly used Social Support Questionnaire (Caplan, Cobb, French, Harrison, & Pinneau, 1975). Consistent with the stress-buffering hypothesis, Ganster et al. (1986) predicted that the positive relationship between six job stressors (role ambiguity, conflict, and underload, plus lack of variability, skill underutilization, and responsibility for others) and strain variables (depression, somatic complaints, job dissatisfaction, and dissatisfaction in life overall) would be moderated by various sources of support.

Significant direct links were found between lack of social support and all of the strain variables, particularly job dissatisfaction. Of the various sources of support, those in the workplace, especially supervisory support, exhibited the strongest negative relationship with strain. Compared with the stressors, however, a relatively small percentage of variance in strain scores (6%) was accounted for by social support variables. More importantly, hierarchical regressions generated few significant interactions between stressors and support, indicating that evidence for the proposed stress-buffering effect of social support was very weak. Ganster et al. suggested that "support for the buffering hypothesis appears to be more prevalent in studies concerning life events as sources of stress than in studies concerning work stressors" (1986, p. 109).

A study of Japanese bank employees by Iwata and Suzuki (1997) also examined the potential moderating effects of support from supervisors, colleagues, family members, and "significant others." Role stressors included in this study were overload, ambiguity, and conflict, and strain was assessed via the General Health Questionnaire (GHQ-28). Supervisory support and support from significant others were directly (negatively) related to strain. However, of 12 interaction terms between stressors and support variables, only one attained statistical significance, again illustrating a lack of buffering effects for social support on stressor-strain relationships.

Similar conclusions were reached by Frone, Russell, and Cooper (1995) from their study of the effects of job-related and family stressors. Perceived availability of social support was significantly correlated with reduced depression and somatic symptoms but displayed no interaction with job stressors, family stressors, or work-family conflict. Frone et al. raised two critical issues from their findings. First, "A conceptual fit may be necessary between a stressor and a moderator before any person-environment interaction is observed" (p. 145). This suggests that specific forms of support should be explored, along with the potential relevance of that support for alleviation of the stressor in question. Second, the importance of social support to the individual must be considered. Some people may place higher value than others on social support as a resource for counteracting the negative consequences of stressors. Very few studies have measured the salience of support to individuals; rather, it has been implicitly assumed that social support is important to everyone.

In contrast, two recent studies have obtained evidence in favor of the stress-buffering role of social support from significant others. In the first of these studies, Lim (1996) assessed the relationship between job insecurity and several work-related outcomes, including job and life satisfaction. Significant, albeit relatively small, increments in percentage variance accounted for were obtained for both work support and off-the-job support, in terms of job satisfaction and life satisfaction respectively. Lim concluded that support from colleagues and supervisors, as well as from family and friends, helped buffer individuals from the strain of job insecurity.

Moyle and Parkes (1999) also observed a moderating effect for social support on the relationship between "transition" stressors and psychological strain among supermarket employees having to make a compulsory move to another store. Where individuals received support from their manager, the extent of strain experienced due to the forced relocation was significantly reduced.

A few studies have investigated the relevance of social support for the experience of burnout (see our discussion of this variable in Chapter 4). Etzion (1984) explored job-related stressors, off-the-job stressors, and burnout among Israeli managers and social service professionals. The moderating effects of support on the job (from colleagues, supervisors, and subordinates) and in life generally (from spouses, family, and friends) were also assessed via self-reports of the availability of various forms of support in each area. Hierarchical regressions demonstrated significant direct linkages between both sources of support and burnout, although these relationships were in opposite directions, negative for job support and positive for off-the-job support. Significant moderator effects were observed for support in this study, although the patterns of these effects varied between men and women. For men, the relationship between job stressors and burnout was moderated by job support, whereas for women this relationship was moderated by off-the-job support. Etzion suggested that job and off-job sources of support may have differential salience for men and women.

Russell, Altmaier, and van Velzen (1987) also looked at the impact of social support on burnout in a sample of elementary and secondary school teachers. They hypothesized that support received from supervisors and colleagues may have important stress-amelioration effects. Their results demonstrated a main effect of supervisor support on emotional exhaustion, depersonalization, and personal accomplishment and an interaction effect between job stressors and supervisor support, but only for the depersonalization subscale of the Maslach Burnout Inventory (see Chapter 4 for a discussion of this measure). No direct or moderating influence was observed for social support from coworkers, spouses, friends, or relatives. At best, these findings provide only marginal support for the stress-buffering hypothesis.

In contrast to the above, Greenglass, Fiksenbaum, and Burke (1995) did obtain a significant moderating influence of friends and family support on teacher burnout (using total scores on the MBI). However, the beta weight for the interaction between family/friend support and job stressors was just .03, and the authors did not report the percentage variance (R^2) accounted for by the interaction term; hence, the relative contribution of the moderator effect in this study is indeterminate. In a more extended investigation of teacher burnout, however, Greenglass, Fiksenbaum, and Burke (1996) presented data showing significant moderator effects of support from colleagues and supervisors on both the emotional exhaustion and depersonalization subscales of the MBI.

Type of Support Provided

In addition to consideration of the impact of different sources of support, research has also explored the effects of different types of support. As outlined earlier, commonly investigators have compared instrumental (practical) and emotional support. In the Greenglass et al. (1996) study referred to above, buffering effects for informational support were also observed.

Fenlason and Beehr (1994) argued that it is important to examine the nature of support provided, rather than assuming common effects across various forms of support. Their study differentiated between global measures of emotional and instrumental support and more specific verbal support, as well as assessing support from different sources (supervisors, colleagues, and family/friends). The types of support were further distinguished as non-work-related, positive work-related, and negative work-related communications. Examples of each of these communications were "We discuss things that are happening in our personal lives" (non-work related), "We talk about how this organization is a good place to work" (positive work related), and "We talk about how we dislike some parts of our work" (negative work related). As anticipated, the three types of communication were more closely related to emotional than to instrumental support. More importantly, specific communications accounted for more reduction in strain (job dissatisfaction, boredom, depression, and anxiety) than did the global support measures, suggesting that the contents of communication may be important aspects of the support process, not just the frequency with which emotional and/or instrumental support is received.

Also of interest, Fenlason and Beehr found that support had both buffering and *reverse buffering* effects. Whereas support is typically viewed as having a positive impact on individuals, the concept of reverse buffering was identified in earlier research by LaRocco, House, and French (1980) and then more directly by Kaufmann and Beehr (1986), who found that under certain circumstances higher levels of support exacerbated rather than alleviated the amount of strain experienced by workers. In particular, Kaufmann and Beehr noted that where support from others reaffirms the aversive nature of the work environment (e.g., "We talk about the bad things in our work"), the person's negative attitudes and reactions (such as strain) are likely to be heightened rather than mitigated by increased levels of support.

Findings such as these suggest that the impact of social support is neither simple nor unilinear. Though most research has typically examined only the frequency or amount of support provided, the research of Beehr and his colleagues illustrates that it is important to unravel the multidimensional character of support, to examine both the nature and source(s) of support. In the Fenlason and Beehr (1994) study, for instance, although positive communications from supervisors, colleagues, and family/friends all showed a negative relationship with psychological strain, and although negative communications were positively linked with strain, between-source variations suggested that the contents of supportive communications and the origin of support are both critical factors to consider. In a similar vein, Chen, Popovich, and Kogan (1999) have suggested that the moderating effects of social support may depend on factors such as the sources of support, the foci or targets of support, and the types of strain outcome investigated. Clearly, more systematic and extensive exploration of these factors is needed to generate a complete understanding of the role of this important, yet complex variable.

Job Demands-Control-Support Model

Johnson and Hall (1988) proposed an extension of Karasek's demands-control model of stress to incorporate social support as a moderator of the linkage of job demands and control with strain, and research has provided some empirical confirmation of a three-way interaction between job demands, control or discretion, and support (Jones & Fletcher, 1996; Schaubroeck & Fink, 1998). A study by Parkes et al. (1994) exemplifies this line of research on the expanded demands-control perspective. The authors tested two alternative hypotheses of the effects of social support. The *additive* hypothesis proposes that support functions independently of job stressors to promote well-being; hence, strain would be predicted by a combination of the demands-control interaction and low social support. This parallels the "direct effect" of social support described above (see Figure 5.3). On the other hand, the *interactive* hypothesis suggests a three-way interaction of job demands × control (or discretion) × support. "Low support combined with high strain conditions would be predicted to give rise to disproportionately adverse health outcomes, relative to either low support and low strain conditions, or high support and high strain" (Parkes et al., 1994, p. 93).

Research along these lines has generated inconsistent findings. For instance, although Landsbergis, Schnall, Dietz, Friedman, and Pickering (1992) obtained evidence of a three-way interaction involving social support, their results indicated a reverse buffering effect, where support appeared to exacerbate rather than ameliorate the effects of stressors. Moreover, data presented by Melamed et al. (1991), and more recently by Dollard and Winefield (1998), confirmed an additive, rather than interactive, influence for support.

Parkes et al. (1994) incorporated Karasek's (1979) measures of demands (time pressure and workload) and discretion (opportunities for control and decision making) and examined the buffering influence of support from coworkers. Strain was assessed by levels of job dissatisfaction and somatic symptoms. Moderated regressions yielded a significant direct link between social support and job satisfaction but not somatic symptoms, and a two-way interaction effect of demands × discretion on job satisfaction. Significant three-way interactions were also obtained for somatic symptoms, lending some support to the stress-buffering model, although the percent variance accounted for by the triple interaction (3% in one study and 1% in another) indicated that the effects were not substantial in scope. From their analyses, Parkes and her colleagues concluded that their job satisfaction results verified the additive effects hypothesis concerning social support and were also consistent with Karasek's demands-control model. For somatic symptoms, there was some confirmation of the interactive model, but Parkes et al. suggested that this result was unlikely to be of great practical importance because the size of the moderator effect was relatively small.

Schaubroeck and Fink (1998) also obtained mixed evidence for the demands-control-support model. These investigators obtained employee self-reports of the amount of social support they received from both their supervisor and their coworkers. Significant demands-control-support interactions were observed more consistently for supervisory support than for support from coworkers. Overall, however, plots of the interaction terms did "not support the prevailing perspective that support buffers the effects of high strain (i.e., low control, high demand) jobs" (p. 167). Schaubroeck and Fink concluded that when low levels of control cannot be avoided, increased social support may not have the predicted stress-buffering effect.

Erosion of Buffering Effects

Although their research was not conducted on job stress per se, Lepore, Evans, and Schneider (1991) found that although social support may exert buffering effects initially, these effects can be eroded by continuation of the stressor(s). Their longitudinal study of college students found a buffering influence of support from roommates on the effects of household crowding on distress at a 2-month time period, but that continued crowding led to a deterioration in perceptions of support and a corresponding increase in strain. Lepore et al. suggested that, with continued exposure to a stressor, the role of support may shift from being a moderator (buffer) to being a mediator in the stressor-strain relationship (see Figure 5.5). This would have significant theoretical and methodological implications for the study of support processes, in that the buffering role of social support may be "washed out" in the presence of chronic (ongoing) stressors. Lepore et al.'s findings also confirm the importance of distinguishing between the impact of acute and chronic stressors. It is possible that support may play a buffering role in respect of the former but not the latter, although more systematic exploration of this suggestion is required.

Unresolved Issues

From this brief overview of research on the role of social support in the stress process, data on the moderating (buffering) effect of support are inconclusive. Though some studies (e.g., Parkes et al., 1994) have obtained evidence of stress buffering, these effects typically have been quite small and of questionable practical importance. More often, social support has displayed a significant direct relationship with lower levels of psychological strain, suggesting that having support is generally beneficial to well-being, irrespective of the stressors encountered.

Having said this, several issues require deeper examination in social support research. First, as noted by Frone et al. (1995) and Winnubst and Schabracq (1996), there needs to be a closer matching between the types of support and the particular stressors encountered by individuals. Not all forms of support are likely to buffer the impact of all stressors. More likely, the effectiveness of support will vary across situations, as well as across individuals. Although some studies have controlled for some individual differences (particularly demographic variables), there has been no systematic effort to determine critical dispositional factors that may themselves moderate the effects of support in stressor-strain relationships. Along with this is a need to examine the importance of support to different individuals, rather than assuming that social support is always relevant to everyone.

A second issue needing resolution is the level of specificity of support. Fenlason and Beehr (1994) found that specific types of support predicted affective outcomes better than did more global measures of instrumental and emotional support. Although the latter may be useful in terms of describing and classifying support types, more detailed investigation of the form and nature of social supports and their utilization is necessary to better understand how and when support functions as a buffer.

Third, as we noted earlier, there is sometimes a confounding in research between support available, support received or used, and support effectiveness. For example, the most commonly used measure of support in studies of job stress, the Caplan et al. (1975) scale, focuses on received support, but other measures are somewhat ambiguous in terms of whether they assess support used or support that may be available but not actually used. Whether support availability per se is sufficient to moderate stressor-strain relations has not been established, but the distinction between availability and usage may have significant implications for the stress-buffering hypothesis.

Finally, there is debate in the literature on the distinction between *perceived* support and *objective* support from others. Most studies of the role of support in the stress-coping process tap individuals' perceptions of support available or received rather than more objective indexes of support. This leaves open the question as to which is more important: subjective perceptions or "objective" reality. In the transactional perspective, what the individual perceives is considered to be paramount, but there would appear to have been little effort in studies of job stress to compare the effects of perceived and objective support.

Conclusion

In this chapter, we examined three broad categories of potential moderators of the relationship between job stressors and strain indexes. First, we considered the stress-buffering effects exerted by several personality or dispositional factors. In recent years, there has been an upsurge of interest in personality variables as predictors of employee attitudes, affective reactions, and behaviors, and the field of job stress has mirrored research in other areas. However, evidence for the moderating effects of specific dispositions is, at this point anyway, less than conclusive. Of the variables reviewed here, self-esteem and self-efficacy are perhaps the most likely candidates, and recent data appear to support the behavioral plasticity hypothesis advanced by Brockner (1988). Other dispositional variables have displayed less consistent buffering effects, suggesting that further research is needed on the specific circumstances under which they may function in this capacity.

The second line of research that we have examined focuses on control over the work environment, which is a major "situational" factor in job-related stress. Research on this topic has been predominantly built around Karasek's (1979) demands-control model, which predicts that high levels of perceived control will ameliorate the aversive consequences of excessively demanding jobs. Again, although there has been some support for this perspective, several studies have failed to obtain the predicted demands × control interaction. From existing evidence, it is clear that closer matching between the types of stressors and specific forms of control is needed to enable appropriate assessment of the buffering effects of control.

The third category of potential moderators reviewed in this chapter was social support. Individuals' stress-coping endeavors (which we discuss in Chapter 6) may be assisted by support from significant others in both their work and off-the-job settings, and there has been considerable research on the moderating functions of social support. As with the two previous kinds of moderators, however, empirical data have not uniformly demonstrated a buffering effect for this variable. More often, it has been found that support has a direct relationship with well-being and job attitudes, rather than moderating the relationship between work stressors and these outcomes. Several suggestions for further research on the potential buffering role of social support were discussed.

In conclusion, we believe that the search for moderators of stressor-strain relationships is important and can yield significant information about the stress process overall. However, the ability to detect moderator effects in organizational research, especially studies conducted in field settings, is constrained by a number of factors. One potential explanation for the lack of significant moderator effects in several of the studies cited in this chapter is that the demonstration of moderation requires the inclusion of individuals (respondents) who exhibit more than just "average" scores on the criterion variable(s)—that is, people who are experiencing reasonably high levels of strain.[1] Given that individuals with high strain are likely to withdraw from the environment (see Chapter 3 for a discussion of the linkage between strain and withdrawal) or may be too "stressed" to contemplate involvement in a research project on job-related strain, it may be difficult to capture these individuals for this type of research. Finally, it is crucial that moderator variables be investigated within the framework of the transactional model of stress, rather than as peripheral issues that may or may not impinge upon stress-coping mechanisms. This means that the focus on moderators must not be at the expense of attention to the transactional process itself; rather, the role of moderators must be considered within the context of the dynamic transaction between the individual and the environment. This will require theoretical models that integrate moderators more explicitly into the coping process, to which we turn in Chapter 6.

Note

1. We wish to thank Ben Schneider for this suggestion.

References

Allred, K., & Smith, T. (1989). The hardy personality: Cognitive and physiological responses to evaluative threat. *Journal of Personality and Social Psychology, 56,* 257-266.

Baron, R., & Kenny, D. (1986). The moderator-mediator variable distinction in social psychological research: Conceptual, strategic and statistical considerations. *Journal of Personality and Social Psychology, 51,* 1173-1182.

Benishek, L., & Lopez, F. (1997). Critical evaluation of hardiness theory: Gender differences, perception of life events and neuroticism. *Work and Stress, 11,* 33-45.

Bolger, N., & Zuckerman, A. (1995). A framework for studying personality in the stress process. *Journal of Personality and Social Psychology, 69,* 890-902.

Brief, A., Burke, M., George, J., Robinson, B., & Webster, J. (1988). Should negative affectivity remain an unmeasured variable in the study of job stress. *Journal of Applied Psychology, 73,* 193-198.

Brockner, J. (1988). *Self-esteem at work: Research, theory and practice.* Lexington, MA: Lexington.

Burke, R. (1988). Type A behavior, occupational and life demands, satisfaction, and well-being. *Psychological Reports, 63,* 451-458.

Caplan, R., Cobb, S., French, J., Harrison, R., & Pineau, S. (1975). *Job demands and worker health.* Ann Arbor: University of Michigan, Institute for Social Research.

Chang, E. (1998). Dispositional optimism and primary and secondary appraisal of a stressor: Controlling for confounding influences and relations to coping and psychological and physical adjustment. *Journal of Personality and Social Psychology, 74,* 1109-1120.

Chen, P., Popovich, M., & Kogan, M. (1999). Let's talk: Patterns and correlates of social support among temporary employees. *Journal of Occupational Health Psychology, 4,* 1-8.

Chen, P., & Spector, P. (1991). Negative affectivity as the underlying cause of correlations between stressors and strains. *Journal of Applied Psychology, 76,* 398-407.

Cohen, S., & Edwards, J. (1989). Personality characteristics as moderators of the relationship between stress and disorder. In W. Neufeld (Ed.), *Advances in the investigation of psychological stress* (pp. 235-283). New York: John Wiley.

Cohen, S., & Wills, T. (1985). Stress, social support and the buffering hypothesis. *Psychological Bulletin, 92,* 257-310.

Davidson, M., & Cooper, C. (1980). Type A coronary-prone behavior in the work environment. *Journal of Occupational Medicine, 22,* 375-383.

Dollard, M., & Winefield, A. (1998). A test of the demand/control/support model of work stress in correctional officers. *Journal of Occupational Health Psychology, 3,* 243-264.

Edwards, J. (1996). An examination of competing versions of the person-environment fit approach to stress. *Academy of Management Journal, 39,* 292-339.

Edwards, J., Baglioni, A., & Cooper, C. (1990). Stress, type-A, coping and psychological and physical symptoms: A multi-sample test of alternative models. *Human Relations, 43,* 919-956.

Etzion, D. (1984). Moderating effect of social support on the stress-burnout relationship. *Journal of Applied Psychology, 69,* 615-622.

Fenlason, K., & Beehr, T. (1994). Social support and occupational stress: Effects of talking to others. *Journal of Organizational Behavior, 15,* 157-175.

Fletcher, B. C. (1991). *Work, stress, disease and life expectancy.* New York: John Wiley.

Fox, M., Dwyer, D., & Ganster, D. (1993). Effects of stressful job demands and control of physiological and attitudinal outcomes in a hospital setting. *Academy of Management Journal, 36,* 289-318.

Frone, M., Russell, M., & Cooper, M. (1995). Relationship of work and family stressors to psychological distress: The independent moderating influence of social support, mastery, active coping and self-focused attention. In R. Crandall & P. Perrewe (Eds.), *Occupational stress: A handbook* (pp. 129-150). Washington, DC: Taylor & Francis.

Ganster, D., Fusilier, M., & Mayes, B. (1986). Role of social support in the experience of stress at work. *Journal of Applied Psychology, 71,* 102-110.

Ganster, D., & Schaubroeck, J. (1995). The moderating effects of self-esteem on the work stress-employee health relationship. In R. Crandall & P. Perrewe (Eds.), *Occupational stress: A handbook* (pp. 167-177). Washington, DC: Taylor & Francis.

Ganster, D., Schaubroeck, J., Sime, W., & Mayes, B. (1991). The nomological validity of the type A personality among employed adults. *Journal of Applied Psychology, 76,* 143-168.

Gentry, W., & Kobosa, S. (1984). Social and psychological resources mediating stress-illness relationships in humans. In W. D. Gentry (Ed.), *Handbook of behavioral medicine* (pp. 87-116). New York: Guilford.

George, J. (1992). The role of personality in organizational life: Issues and evidence. *Journal of Management, 18,* 185-213.

Greenglass, E., Fiksenbaum, L., & Burke, R. (1995). The relationship between social support and burnout over time in teachers. In R. Crandall & P. Perrewe (Eds.), *Occupational stress: A handbook* (pp. 239-248). Washington, DC: Taylor & Francis.

Greenglass, E., Fiksenbaum, L., & Burke, R. (1996). Components of social support, buffering effects and burnout: Implications for psychological functioning. *Anxiety, Stress, and Coping, 9,* 185-197.

Hackman, J., & Oldham, G. (1976). Motivation through the design of work: Test of a theory. *Organizational Behavior and Human Performance, 16,* 250-279.

Hofstede, G. (1980). *Culture's consequences: International differences in work-related values.* Beverly Hills, CA: Sage.

House, J. (1981). *Work stress and social support.* Reading, MA: Addison-Wesley.

Hull, J., van Treuren, R., & Virnelli, S. (1987). Hardiness and health: A critique and alternative approach. *Journal of Personality and Social Psychology, 53,* 518-530.

Iwata, N., & Suzuki, K. (1997). Role stress-mental health relations in Japanese bank workers: A moderating effect of social support. *Applied Psychology: An International Review, 40,* 207-218.

Jamal, M. (1999). Job stress, Type-A behavior and well-being: A cross-cultural examination. *International Journal of Stress Management, 6,* 57-67.

Jenkins, C., Zyzanski, S., & Rosenman, R. (1971). Progress toward validation of a computer-scored test for the Type A behavior pattern. *Psychosomatic Medicine, 33,* 193-202.

Jex, S., & Gudanowski, D. (1992). Efficacy beliefs and work stress: An exploratory study. *Journal of Organizational Behavior, 13,* 509-517.

Jex, S., & Spector, P. (1996). The impact of negative affectivity on stressor-strain relations: A replication and extension. *Work and Stress, 10,* 36-45.

Jimmieson, N., & Terry, D. (1998, April). *The role of informational control in the stress-strain relationship.* Poster session at the 13th Annual Conference of the Society for Industrial and Organizational Psychology, Dallas, TX.

Johnson, J., & Hall, E. (1988). Job strain, work place social support and cardiovascular disease: A cross-sectional study of a random sample of the working population. *American Journal of Public Health, 78,* 1336-1342.

Jones, F., & Fletcher, B. C. (1996). Job control and health. In M. Schabracq, J. Winnubst, & C. Cooper (Eds.), *Handbook of work and health psychology* (pp. 33-50). New York: John Wiley.

Karasek, R. (1979). Job demands, job decision latitude and mental strain: Implications for job redesign. *Administrative Science Quarterly, 24,* 285-308.

Kaufmann, G., & Beehr, T. (1986). Interactions between job stressors and social support: Some counterintuitive results. *Journal of Applied Psychology, 71,* 522-526.

Kobosa, S. (1979). Stressful life events, personality and health: An inquiry into hardiness. *Journal of Personality and Social Psychology, 37,* 1-11.

Kobosa, S. (1982). The hardy personality: Toward a social psychology of stress and health. In G. Sanders & J. Suls (Eds.), *Social psychology of health and illness* (pp. 3-32). Hillsdale, NJ: Lawrence Erlbaum.

Kohn, M., & Schooler, C. (1983). *Work and personality: An inquiry into the impact of social stratification.* Norwood, NJ: Ablex.

Kristensen, T. (1996). Job strain and cardiovascular disease: Theoretic critical review. *Journal of Occupational Health Psychology, 1,* 246-260.

Kushnir, T., & Melamed, S. (1991). Work-load, perceived control and psychological distress in Type A/B industrial workers. *Journal of Organizational Behavior, 12,* 155-168.

Landsbergis, P., Schnall, P., Dietz, D., Friedman, R., & Pickering, T. (1992). The patterning of psychological attributes and distress by "job strain" and social support in a sample of working men. *Journal of Behavioral Medicine, 15,* 379-405.

LaRocco, J., House, J., & French, J. (1980). Social support, occupational stress and health. *Journal of Health and Social Behavior, 21,* 202-218.

Lee, C., Ashford, S., & Bobko, P. (1990). Interactive effects of "Type A" behavior and perceived control on worker performance, job satisfaction, and somatic complaints. *Academy Management Journal, 33,* 870-881.

Lee, C., Ashford, S., & Jamieson, L. (1993). The effects of Type A behavior dimensions and optimism on coping strategy, health, and performance. *Journal of Organizational Behavior, 14,* 143-157.

Lepore, S., Evans, G., & Schneider, M. (1991). Dynamic role of social support in the link between chronic stress and psychological distress. *Journal of Personality and Social Psychology, 61,* 899-909.

Lim, V. (1996). Job insecurity and its outcomes: Moderating effects of work-based and nonwork-based social support. *Human Relations, 49,* 171-194.

Marshall, G., & Lang, E. (1990). Optimism, self-mastery, and symptoms of depression in women professionals. *Journal of Personality and Social Psychology, 59,* 132-139.

Melamed, S., Kushnir, T., & Meir, E. (1991). Attenuating the impact of job demands: Additive and interactive effects of perceived control and social support. *Journal of Vocational Behavior, 39,* 40-53.

Mossholder, K., Bedeian, A., & Armenakis, A. (1981). Role perceptions, satisfaction and performance: Moderating effects of self-esteem and organizational level. *Organizational Behavior and Human Performance, 28,* 224-234.

Moyle, P., & Parkes, K. (1999). The effects of transition stress: A relocation study. *Journal of Organizational Behavior, 20,* 625-646.

O'Driscoll, M., & Beehr, T. (2000). Moderating effects of perceived control and need for clarity on the relationship between role stressors and employee affective reactions. *Journal of Social Psychology, 140,* 151-159.

Parkes, K. (1990). Coping, negative affectivity, and the work environment: Additive and interactive predictors of mental health. *Journal of Applied Psychology, 75,* 399-409.

Parkes, K., Mendham, C., & von Rabenau, C. (1994). Social support and the demand-discretion model of job stress: Tests of additive and interactive effects in two samples. *Journal of Vocational Behavior, 44,* 91-113.

Payne, R. (1988). Individual differences in the study of occupational stress. In C. Cooper & R. Payne (Eds.), *Causes, coping and consequences of stress at work* (pp. 209-232). New York: John Wiley.

Perrewe, P. (1987). The moderating effects of activity level and locus of control in the personal control-job stress relationship. *International Journal of Psychology, 22,* 179-193.

Perrewe, P., & Ganster, D. (1989). The impact of job demands and behavioral control on experienced job stress. *Journal of Organizational Behavior, 10,* 213-229.

Pierce, J., Gardner, D., Dunham, R., & Cummings, L. (1993). Moderation by organization-based self-esteem of role condition-employee response relationships. *Academy of Management Journal, 36,* 271-288.

Rhodewalt, F., & Zone, J. (1989). Appraisal of life change, depression and illness in hardy and nonhardy women. *Journal of Personality and Social Psychology, 56,* 81-88.

Rosenman, R., Friedman, M., Straus, R., Wurm, M., Kositchek, R., Hahn, W., & Werthessen, N. (1964). A predictive study of coronary heart disease. *Journal of the American Medical Association, 189,* 15-22.

Roth, D., Wiebe, D., Fillingham, R., & Shay, K. (1989). Life events, fitness, hardiness and health: A simultaneous analysis of proposed stress-resistance effects. *Journal of Personality and Social Psychology, 57,* 136-142.

Russell, D., Altmaier, E., & van Velzen, D. (1987). Job-related stress, social support, and burnout among classroom teachers. *Journal of Applied Psychology, 72,* 269-274.

Sargent, L., & Terry, D. (1998). The effects of work control and job demands on employee adjustment and work. *Journal of Occupational and Organizational Psychology, 71,* 219-236.

Schaubroeck, J., & Fink, L. (1998). Facilitating and inhibiting effects of job control and social support on stress outcomes and role behavior: A contingency model. *Journal of Organizational Behavior, 19,* 167-195.

Schaubroeck, J., Ganster, D., & Fox, M. (1992). Dispositional affect and work-related stress. *Journal of Applied Psychology, 77,* 322-335.

Schaubroeck, J., & Merritt, D. (1997). Divergent effects of job control on coping with work stressors: The key role of self-efficacy. *Academy of Management Journal, 40,* 738-754.

Scheck, C., Kinicki, A., & Davy, J. (1997). Testing the mediating processes between work stressors and subjective well-being. *Journal of Vocational Behavior, 50,* 96-123.

Scheier, M., & Carver, C. (1992). Effects of optimism on psychological and physical well-being: Theoretical overview and empirical update. *Cognitive Therapy and Research, 16,* 201-228.

Schreurs, P., & Taris, T. (1998). Construct validity of the demand-control model: A double cross-validation approach. *Work & Stress, 12,* 66-84.

Schwalbe, M. (1985). Autonomy in work and self-esteem. *Sociological Quarterly, 26,* 519-535.

Semmer, N. (1996). Individual differences, work stress and health. In M. Schabracq, J. Winnubst, & C. Cooper (Eds.), *Handbook of work and health psychology* (pp. 51-86). New York: John Wiley.

Spector, P. (1986). Perceived control by employees: A meta-analysis of studies concerning autonomy and participation at work. *Human Relations, 39,* 1005-1016.

Spector, P. (1998). A control theory of the job stress process. In C. Cooper (Ed.), *Theories of organizational stress* (pp. 153-169). New York: Oxford University Press.

Spector, P., Fox, S., & van Katwyk, P. (1999). The role of negative affectivity in employee reactions to job characteristics: Bias effect or substantive effect? *Journal of Occupational and Organizational Psychology, 72,* 205-218.

Spector, P., Jex, S., & Chen, P. (1995). Personality traits as predictors of objective job characteristics. *Journal of Organizational Behavior, 16,* 59-65.

Spector, P., Zapf, D., Chen, P., & Frese, M. (2000). Why negative affectivity should not be controlled in job stress research: Don't throw the baby out with the bath water. *Journal of Organizational Behavior, 21,* 79-95.

Spielberger, C., Gorsuch, R., & Lushene, R. (1970). *State-Trait Anxiety Inventory test manual for Form X.* Palo Alto, CA: Consulting Psychologists Press.

Sutton, R., & Kahn, R. (1987). Prediction, understanding and control as antidotes to organizational stress. In J. W. Lorsch (Ed.), *Handbook of organizational behavior* (pp. 272-285). Englewood Cliffs, NJ: Prentice Hall.

Tetrick, L., & LaRocco, J. (1987). Understanding, prediction, and control as moderators of the relationships between perceived stress, satisfaction, and psychological well-being. *Journal of Applied Psychology, 72,* 538-543.

Wall, T., Jackson, P., Mullarkey, S., & Parker, S. (1996). The demands-control model of job strain: A more specific test. *Journal of Occupational and Organizational Psychology, 69,* 153-166.

Warr, P. (1987). *Work, unemployment and mental health.* New York: Oxford University Press.

Watson, D., & Clark, L. (1984). Negative affectivity: The disposition to experience negative aversive emotional states. *Psychological Bulletin, 96,* 465-498.

Watson, D., & Pennebaker, J. (1989). Health complaints, stress and distress: Exploring the central role of negative affectivity. *Psychological Review, 96,* 234-254.

Westman, M. (1992). Moderating effect of decision latitude on stress-strain relationship: Does organizational level matter? *Journal of Organizational Behavior, 13,* 713-722.

Winnubst, J., & Schabracq, M. (1996). Social support, stress and organization: Toward optimal matching. In M. Schabracq, J. Winnubst, & C. Cooper (Eds.), *Handbook of work and health psychology* (pp. 87-102). New York: John Wiley.

Xie, J. (1996). Karasek's model in the People's Republic of China: Effects of job demands, control, and individual differences. *Academy of Management Journal, 39,* 1594-1618.

Yoon, J., Han, N.-C., & Seo, Y.-J. (1996). Sense of control among hospital employees: An assessment of choice process, empowerment, and buffering hypotheses. *Journal of Applied Social Psychology, 26,* 686-716.

Zellars, K., Perrewe, P., & Hochwarter, W. (1999). Mitigating burnout among high-NA employees in health care: What can organizations do? *Journal of Applied Social Psychology, 29,* 2250-2271.

6   Coping With Job Stress

R esearch in the field of stress illustrates the growing belief that coping
is a fundamental element in the relationship between stressors and
strain (Oakland & Ostell, 1996), but reviewers have often concluded
that there is still little known about how individuals cope (O'Driscoll &
Cooper, 1994, 1996) or the factors important to coping (Newton &
Keenan, 1985). Indeed, the accumulated research on work stress and
coping has been described as disappointing (Bar-Tal & Spitzer, 1994)
and limited in its ability to determine the role of coping in the connection between stressors and strain (Erera-Weatherley, 1996). The present
chapter draws attention to conceptual (definitional) and methodological (measurement) issues surrounding the study of coping in workplace
contexts, points to some of the limitations and concerns about existing
coping research, and offers some suggestions for future research in
this area. Our aim is not to present final solutions to all the problems
and dilemmas associated with research on stress coping but (more
modestly) to contribute to the debate on how these difficulties may be
resolved.

Definitions and the Research Context

Like the concept of stress itself, various definitions of coping have been proposed, including coping as a psychoanalytic process; as a personal trait, style, or disposition; as a description of situationally specific strategies; and as a process. Traditional approaches to conceptualizing coping defined it in terms of a relatively stable trait or some enduring behavior or characteristic of the person (Stone, Greenberg, Kennedy-Moore, & Newman, 1991). The notion that coping is a stable dispositional characteristic is still vigorously debated (Lazarus, 1991). This debate needs to be kept separate from the role of individual differences and their moderating effect on coping. However, Lazarus (1991) has suggested that the static model implied by a dispositional definition of coping does not fit well with the dynamic, process-oriented nature of coping and tends to overlook the situational context in which coping behaviors occur.

As was highlighted in Chapter 1, there is growing acceptance that stress should be defined relationally (Lazarus & Launier, 1978), as involving transactions between the person and the environment. Transaction theory views coping as thoughts and actions that are initiated in response to a specific encounter and that change over time as efforts are reappraised and outcomes are evaluated. This implies a dynamic interaction between the person and the environment, whereby the individual imposes a particular appraisal on the environment, while the environment is also influential in shaping that appraisal (Dewe & Guest, 1990). It also highlights the fact that efforts initiated in relation to a particular encounter will affect subsequent appraisals of the demand and hence further coping efforts. Clearly, if our interest in coping is to capture what individuals actually think and do in any encounter, then definitions and assessments of coping need to express a breadth and range of strategies that reflects the diversity and complexity of coping behaviors (Holroyd & Lazarus, 1982). Definitions that reflect a static approach are simply not designed to do this or to deal with the empirical issues raised by the process-oriented perspective (Stone et al., 1991).

Using a transactional perspective, one can define coping as "cognitive and behavioral efforts to master, reduce or tolerate the internal or external demands that are created by the stressful transaction"

(Folkman, 1984, p. 843). Coping efforts can be conceptually distinguished from the results (success or failure) of these efforts. The three key features of this definition are (a) the emphasis it places on the process in contrast to the more interactional (cause-effect) nature of traditional approaches (Cox, 1987; Edwards, 1988), (b) the positioning of coping in the relationship between the person and the environment (Folkman, 1982), and (c) the link it provides with other components of the stress process. Central to this definition of coping is the integrating role of cognitive appraisal. Defined in this way, coping is offered as a conceptually distinct variable, capable of assessment independently of stressors and resultant strains (Folkman, 1982).

As a result of ongoing transactions with the environment, individuals are confronted with demands that impinge on their cognitive processes and activate a requirement to cope or adapt. The unit of analysis that captures the transactional nature of stress is appraisal, of which there are two kinds (Lazarus, 1991). The first is *primary appraisal*—where individuals give meaning and significance to the situation and evaluate what is at stake for them and whether the situation (or events within it) pose a potential or actual threat to their well-being. *Secondary appraisal*, on the other hand, refers to the perceived availability of coping resources for dealing with a stressful encounter. At this stage, coping options are evaluated in terms of available social, personal, economic, and organizational resources and the level of control that individuals perceive they have over the situation.

Coping behaviors are initiated as a consequence of primary and secondary appraisal. These processes are interdependent, influencing each other and shaping the nature of any encounter (Folkman, 1984). Identifying them as the processes that link the individual to the environment shifts the focus of research toward developing an understanding of what people actually think and do in a stressful encounter (Holroyd & Lazarus, 1982). Understanding coping therefore requires researchers to focus at the individual level. As we shall see in Chapter 7, this by no means undermines the importance of investigating organization-level stress management interventions, which may be necessary to deal with certain kinds of stressors, especially those over which individuals can exert little or no control. Nevertheless, even in these interventions, individual appraisals and activities must be taken into account.

Applying the Transactional Model Within Work Settings

The application of the transactional model to work settings has raised some concerns (Harris, 1991), especially about whether this model can provide a mechanism for identifying and delineating the workplace conditions associated with stress. One concern is that the transactional model argues that stress essentially occurs at the individual level and involves the need to focus on and understand individual patterns and intraindividual processes. The difficulty with this focus, according to Brief and George (1991), is that it may not provide the level of analysis necessary to identify "those working conditions that are likely to affect the well-being of *most* workers" (p. 16). The essence of this concern is whether work stress researchers better fulfill their social responsibilities to those whose work they research by creating a taxonomy of stressful job conditions that affect most workers or by improving an understanding of job stress by more fully investigating the intraindividual processes at the heart of the transactional approach.

These goals are not mutually exclusive, nor are they incompatible. Exploring the factors that most people would appraise as threatening or harmful and would have difficulty coping with to the extent that their well-being was impaired would enable researchers to gain information not only about stressful working conditions that affect most workers but also on whether individuals appraise those situations in similar ways. By using this approach, it would appear possible (a) to identify those features of the work environment that are stressful to most workers, (b) to explore qualitative differences between those features and how they are appraised, (c) to consider whether there is any commonality between appraisals—that is, whether some appraisals are common across encounters, and (d) to use the theoretical orientations of the transactional approach to frame questions that do provide information that may benefit most workers.

Brief and George (1991) have argued that work represents a unique context because of its economic instrumentality and that how we study stress and coping processes should therefore reflect the fundamental importance of work in people's lives. In a similar vein, Harris (1991) questioned whether organizations expect certain types of behavior from their employees and therefore whether the range of coping strategies available to individuals may to a considerable extent be determined by organizational values, culture, and norms. That is, the structure, culture, functions, and strategies of the organization may determine the meaning of a particular encounter (primary appraisal). This organizational impact may also extend to the availability of coping resources (control, power, and authority) during the secondary appraisal process. Therefore, the effects of organizational factors on these processes need to be appropriately determined. As Harris (1991) has illustrated, these effects have implications for the assessment of cognitive appraisals and coping activities.

The transactional perspective can be found in other approaches, albeit at times implicitly, through the idea of person-environment fit. Karasek's (1979) model of job demands, for example, suggests that strain occurs when high demands are combined with low decision latitude (see Chapter 5). McGrath's (1976) discussion of the fit between environmental demands and personal skills and abilities also encompasses transactional elements. In their cybernetic framework of stress, Cummings and Cooper (1979) suggested that the misfit between an individual's preferred and actual state would result in strain, and Schuler (1980) modeled stress in terms of a state that emerges when individuals are potentially prevented from having, being, or doing what they desire. Despite some differences in approach, on the whole these perspectives reflect a conceptualization of the stress process that entails the same basic sequence of events: (a) the encountering of a taxing demand, (b) a set of psychological thoughts and behaviors triggered by that demand, and (c) a more or less complex array of consequences in which the well-being of the individual is involved (Kahn & Byosiere, 1992).

It is within this context that coping research has taken place. The development of work stress research is similar to other areas of investigation in that there is not always a consistent sequence to the direction it has taken. This stems partly from researchers pursuing their own areas of interest and partly because a number of avenues for research are, more often than not, being explored in parallel, with little felt need for convergence. However, it is possible to construct some broad stages that researchers have worked through in an attempt first to develop a body of knowledge about the different constructs in the stress process and then to consider the relationships between those constructs. With regard to this latter stage, over time researchers have moved from simply investigating the interaction between stressors and strain to exploring the variables that may moderate the relationship, to identifying the nature of the stress process and the relationship between those variables that best express the nature of that process.

Where variables have been found to moderate the stressor-strain relationship, there has been a tendency to infer that such moderators reflect a style or way of coping. For example, if age were found to moderate the stressor-strain relationship, one possible explanation could be that older people cope differently than younger people. However, this could only be inferred from the moderating effect of age. The result is that coping becomes by inference the by-product of the relationship rather than a primary focus of research. This is not to say that coping has been considered unimportant. Where coping has been investigated in a work setting, researchers seem to be overly concerned with investigating "coping effectiveness" rather than concentrating on what would appear to be the primary goal, developing an understanding of the coping construct through systematic measurement (Dewe, 1989). The issue of systematic measurement is, of course, one that could be applied to all stress research, irrespective of whether the focus is on stressors, strains, or coping. We raise this issue here to signal that there seems to be a much greater sense of urgency to research coping effectiveness without first considering how best to assess coping strategies.

A conclusion that emerges from this is that although at the conceptual level researchers may agree that stress is relational, involving some sort of transaction between the individual and the environment, at the empirical level the tendency is still to research the relationship between the specific constructs of the transaction rather than to explore the nature of the transaction itself and the processes that link the individual to the environment (Dewe, 1991). Progress toward a better understanding of the transactional process can come only by reconsidering the way in which work stress is conceptualized, along with the implications of such reconceptualization for measurement, analysis, and the evaluation of research findings.

To summarize how research on coping with job-related stressors has developed:

- The stressor-strain (stimulus-response) model of stress has been central in the development of work stress research. There is now a considerable body of knowledge on these constructs and on their interaction (Sutherland & Cooper, 1988).
- Though this approach has been important in developing our understanding of the different constructs and their interrelationships, it is now generally recognized that such an approach cannot contribute in a significant way to an understanding

of the transactional nature of stress (Lazarus, 1990). Working conditions do create strain, but, as Lazarus (1991) pointed out, "This idea alone is no longer enough to substantiate an adequate theory of stress" (p. 5).

- Though attention has been given to work structures and individual-difference variables and their moderating effects, this has tended to obscure the role of coping or at best has provided only a limited context for understanding the coping process. In many cases, where the moderator variable has been shown to have a significant effect, it is simply inferred that its effect can be best explained in terms of how individuals cope, so coping assumes the role of an inferred explanatory tool rather than being the focus of explicit research attention.
- Though researchers accept the transactional nature of stress at the conceptual level, at the empirical level they need to continue to explore how best this can be applied to a work setting.
- The transactional model points to two processes that link the individual to the environment. These are operationalized in terms of primary and secondary appraisal. Further research efforts are needed to explore the explanatory potential of these concepts and their role in the stress process.
- The first priority should be to develop assessments of coping that are refined enough to capture the actual responses of individuals to demands confronted in their work settings.

In the remainder of this chapter, we explore the measurement of coping efforts in organizational contexts and issues relating to the assessment of coping effectiveness. We begin with a discussion of how coping behaviors are determined and classified.

Taxonomies of Coping

The most common approach to the study of coping in work settings has been described as *taxonomic* (Cox, 1987), where researchers describe and categorize coping behaviors that are broadly applicable to all (or most) work situations. This line of research (based on the work of Lazarus and his colleagues) has identified two broad categories of coping strategies: *problem focused*, in which attempts are made to deal with the demands of the encounter, and *emotion focused*, in which attempts are made to deal with the emotional disturbance resulting from those demands. However, no consensus has been reached as to how best to classify coping strategies. As Fleishman (1984) pointed out, a clear-cut and universally accepted typology has yet to be achieved. Several alternative proposals have been suggested (see Cox & Ferguson, 1991; Dewe & Guest, 1990; Latack, 1986), but these too do not appear to satisfy the precision required, to encapsulate the different functions that coping strategies may perform, or to adequately capture the range of potential coping responses. Any schema for classifying coping strategies must take into account not just the focus (problem vs. emotion) of a particular strategy but also its form (cognitive/behavioral) and the variety of different strategies used (Latack & Havlovic, 1992). More comprehensive approaches to understanding coping are needed to facilitate the development of valid coping measures.

Deductive Versus Inductive Approaches

Classifying coping strategies is not the only topic on which there appears to be debate. The research methods employed to generate measures of coping are also of some concern. In particular, there has been debate over the merits of using deductive or inductive methods for constructing coping instruments. Coping measures have been constructed both deductively—that is, from existing literature and research on coping (e.g., Latack, 1986)—and inductively (e.g., Dewe & Guest, 1990), by examining, describing, and developing coping items based on strategies that individuals report using. The major advantage of the inductive method is that it makes no assumptions about how individuals might respond and does not prescribe the range or type of response that individuals may engage in during a stressful encounter (O'Driscoll & Cooper, 1994). Coping measures constructed inductively are based on what individuals actually think and do and therefore expose meaning rather than impose it (Erera-Weatherley, 1996). However, it is this very feature—the classification of such information into meaningful and reliable self-report categories—that may also be its greatest weakness: Such classification may prove to be impossible without losing the very richness of the data, the dynamic nature of the coping process (Oakland & Ostell, 1996), and perhaps the very advantage of using the inductive approach in the first place.

Difficulties when constructing coping measures are not limited just to identifying and classifying coping strategies. A number of reviewers (Dewe, Cox, & Ferguson, 1993; O'Driscoll & Cooper, 1994; Parkes, 1994) have drawn attention to a range of other issues that confront researchers wishing to measure coping. These include (a) whether measures should focus on how individuals cope with stress in general or on assessing coping with specific encounters; (b) whether the response category should ask individuals to rate how frequently they used a particular strategy or whether to obtain ratings of coping effectivness (Bar-Tal & Spitzer, 1994); and (c) whether self-report rating scales are the most appropriate vehicle for measuring how people actually cope (Erera-Wetherley, 1996), whether a combination of qualitative and quantitative measures should be used (Stone & Neale, 1984), or whether coping is best tested indirectly, asking no direct questions about coping at all but capturing how people cope by having them describe the nature of stressful encounters and their responses within those situations (O'Driscoll & Cooper, 1994, 1996).

The above issues raise two significant questions. First, are coping strategies best determined deductively (from existing research and the literature on coping) or inductively (from individuals' own accounts of what they have done to manage stressors in their work environment)? If researchers rely on the former, how can they ensure that the coping responses identified through the literature actually reflect the experiences and responses of the population under investigation (Dewe, 2000)? On the other hand, if inductive procedures are favored, how should questions be framed to elicit valid accounts of individuals' actual responses to various environmental demands, bearing in mind the constraints of social desirability and selective recall of behaviors?

In terms of this latter issue (how questions should be framed), researchers may, depending on their research objectives, want to consider a number of points. For example, the most common approach is to use a critical-incident technique to derive coping strategies. With this method, individuals are usually asked, "Can you think of a particular time at work when you felt under stress? Can you tell me what happened and how you managed to cope with it?" Frequently coupled with this question is one that asks, "If, like most people, you occasionally get fed up with your job and feel tense and frustrated, how do you cope?" Although such questions have identified a range of coping strategies and capture what individuals actually do, they are sometimes criticized because they fail to build in some time limit to reduce memory bias (Newton, 1989); because they identify only "successful-effective" strategies because of the connotations associated with the word *cope;* because they cannot easily identify those coping behaviors that are antisocial, those that an individual is not prepared to talk about, and those that they are not aware of (Dewe, Guest, & Williams, 1978); and because they are at times limited in scope and range due to the nature of the incident being described. Nevertheless, the strength of such questions lies in their ability to capture the reality of individual experience and, for those engaged in analysis, a sense of relevance and attachment to those whose working lives are being explored.

If, on the other hand, as some researchers suggest (Oakland & Ostell, 1996), coping strategies cannot be understood without reference to the context in which they are used, then what are required are questions that best reflect or "parallel the diagnostic approach of a therapist building a model of a client's problem situation" (Oakland & Ostell, 1996, p. 142). With this approach, individuals, once they had described two recent "stressful" situations (one with a successful outcome and one with an unsuccessful outcome), would be asked probing questions: "Who else was involved?" "How did you feel when the situation first arose?" "What was it about the situation that made you feel angry, guilty, anxious, etc.?" "What, if anything, did you do when you felt angry, anxious, etc.?" "What did you do initially to deal with the situation?" This sort of approach, while identifying different coping behaviors and actions, also points to a broader methodological question of whether quantitative methods can actually assess the dynamic nature of coping. So qualitative approaches to researching coping provide both a method for identifying how individuals cope and a context for better understanding the nature of the coping process itself. Finally, Erera-Weatherley (1996) suggested that, in line with earlier recommendations, coping strategies are best identified indirectly by focusing on the causes of stress that evoke them. In this way, open-ended questions would be used to explore the nature of the stressful encounter, and subsequent analysis would provide an independent confirmation of the connection between sources of stress and coping. Though of course the selection of one approach over another will depend on the nature of the research and the research objectives, the thoughtful use of open-ended questions can only add to our understanding of the stress process and more particularly to the way in which measures of coping behaviors are constructed and refined.

The second question emerging from critiques of coping research focuses on the nature of self-rating instruments for assessing coping responses. The most common approach used is to obtain ratings of response frequency. However, whereas some studies have focused on coping with specific stressors (e.g., Folkman & Lazarus, 1985; Folkman,

Lazarus, Dunkel-Schetter, DeLongis, & Gruen, 1986), others have asked respondents how they "usually coped" with stress (Pearlin & Schooler, 1978). The latter approach generates information on more general "styles" of coping, or at least individuals' reports of their coping styles, rather than details of the actual strategies used to cope with specific demanding encounters. It cannot be assumed that these data are equivalent (O'Driscoll & Cooper, 1994).

The Role of Coping

The functions of coping in the stress process have also been of considerable interest to job stress researchers, who have endeavored not simply to describe variations in coping responses but also to delineate the conditions under which different coping strategies are used and to assess the effectiveness of such strategies. One of the dilemmas facing researchers doing this type of research is that the relationship between coping and other stress-related constructs is reciprocal. Coping operates as both a cause (an independent variable) and an effect (a dependent variable) of other stress-related constructs (Kinicki & Latack, 1990). Similarly, coping responses may function as both mediators and moderators of stressor-strain relationships (Kinicki, McKee, & Wade, 1996). Consequently, researchers have examined, for example, (a) the influence of personality, gender, and race on the use of different coping strategies; (b) strategies used when coping with specific stressful work experiences; (c) the relationship between coping and adaptational outcomes; (d) the effectiveness of coping strategies; and (e) the mediational properties of coping strategies. According to Kinicki et al.'s (1996) review, the basic proposition that environmental and personality variables influence the choice of coping strategies has been generally supported in empirical research, but the relationships between coping strategies and outcomes are inconsistent, and moderating effects of coping have not always been demonstrated.

To understand these results, it is important to consider the theoretical role of coping in the stress process. A number of themes emerge. The first is whether coping functions as a mediator or moderator. The transactional model of stress views coping as a mediating variable (Lazarus & Folkman, 1984). Treating coping as mediating the link between stressors and strain entails a different research design from considering it as as moderating the stressor-strain relationship (Cox & Ferguson, 1991). Small effects and mixed findings may well be the result not just of design and methodological limitations (Parkes, 1994) but also of the difficulties involved in deciding how to research the complexities of the transactional relationship.

Another reason for the confusion surrounding the mediating-moderating effects of coping may be that such effects are present only under fairly specific conditions (Trenberth, 1996). In many studies, little information is provided on why coping was expected to moderate a particular relationship or on the basis for selecting the dependent and independent variables (Parkes, 1994). Finally, as noted above, there is sometimes both theoretical and methodological confusion between coping "behaviors" and coping "styles." Whereas dispositional styles are more likely to moderate linkages between environmental conditions (stressors) and individual reactions (strains), specific behaviors may function as mediators between these variables. For instance, increased work demands may lead to an individual's working harder to achieve required goals, which in turn reduces the strain associated with the initial demands.

Inferential support for this distinction comes from studies that have demonstrated a clear relationship between personality and coping (Parkes, 1994). Although there are powerful arguments for measuring coping behaviors rather than style or personality variables (Lazarus, 1990; Parkes, 1994), equally strong arguments can be mounted for considering the relationship between personality and coping. For example, secondary appraisals (of what coping resources are available to the person) include assessment of dispositional factors such as the person's resilience or hardiness and self-efficacy as possible buffers of the impact of stressors on an individual's well-being (see Chapter 5). Clearly, individual differences may play an important role in both the selection of coping strategies and their effectiveness.

Coping as a Dependent or Independent Variable

Whether coping operates as a dependent or an independent variable is another issue of theoretical and empirical importance. The reciprocal nature of the transactional process positions coping responses as both, at different stages in the process. Unfortunately, the reliance on cross-sectional design in many stress-coping studies precludes further specification of the status of coping behaviors because it is impossible to identify which stage of that process has been measured. Furthermore, traditional assessment approaches, especially self-ratings of coping behaviors, may not discriminate between the dual roles that coping can play. Consequently, there is a tendency to emphasize a unidimensional causal pattern, whereas the relationship between coping, appraisal, and outcome variables is bidirectional, with each affecting the other (Folkman & Lazarus, 1988). Coping research should address both the effects of appraisal and strain on coping and the effects of coping on appraisal and strain (Harris, 1991).

Assessment and Analysis of Coping

A fundamental issue pervading coping research as well as stress research generally, is one of measurement. Despite efforts to achieve agreement on how best to measure coping, no consensus has emerged as to how this should be done, other than to suggest that any measure should (a) capture what individuals actually think and do in any encounter; (b) be nonevaluative, making no prior judgment about whether a strategy is effective or not; and (c) ensure a range and breadth of strategies that not only capture the variety and complexity of coping but provide a valid framework for exploring the role of coping in the stress process (Dewe, 1991, 2000). Resolving these measurement issues is critical to increasing our understanding of the structure of coping and its role in the stress process. Stone and Kennedy-Moore (1991) have summarized the thrust of this research, highlighting that "exploring these issues stems from a desire to understand how well current coping instruments are fulfilling their intended function and to identify areas for improvement" (p. 204). The last decade has seen the development of a number of coping questionnaires specifically designed for work settings (e.g., Dewe & Guest, 1990; Latack, 1986; Schwartz & Stone, 1993) and although there has been considerable variation in how these and other coping instruments (e.g., Billings & Moos, 1984; Folkman & Lazarus, 1980) have been used to assess coping, these self-report measures have been the principal tool for determining the extent of use and the effectiveness of different coping strategies.

However, as interest in coping has grown and as the need to adequately measure coping strategies has increased in importance, the way the different measures have been used (Dewe et al., 1993), the inconsistencies in the findings (O'Driscoll & Cooper, 1994), and conceptual concerns underlying their development (Stone, Helder, & Schneider, 1988) have raised questions about how these difficulties affect the assessment of coping, as well as the validity and interpretation of results. Many coping measures have been constructed and adapted with only passing reference to theory and apparently with little hope of agreeing upon a standardized set of measures or even considering measure replication (Trenberth, Dewe, & Walkey, 1996). This has led some reviewers to question the value of persevering with standardized self-report rating scales and to conclude that progress toward understanding coping and its role in the stress process may now be achieved only through pursuing alternative approaches to measurement (Erera-Weatherley, 1996; Oakland & Ostell, 1996; O'Driscoll & Cooper, 1994, 1996).

Proponents of alternative approaches to the measurement of coping have queried whether existing quantitative (self-rating) measures adequately represent the coping process. It has been suggested that rating scale response formats may obscure, distort, or fail to provide adequate information on the coping process (Oakland & Ostell, 1996). This may occur in two ways, each challenging the internal validity of the measures themselves. First, the perceived limitations of self-reports include (Stone et al., 1988) (a) how questionnaire items are derived, expressed (in terms of their clarity), and interpreted; (b) the appropriateness of the rating scale—whether the preoccupation with how often a strategy is used actually increases our understanding of coping efficacy (Oakland & Ostell, 1996); and (c) how best the data should be analyzed and whether techniques such as factor analysis capture the essence and subtlety of different coping strategies (Stone & Kennedy-Moore, 1991).

Process concerns are not entirely separate from the issues listed above. The essence of these concerns is the need to ensure that coping measures are providing comprehensive information about the coping process. This includes a more integrated analysis of stressful encounters, individual responses to those events, and the consequences of coping actions (O'Driscoll & Cooper, 1994). It requires a measure or technique that captures the unfolding and variability of the factors that influence coping actions, the temporal nature of the process, and the dynamics of reappraisal and coping effectiveness (Oakland & Ostell, 1996). One way to fulfill these requirements would be to measure coping indirectly by focusing on the strain that initiates coping and then exploring how such encounters were responded to. The advantages of doing this would be that a direct link between stressor and coping could be established, coping and strain would not need to be artificially separated, and, consequently, coping could be examined within a specific context (Erera-Weatherley, 1996).

Researchers wishing to investigate coping with work stress may need to consider alternative qualitative methods that capture the richness and idiographic nature of the process in order to overcome some of the structural limitations imposed by self-report quantitative measures. Examples of alternative approaches include critical-incident analysis (O'Driscoll & Cooper, 1996), the use of open-ended questioning (Erera-Weatherley, 1996), and a combination of qualitative and quantitative approaches (Stone & Neale, 1984). Use of multimethod approaches would enable simultaneous exploration of the extent of use of various coping strategies, as well as the meaning and relevance of those strategies for the individual under study, thereby producing a more complete understanding of the stressor-coping-strain process. The hostility between qualitative and quantitative approaches will need to be overcome, and the challenge will be to achieve precision in measurement while at the same time considering how best to capture the richness and complexity of the coping process (Folkman, 1991).

Refining Self-Report Measures of Coping

Several steps can be taken to ensure precision in the assessment of coping. As discussed earlier, consideration must be given to what is being measured, coping styles or coping behaviors. Coping measures are generally used in two different ways to identify how individuals cope. The first asks individuals to indicate in general terms how they use different coping strategies when confronted with a stressful situation. This approach generates information on how individuals report that they typically cope, capturing a style or pattern or a disposition toward coping in a particular way (Parkes, 1994). However, using this approach means that the nature of the encounter (stressor) is unknown. Alternatively, individuals may be asked to think of a recent stressful event, describe it, and then indicate how they responded to it. The intention here is to capture a set of behaviors that reflect what was actually used to deal with a particular encounter. The point of thinking about whether coping measures are measuring style or behavior lies in the fact that this distinction is frequently ignored by researchers, with the effect that measures that are believed to be measuring coping behaviors are, more often than not, measuring coping style (Newton, 1989). Added to this is the issue of whether "coping styles" exist at all. What is needed is research that examines patterns of coping responses across stressors.

Perhaps the main reason for considering this distinction between style and behavior is that general approaches to the measurement of coping may generate responses that are more likely to reflect how individuals think they cope than how they cope in reality (Newton, 1989). On the other hand, measuring coping in relation to a specific event rather than as an isolated construct, though well supported by theory and likely to get closer to the actual behaviors that people exhibit, involves some difficulties as well. For example, using this approach to measurement, researchers would need to consider the nature and significance of the encounter described, what and who was involved, the duration of the encounter, and the stage that was reached in dealing with the stressor(s). Also, careful thought would need to be given to how the data should be analyzed, especially if the aim was to relate specific coping strategies to different aspects of the encounter. Focusing on specific events, one question that arises is whether coping strategies differ depending on whether the event is chronic or acute (Newton, 1989). The longer an encounter lasts, the greater the likelihood that a wider range of coping strategies will be used (Stone et al., 1991). Finally, different coping strategies are likely to be used at different stages of the encounter (Stone & Kennedy-Moore, 1991).

In sum, when measuring coping behaviors by getting individuals to describe a potentially stressful encounter, it is as important to understand the "event" as it is to acknowledge the distinction between coping behaviors and style. Conversely, a specific event may not necessarily involve an individual's full coping repertoire (Parkes, 1994), and what is gained in terms of specificity may be lost in terms of breadth, so researchers must decide clearly what they want to measure—style or behavior.

Selection of items to include in self-report coping instruments poses another major challenge for researchers. The overall aim must be to identify and describe what individuals actually think and do. Two broad approaches can be identified in terms of item generation. The first (deductive) approach generates items from a review of the literature and selects items on an a priori basis to reflect a range of coping strategies. The second (inductive) approach entails asking individuals to respond to open-ended questions about how they cope. Coping strategies are then generated from the content analysis of these responses. There are no simple answers as to which approach is best (Cohen, 1987). However, when considering which approach to adopt, the deciding criterion should be comprehensiveness (Stone & Kennedy-Moore, 1991) and thus the need to ensure as wide a range of coping strategies as possible. Coupled with this is the issue of whether comprehensiveness is best achieved by allowing coping strategies to emerge from what individuals say they think and do, thereby capturing their reality, or whether the same results can be achieved by a priori selection of coping behaviors from the literature and previous research, where the reality is imposed. Concern that current research methods have become somewhat divorced from the constructs they are purporting to measure has led to a questioning of the structured reality imposed by such measures (Jick, 1979; Payne, Jick, & Burke, 1982).

Researchers have also concluded that many of the items used in coping scales are ambiguous (Stone et al., 1988), lack a clear focus (Oakland & Ostell, 1996), and do not always differentiate coping strategies from emotional outcomes (Stanton, Danoff-Burg, Cameron, & Ellis, 1994). In the case of ambiguous items, the issue is that some coping items can, in the mind of those completing the measure, be interpreted to mean different things, so that a particular item may reflect a variety of coping functions. For example, an item like "went for a walk" could be interpreted as distraction, relaxation, or problem solving, depending on how an individual imagined using it and the nature of the stressful encounter being confronted (Stone et al., 1988). This problem is compounded because simply asking individuals if they engaged in a particular behavior (e.g., "went for a walk") yields no information on *why* this behavior was undertaken and what the person was hoping or intending to achieve with it (Oakland & Ostell, 1996).

A further source of confusion is that some items in existing coping instruments (e.g., "I get upset and let my emotions out") include both coping behaviors (letting one's feelings out) and their outcomes (getting upset), which may lead to problems of confounding and redundancy in measurement (Stanton et al., 1994). The difficulties associated with expressing coping items in an unambiguous way, along with the variability in the functions that different coping items perform and the reliability of coping measures, all help to explain why classifying coping strategies is such a problem. Finally, coping measures often ask people, "How did you cope?" which implies that the person did in fact cope successfully. Whether self-report measures of coping can provide meaningful and reliable coping categories and adequately express what people actually think and do appears to be a contested point (Erera-Weatherley, 1996; Oakland & Ostell, 1996) and once again raises the issue of whether adherence to single-method research designs limits our understanding of the coping process.

Scaling Techniques

If the overall goal is to achieve more precision when using self-report coping measures, increased attention must be given to the scoring of coping responses. At times, the use of a coping strategy has been determined through the analysis of open-ended data (Erera-Weatherley, 1996) or through getting participants to consider a number of different coping approaches (e.g., emotional relief, rational task-oriented behavior) and then to describe the sorts of coping strategies that they believe best fall within each approach (Schwartz & Stone, 1993). By far the most common approach is to get respondents to indicate "how frequently" they have used specified coping strategies. However, other response formats have also been used, including the degree to which different coping strategies have been engaged in, the extent to which strategies are used, and the likelihood of using particular strategies. Scoring keys also differ in terms of the number of points on the scale and anchor points. As a result, response ranges may vary from 5 to 7 points and begin with a 1 or 0; and even when different researchers are measuring the same thing (e.g., frequency), the descriptors they use to identify scale intervals vary considerably. Furthermore, interval scales are not the only methods employed to measure coping strategies (see Dewe, 2000).

A difficulty emerging from the multiplicity of response formats is the interpretation of findings from different studies. For example, Stone and his colleagues concluded that the term *extent,* when used in relation to coping, can variously mean duration, frequency, usefulness, and effort involved. They have argued that terminological ambiguity undermines efforts to ensure consistency of measurement because individual respondents may interpret response options in different ways. Stone and Kennedy-Moore (1991) suggested that individuals should be asked to respond on clearly defined dimensions; the difficulty is which dimension to choose and how best to describe it.

A further issue with respect to response options is the confusion between usage and effectiveness of coping strategies. Oakland and Ostell (1996) have argued that asking respondents how frequently they engaged in a particular behavior is futile because this approach provides no information on how effective each strategy was. Nevertheless, we believe that it is important to maintain a distinction between coping use (whether measured in terms of frequency or some other dimension) and coping effectiveness. Part of the problem may be that the word *coping* itself implies a satisfactory outcome. Bar-Tal and Spitzer (1994) argued that using scoring keys like "extent" or "helpfulness" on their own fails to reflect the multidimensional nature of coping. To them, a better and more useful key, and one that captures the complexity of coping, is "effectiveness." In support of this view is the research of Stone et al. (1991). Their results showed that, when asked to rate the extent to which they used a coping strategy, respondents interpreted *extent* to mean "usefulness" and so were in essence rating the effectiveness of a strategy.

Whether "effectiveness" is the appropriate scoring key, and whether this dimension will bring precision to how coping actions are measured, is a debate that has only just begun. Clearly, there are theoretical issues that need to be resolved. A transactional approach to coping requires that coping be measured independently of its effectiveness. So, however the issue of precision in measurement is approached, fundamental theoretical and methodological questions will still need to be resolved, not the least of which is whether self-report measures actually have the capacity to capture the subtlety of the coping process, let alone whether people report accurately. Social desirability may mean that people are reluctant to describe antisocial behaviors, are not prepared to admit to how emotional they may get, or cannot report certain behaviors due to lack of behavioral awareness.

What emerges from the debate surrounding how coping should best be measured is the question of whether traditional methodologies have provided an adequate basis for exploring and understanding the coping process. There is now a growing body of opinion and research that suggests that greater use of qualitative methods will enhance our understanding of coping. On the other hand, as researchers become more experienced in the use of self-report measures—the traditional approach to measuring coping—it becomes possible to identify an array of measurement issues that will continue to impede our understanding of coping and our ability to adequately assess the efficacy of this approach to the measurement of coping. The issue is not abandoning one approach in favor of another. A balance of quantitative and qualitative approaches may provide the conceptual richness and generalization that coping researchers are seeking.

Analysis of Coping Responses

Analyses of responses to questionnaire items on coping typically employ one or another form of factor analysis to group coping behaviors into themes or categories. Although factor analysis is a commonly used statistical technique in numerous areas of organizational behavior research, several issues concerning its application need to be considered, especially in relation to the development of coping "scales." Following our earlier discussion, one issue that arises is whether this procedure actually clusters together items that represent "coping styles" rather than "coping behaviors" (Dewe, 1989). Whether this is the case depends in part on the way individuals have been asked to respond to coping items. However, the variety of different factor structures, and hence the range of coping categories that have emerged from coping research, casts some doubt on the generality of coping responses identified by researchers and suggests that careful thought needs to be given to the identification and labeling of coping dimensions.

Another issue that has been raised (see Trenberth et al., 1996) when factor analysis has been used to identify categories of coping is whether the factors developed to describe different coping categories represent replicable categories of coping strategies or merely strategies that reflect the idiosyncrasies of the sample group (e.g., influenced by the type of occupation, the organization's culture, and the different resources available to help them cope). The number of factors to rotate and their replicability are issues that have captured the attention of researchers and that reflect the continuing need to review the methods used to explore the dimensions of coping.

Third, factor analyses of coping instruments typically use orthogonal rotation to maximize differences between emergent factors (coping strategies). This approach makes sense if the aim is to compare the outcomes of conceptually distinct coping strategies or to examine relationships between specific strategies and individual well-being. Empirically, however, it may not be possible to differentiate coping strategies in this manner, especially if there is an overlap in their functions (e.g., the same coping behavior may serve several functions for an individual). Similar arguments can be made with respect to assigning items to specific factors. In short, although it is empirically "cleaner" to identify and describe distinct coping factors, this may be an unrealistic goal, given the overlapping purposes fulfilled by various coping behaviors and strategies.

Finally, the use of factor analysis to identify coping categories has typically resulted in the derivation of composite coping scales. Mean scale scores are then obtained to reflect the frequency with which different coping categories are used. Stone et al. (1991), however, questioned whether these mean scores adequately represent the actual coping behaviors displayed by individuals. For example, the nature of a stressful encounter may mean that only one or a small number of responses in a scale are applicable. A low mean scale score does not necessarily indicate that one person used that coping strategy less than another individual who obtained a higher mean score; perhaps it might mean that the type of encounter faced imposed a limit on the score that could be obtained or that some of the strategies were not relevant to the particular encounter.

Similarly, though two people may obtain the same mean score on a particular coping scale, the items they checked to derive their score might differ considerably, so that despite having the same score they coped quite differently. Though the idea of score profiles is not new in coping research, the quite natural focus on mean scores does raise the issue that such scores may distort the way in which the different scales are interpreted. This is not an argument to stop using mean scores, but it does suggest that researchers need to consider alternative methods that may be more consistent with the constructs under investigation. If it does nothing else than force us to consider the way in which mean scores are derived and the variation in coping items that may be used to make up similar scores, it may go some way toward explaining the low reliability of some coping scales, as some researchers have pointed out (O'Driscoll & Cooper, 1994; Parkes, 1994).

For example, are there some coping strategies that, once used, simply inhibit or prevent the use of others? Could it be that "losing your temper" results in being cut off from a range of coping strategies that offer support or other forms of emotional relief? Are some coping strategies used in combination with each other (e.g., "setting priorities" and "working harder")? Do some coping strategies depend on the availability of resources (e.g., "delegating work" and "drawing on the support of others")? Are there individual coping strategies that immediately resolve the problem or dissipate the emotional discomfort? There is an assumption when using Likert-scored self-report measures "that endorsement of more items necessarily implies greater coping effort and hence a greater effect on outcome" (Parkes, 1994, p. 120). The nature of the coping process itself and the ways in which different coping strategies are used may not justify such an assumption (see Parkes, 1994). Therefore, researchers, to understand the coping process, may need to think more in terms of how best to investigate coping score profiles and, by association, the patterns in which different coping strategies are used; recognize that a low mean score does not necessarily reflect ineffective coping; and come to accept that low internal consistency scores may reflect the way in which coping strategies are used rather than poor internal consistency.

In sum, the argument is not about abandoning factor analysis and the subsequent computation of mean coping scores. As Folkman (1991) has indicated, this would be imprudent because factor analytical techniques do produce coping categories that have empirical, as well as conceptual, integrity. However, it is imperative to consider the most appropriate ways of using such techniques to ensure that optimal benefits are obtained.

Classification of Coping Strategies

An issue that has attracted considerable debate is the classification of coping strategies. Typically, coping strategies have been classified on the basis of the "function" they perform. This has already been noted in our discussion on the merits of the distinction between "problem-focused" and "emotion-focused" strategies. An examination of coping scales by Ferguson and Cox (1997) suggests that there may now be some agreement that coping performs four major functions, classified as emotional regulation, approach, reappraisal, and avoidance.

Whether these are distinct functions or merely subsets of the problem-focused/emotion-focused distinction can be debated. What may be more critical is to recognize that function and form are both important when considering the nature of coping strategies and that although it may be possible to classify coping scales through simple inspection, this fails to recognize the context within which coping takes place. Further research is needed to explore how characteristics of the transactional encounter combine to determine the functions that a coping strategy performs (Ferguson & Cox, 1997). For example, the coping strategy "working harder" might be viewed, in most classification systems, as a problem-solving behavior. However, working harder may also be used as a mechanism for reducing emotional discomfort by taking one's mind off a particular problem, in which case it might be classified as an emotion-focused coping strategy.

Coping Effectiveness

Another approach to conceptualizing the functions of coping behaviors is to consider whether they are effective or ineffective in removing stressors or alleviating strain (Folkman, 1982): that is, to evaluate them on the basis of their outcomes, with effective coping strategies resulting in outcomes that are favorable for the individual and ineffective strategies not producing favorable outcomes or, worse, leading to unfavorable outcomes. As Folkman (1982), among others, has illustrated, a major pitfall of this distinction is that it has tended to link problem-focused coping with encounters that are controllable (by the individual), whereas emotion-focused coping has been associated with situations where there is little opportunity for the individual to exert control over the transaction and hence where there is a lower likelihood of a favorable outcome. Thus, by extension, problem-focused coping is considered more effective than emotion-focused coping. The dubiousness of this conclusion has been pointed out by several researchers (e.g., Bar-Tal & Spitzer, 1994; Folkman, 1992; Oakland & Ostell, 1996). In particular, differences between situations and individuals make it impossible to judge a priori whether a coping effort has been successful or unsuccessful.

Furthermore, definitions and measures of "effectiveness" must be based upon the perceptions and goals of the individuals enacting the behaviors rather than developed around so-called objective indexes. Pursued in this manner, it is clear that both problem-focused and emotion-focused coping may contain both effective and ineffective strategies (Erera-Weatherley, 1996). Studies of coping effectiveness must assess the cognitive processes that individuals engage in when evaluating their coping efforts. How individuals themselves define effectiveness is an issue that has yet to be explored and raises the interesting questions of effectiveness for whom and at what cost, in addition to consideration of the best methodology to tease out such distinctions.

An alternative approach to judging coping effectiveness is to examine the notion of goodness of fit (Folkman, 1992). Using this approach, the focus shifts to considering the fit between situational appraisals and coping. The greater the misfit between how a situation is appraised and a coping response, the greater the probability that coping will not be effective. This approach requires measures of both primary appraisal and coping, and perhaps for this reason it has received less attention in settings involving work stress.

When coping effectiveness is being explored, researchers should carefully consider (a) the context within which coping is being judged, particularly the level of control individuals have over the situation (Folkman, 1992); (b) the outcome that is being used as the criterion variable, given that different outcomes are associated with different coping strategies (Oakland & Ostell, 1996); (c) the role of individual differences in the selection of a coping strategy (Erera-Weatherley, 1996); (d) the nature of the situation and the demands it places on the individual (Newton, 1989), together with how such demands are appraised (Dewe, 1989); (e) the impact of confounding between coping and outcomes, as measures developed to explore emotion-focused coping often include items that reflect emotional outcomes (Stanton et al., 1994); (f) the merits of longitudinal versus cross-sectional research design, including issues like the episodic or chronic nature of demands and short-term versus long-term effects (Folkman, 1992); and, finally, (g) whether contradictory findings concerning coping effectiveness are due more to the difficulties inherent in self-report measures of coping than to the nature of the coping strategy being judged (Oakland & Ostell, 1996).

Conclusion

There is no doubt that the intensity of the debate surrounding coping as a field of study reflects its fundamental importance to our understanding of the stress process. The research literature is dominated by the issue of how coping should best be measured and how coping strategies should be classified. Even when the primary aim of researchers has been to explore the broader context within which coping takes place, concerns over measurement issues have dominated their approach and influenced their results. Three schools of thought on coping measurement have emerged. The first recognizes the difficulties inherent in self-report measures of coping and argues that research should focus on how such measures can be refined to enhance precision in measurement. Only then will our understanding of coping be advanced. The second argues that the complexity of the coping process cannot be understood by using quantitative self-ratings because these are too blunt to capture the subtlety of stressful encounters. Coping should be investigated using qualitative techniques, as these are free of the structural limitations imposed by the more traditional approaches. To ensure that coping measures provide comprehensive information on the coping process, a more integrated analysis of coping is required that captures the reality of those undergoing such an experience. This can be achieved only by considering qualitative methods that capture the richness of the process and the idiographic nature of the experience.

What is apparent is that both schools of thought have as their rationale the desire to better understand coping and its role in the coping process. However, a third school is emerging that suggests that the way forward may be to use a combination of both qualitative and quantitative techniques. How coping with job-related stress will be investigated in the future will be decided by how well the strengths of all methods can be integrated into research designs. The importance of coping and how it should best be measured is too important an issue to allow the debate to degenerate into mutual antagonism and distrust between advocates of alternative methodologies. Research on coping and the appraisal process represents the most likely means of enhancing our understanding of the stress process and for fulfilling our obligations to those whose working lives we research. We should not allow it to be obstructed by arguments about the superiority of one approach over another.

References

Bar-Tal, Y., & Spitzer, A. (1994). Coping use versus effectiveness as moderating the stress-strain relationship. *Journal of Community and Applied Social Psychology, 4,* 91-100.

Billings, A., & Moos, R. (1984). Coping, stress and social resources among adults with unipolar depression. *Journal of Personality and Social Psychology, 46,* 877-891.

Brief, A. P., & George, J. M. (1991). Psychological stress and the workplace: A brief comment on Lazarus' outlook. *Journal of Social Behaviour and Personality, 6,* 15-20.

Cohen, F. (1987). Measurement of coping. In S. V. Kasi & C. L. Cooper (Eds.), *Stress and health: issues in research methodology* (pp. 283-305). New York: John Wiley.

Cox, T. (1987). Stress, coping and problem solving. *Work and Stress, 1,* 5-14.

Cox, T., & Ferguson, E. (1991). Individual differences, stress and coping. In C. L. Cooper & R. Payne (Eds.), *Personality and stress: Individual differences in the stress process* (pp. 7-30). New York: John Wiley.

Cummings, T. G., & Cooper, C. L. (1979). A cybernetic framework for studying occupational stress. *Human Relations, 32,* 395-418.

Dewe, P. J. (1989). Examining the nature of work stress: Individual evaluations of stressful experiences and coping. *Human Relations, 42,* 993-1013.

Dewe, P. J. (1991). Primary appraisal, secondary appraisal and coping: Their role in stressful work encounters. *Journal of Occupational Psychology, 64,* 331-351.

Dewe, P. (2000). Measures of coping with stress at work: A review and critique. In P. Dewe, M. Leiter, & T. Cox (Eds.), *Coping, health and organizations* (pp. 3-28). Washington, DC: Taylor & Francis.

Dewe, P., Cox, T., & Ferguson, E. (1993). Individual strategies for coping with stress and work: A review. *Work and Stress, 7,* 5-15.

Dewe, P., & Guest, D. (1990). Methods of coping with stress at work: A conceptual analysis and empirical study of measurement issues. *Journal of Organisational Behaviour, 11,* 135-150.

Dewe, P. J., Guest, D. E., & Williams, A. R. T. (1978). Methods of coping with work related stress. In C. Mackay & T. Cox (Eds.), *Response to stress: Occupational aspects* (pp. 69-84). New York: Guilford.

Edwards, J. R. (1988). The determinants and consequences of coping with stress. In C. L. Cooper & R. Payne (Eds.), *Causes, coping and consequences of stress and work* (pp. 233-263). New York: John Wiley.

Erera-Weatherley, P. L. (1996). Coping with stress: Public welfare supervisors doing their best. *Human Relations, 49,* 157-170.

Ferguson, E., & Cox, T. (1997). The Functional Dimensions of Coping Scale: Theory reliability and validity. *British Journal of Health Psychology, 2,* 109-129.

Fleishman, L. A. (1984). Personality characteristics and coping patterns. *Journal of Health and Social Behaviour, 25,* 229-244.

Folkman, S. (1982). An approach to the measurement of coping. *Journal of Occupational Behaviour, 3,* 95-107.

Folkman, S. (1984). Personal control and stress and coping processes: A theoretical analysis. *Journal of Personality and Social Psychology, 46,* 839-852.

Folkman, S. (1991). Improving coping assessment: Reply to Stone and Kennedy-Moore. In H. S. Friedman (Ed.), *Hostility, coping and health* (pp. 215-223). Washington, DC: American Psychological Association.

Folkman, S. (1992). Making the case for coping. In B. N. Carpenter (Ed.), *Personal coping: Theory, research and application* (pp. 31-46). Westport, CT: Praeger.

Folkman, S., & Lazarus, R. S. (1980). An analysis of coping in a middle aged community sample. *Journal of Health and Social Behaviour, 21,* 219-239.

Folkman, S., & Lazarus, R. (1985). If it changes, it must be a process: Study of emotion and coping during three stages of a college examination. *Journal of Personality and Social Psychology, 48,* 150-170.

Folkman, S., & Lazarus, R. S. (1988). The relationship between coping and emotion: Implications for theory and research. *Social Science and Medicine, 26,* 309-317.

Folkman, S., Lazarus, R., Dunkel-Schetter, C., DeLongis, A., & Gruen, R. (1986). Dynamics of a stressful encounter: Cognitive appraisal, coping and encounter outcomes. *Journal of Personality and Social Psychology, 50,* 992-1003.

Harris, J. R. (1991). The utility of the transactional approach for occupational stress research. *Journal of Social Behaviour and Personality, 6,* 21-29.

Holroyd, K. A., & Lazarus, R. S. (1982). Stress, coping and somatic adaptation. In L. Goldberger & S. Breznitz (Eds.), *Handbook of stress: Theoretical and clinical aspects* (pp. 21-35). New York: Free Press.

Jick, T. D. (1979). Mixing qualitative and quantitative methods: Triangulation in action. *Administrative Science Quarterly, 24,* 802-811.

Kahn, R. L., & Byosiere, S. (1992). Stress in organizations. In M. Dunnette & L. M. Hough (Eds.), *Handbook of industrial and organizational psychology* (pp. 571-648). Chicago: Rand-McNally.

Karasek, R. A. (1979). Job demands, job decision latitude, and mental strain: Implications for job redesign. *Administrative Science Quarterly, 24,* 285-308.

Kinicki, A. J., & Latack, J. C. (1990). Explication of the construct of coping with involuntary job loss. *Journal of Vocational Behaviour, 36,* 339-360.

Kinicki, A. J., McKee, F. M., & Wade, K. J. (1996). Annual Review 1991-1995: Occupational Health. *Journal of Vocational Behaviour, 49,* 190-220.

Latack, J. C. (1986). Coping with job stress: Measures and future directions for scale development. *Journal of Applied Psychology, 71,* 377-385.

Latack, J. C., & Havlovic, S. J. (1992). Coping with job stress: A conceptual evaluation framework for coping measures. *Journal of Organisational Behaviour, 13,* 479-508.

Lazarus, R. L., & Launier, R. (1978). Stress-related transactions between person and environment. In L. A. Pervin & M. Lewis (Eds.), *Perspectives in international psychology* (pp. 287-327). New York: Plenum.

Lazarus, R. S. (1990). Theory-based stress measurement. *Psychological Inquiry, 1,* 3-13.

Lazarus, R. S. (1991). Psychological stress in the workplace. *Journal of Social Behaviour and Personality, 6,* 1-13.

Lazarus, R. S., & Folkman, S. (1984). *Stress, appraisal and coping.* New York: Springer.

McGrath, J. E. (1976). Stress and behavior in organizations. In M. D. Dunnette (Ed.), *Handbook of industrial and organizational psychology* (pp. 1351-1395). Chicago: Rand-McNally.

Newton, T. J. (1989). Occupational stress and coping with stress: A critique. *Human Relations, 42,* 441-461.

Newton, T. J., & Keenan, A. (1985). Coping with work-related stress. *Human Relations, 38,* 107-126.

Oakland, S., & Ostell, A. (1996). Measuring coping: A review and critique. *Human Relations, 49,* 133-155.

O'Driscoll, M. P., & Cooper, C. L. (1994). Coping with work related stress: A critique of existing measures and proposal for an alternative methodology. *Journal of Occupational and Organisational Psychology, 67,* 343-354.

O'Driscoll, M. P., & Cooper, C. L. (1996). A critical incident analysis of stress-coping behaviours at work. *Stress Medicine, 12,* 123-128.

Parkes, K. R. (1994). Personality and coping as moderators of work stress processes: Models, methods and measures. *Work and Stress, 8,* 110-129.

Payne, R. A., Jick, T. D., & Burke, R. J. (1982). Wither stress research? An agenda for the 1980s. *Journal of Occupational Behaviour, 3,* 131-145.

Pearlin, L., & Schooler, C. (1978). The structure of coping. *Journal of Health and Social Behavior,* *19,* 2-21.

Schuler, R. S. (1980). Definition and conceptualization of stress in organisations. *Organisational Behaviour and Human Performance, 24,* 184-215.

Schwartz, L. E., & Stone, A. A. (1993). Coping with daily work problems: Contributions of problem content, appraisals, and person factors. *Work and Stress, 7,* 47-62.

Stanton, A. L., Danoff-Burg, S., Cameron, C. L., & Ellis, A. P. (1994). Coping through emotional approach: Problems of conceptualization and confounding. *Journal of Personality and Social Psychology, 66,* 350-362.

Stone, A. A., Greenberg, M. A., Kennedy-Moore, E., & Newman, M. G. (1991). Self-report, situation specific coping questionnaires: What are they measuring. *Journal of Personality and Social Psychology, 61,* 648-658.

Stone, A. A., Helder, L., & Schneider, M. S. (1988). Coping dimensions and issues. In L. H. Cohen (Ed.), *Life events and psychological functioning: Theoretical and methodological issues* (pp. 182-210). Beverly Hills, CA: Sage.

Stone, A. A., & Kennedy-Moore, E. (1991). Assessing situational coping: Conceptual and methodological considerations. In H. S. Friedman (Ed.), *Hostility, coping and health* (pp. 203-214). Washington, DC: American Psychological Association.

Stone, L. A., & Neale, L. M. (1984). New measure of daily coping: Development and preliminary results. *Journal of Personality and Social Psychology, 46,* 892-906.

Sutherland, V. J., & Cooper, C. L. (1988). Sources of work stress. In J. J. Hurrell, L. R. Murphy, S. L. Sauter, & C. L. Cooper (Eds.), *Occupational stress: Issues and developments in research* (pp. 3-40). New York: Taylor & Francis.

Trenberth, L. D. (1996). *Principals, deputy principals and work stress: The role of coping and leisure.* Unpublished doctoral thesis, Massey University, Palmerston North, New Zealand.

Trenberth, L. D., Dewe, P. J., & Walkey, F. H. (1996). A factor replication approach to the measurement of coping. *Stress Medicine, 12,* 71-79.

7 Organizational Interventions

As was mentioned earlier in this volume, the human and financial costs of job-related strain can be substantial (De Frank & Ivancevich, 1998; Murphy, 1995). However, despite widespread acknowledgment of the detrimental impact of stress on individuals and organizations, the amount of attention given by employers to understanding the causes (sources) of work-related strain and to alleviating stressful work conditions is relatively small compared with other areas, such as maintaining effective equipment and balancing financial budgets. Each year, organizations invest considerable sums of money in stress management programs (predominantly stress management training), but often there is an incomplete understanding of the sources of strain to be confronted and of the effectiveness of stress management approaches in dealing with these particular stressors.

For some time now, stress researchers have commented on the seeming haphazardness of stress management within organizational settings and the lack of congruence between workplace practices and theoretical and empirical work in this field. Along with personnel selection and employee training, this would appear to be another area where there is a gap between theory and practice in the domain of organizational behavior.

Many reasons can be proffered for the divergence between scientific research on stress management and organizational practices. Predominant among these are (a) managers' perceptions and beliefs about the impact of the work environment on levels of employee strain and general well-being (Cartwright, Cooper, & Murphy, 1995), (b) their beliefs about who is responsible for managing individual employees' levels of strain, and (c) the costs associated with making organization-level changes compared with those related to teaching individuals to cope more effectively (Cooper & Cartwright, 1994; Daniels, 1996; Murphy, 1988). These three factors are linked, and together they promote a climate where stress management is viewed either as the responsibility of individual employees or as best tackled by the provision of stress management training that will enhance individuals' capability to manage their own levels of strain, without requiring substantial changes in jobs or the work environment itself.

Building upon the transactional model of stress outlined in Chapter 1, the present chapter begins with an outline of a conceptual framework for understanding stress management interventions (SMIs). Chapter 6 focused on coping behaviors (strategies) at the individual level; here we will describe examples of interventions that have been carried out either at the level of the specific job or at the broader organizational level. Research on the effectiveness of these interventions will be reviewed, along with some of the major problems associated with conducting good research in this area and guidelines for evaluating SMIs. The chapter concludes with a discussion of practical recommendations for implementing SMIs within organizations.

For simplicity, we will not differentiate here between interventions that are designed to offset the effects of strain in general and those that target burnout (discussed in Chapter 4) specifically. It is important to acknowledge, however, that the type of strain indicator (whether general strain, burnout, or some other specific symptom of strain) is critical to consider when implementing an SMI. (Richardsen & Burke, 1995, have outlined some specific interventions that might follow from the models of burnout described in Chapter 4.)

A Conceptual Framework for Stress
Management Interventions

Efforts to combat job-related strain have been conceptualized in a number of different ways (see Table 7.1). These approaches can be

Table 7.1 A Framework for Stress Management Interventions

Primary Interventions	

Scope: Preventative—Reduce the number and/or intensity of stressors
Target: Alter work environments, technologies, or organizational structures
Underlying assumption: Most effective approach to stress management is to remove stressors
Examples: job redesign; role restructuring; organizational restructuring

Secondary Interventions

Scope: Preventative/reactive—Modify individuals' responses to stressors
Target: Individual
Underlying assumption: May not be able to remove/reduce stressors, so best to focus on individuals' reactions to these stressors
Examples: stress management training; communication and information sharing; "wellness" programs

Tertiary Interventions

Scope: Treatment—Minimize the damaging consequences of stressors by helping individuals cope more effectively with these consequences
Target: Individual
Underlying assumption: Focus is on "treatment" of problems once they have occurred
Examples: employee assistance programs; counseling

differentiated by the level at which an intervention occurs (primary, secondary, or tertiary), the scope of the intervention activity, its target, and the assumptions underlying each intervention. Although the approaches represented in Table 7.1 are not mutually exclusive, to some extent each is distinct, and the choice of approach has considerable implications for individuals and the organization as a whole.

A distinction is frequently drawn between the levels at which SMIs operate. *Primary interventions* are based on the assumption that the most effective way to combat strain is to eliminate or at least reduce the sources of strain (i.e., stressors) in the work environment, hence alleviating the pressures placed upon individual employees. This type of intervention is the most proactive and preventative approach to stress management and has been reported as generally being effective when implemented systematically and as a result of a careful assessment of specific stressors (Burke, 1993; Ivancevich & Matteson, 1987; Murphy, 1988). Considered from the perspective of the person-environment fit model of stress (see, e.g., Edwards & Cooper, 1990), the focus of primary interventions is on modifying or adapting the physical or social-political environment to meet the needs of workers.

Elkin and Rosch (1990) summarized a range of primary preventions that might be implemented to reduce workplace stressors, including structural changes in the organization, job redesign, and changes in social systems within the organization. The following represent illustrations of the types of intervention that would be classified under this heading:

- Reorganization of lines of authority
- Restructuring of organizational units
- Changes in decision-making processes, such as increased employee participation in relevant decisions
- Redesign of job tasks, such as increasing employee autonomy and control over job functions and work schedules
- Redesign of the physical work environment
- Changes in job roles
- Provision of a more supportive climate, including more constructive feedback on job performance
- Establishment of a more equitable system of reward distribution

A key component of many of the strategies listed above is the provision of greater individual control over the work environment. As discussed in Chapter 5, although empirical findings on the moderating (buffering) effects of employee control on the stressor-strain relationship are not totally conclusive, there is substantial evidence that increased personal control is directly linked with higher levels of employee satisfaction and well-being.

In contrast to primary interventions, *secondary interventions* focus on stress management training to alleviate the impact that environmental stressors exert on workers, rather than making changes to work conditions or the organizational environment. Secondary interventions represent the most common form of intervention used by organizations to deal with problems of stress management (Dewe, 1994). They are targeted at individual rather than organizational changes, and they aim primarily to increase individuals' awareness of their levels of strain and to enhance their personal coping strategies. Examples of techniques employed under this banner include meditation, relaxation training, biofeedback, cognitive restructuring, time management, and conflict resolution strategies. A large number of organizations have also introduced health promotion activities (sometimes referred to as "wellness" programs) for their employees (Ganster, 1995).

Secondary interventions may be either proactive (preventative) or reactive. For example, training individuals in conflict resolution skills may help to prevent the onset or development of interpersonal conflict between themselves and their colleagues. On the other hand, utilization of this training after such conflict has already surfaced illustrates a reactive approach to this particular stressor.

Stress management training has been found to be useful for some forms of stressors (Dewe, 1994), although its long-term effectiveness and its impact on organizational outcomes (such as strain-related absenteeism, accidents, and performance) have not been consistently demonstrated (Ganster, 1995). One considerable advantage of this approach over the primary interventions described above is that it can typically be implemented quickly and may cause little disruption to existing work patterns (Murphy, 1995). Furthermore, skills training and increasing employee awareness of strain may play an important role in extending workers' psychosocial resources and in helping people deal with stressors that cannot be changed and hence have to be "lived with." These strategies may also function to strengthen a person's general resilience and resistance to stressors.

Despite these benefits, secondary interventions essentially reflect "damage limitation," often addressing the outcomes rather than the sources of strain that may be inherent in an organization's structure, culture, or climate. Hence, their exclusive use raises several concerns about ethics and control. For instance, the aim of training workers to cope more effectively means that often stress management training is not designed to eliminate or modify stressors in the workplace (Ganster, 1995). The effectiveness of such training depends upon whether any change in individual coping strategies will be adequate to reduce the amount of strain the individual actually experiences, either short or long term. When stressors are systemic or structural (such as continuing excessive workload), individual coping behaviors may be insufficient, and job redesign or role restructuring may be required to alleviate the strain experienced and to prevent the development of burnout.

An even more fundamental issue is that use of stress management training without thorough exploration of the specific sources of strain may entail a shift of responsibility from management to individual workers. As noted earlier, managers exhibit a tendency to attribute the causes of strain to individual employees' own behaviors and to view the responsibility for stress management as resting with workers themselves (Dewe, 1994). In part, this is due to a fear of litigation, with employers wishing to avoid the legal and financial repercussions of admitting responsibility for stressful work environments. Over 10 years ago, Murphy (1988) noted that as long as managers adopt this stance, secondary interventions focusing on individual coping behaviors will continue to be more prevalent than more radical primary interventions. Little has changed in the intervening period.

The *tertiary* level of stress management intervention is concerned with the rehabilitation of individuals who have suffered ill health or reduced well-being as a result of strain in the workplace. Interventions at this level are based on a "treatment" rather than a preventative philosophy and are best illustrated by employee assistance programs (EAPs), which typically encompass some form of counseling to help employees deal with workplace stressors that cannot be changed structurally, as well as examining any potential spillover between work stressors and life off the job (e.g., marital and family difficulties). EAP programs also involve procedures that identify and respond to personal issues that may be interfering with work performance.

EAPs are characterized by a range of services (for an overview, see Davis & Gibson, 1994) and may be provided by the human resource function within the organization or by external consultants. The latter are becoming increasingly utilized for this purpose, as one major issue with respect to EAPs is confidentiality and the protection of individual privacy. Two referral pathways are common in most organizations: (a) self-referral, where the individual employee makes direct contact with the EAP consultant to use his or her services, and (b) referral from a supervisor or manager, which may occur especially when job performance problems have become evident.

Although the financial benefits (to the organization) of EAPs have been scrutinized, there is still little agreement on how best to evaluate this type of intervention (Dewe, 1994; Murphy, 1984). Berridge and Cooper (1993) commented that it is sometimes difficult to reconcile the economic benefits to the organization with a more social therapeutic approach that emphasizes the impact of counseling on individual well-being. Furthermore, evaluation data on EAP schemes are frequently gathered by the consultants or managed care companies that are responsible for the implementation of the program; hence, these data may not be impartial (Smith & Mahoney, 1989).

Nevertheless, there is evidence suggesting that counseling services are effective in many cases in improving the psychological well-being of employees, as well as having benefits for the organization as a whole.

For example, Cooper and Cartwright (1994) analyzed U.S. data that indicated typical savings-to-investment ratios ranging from 3:1 to 15:1. Similarly, Cooper and Sadri (1991) found significant postcounseling improvements in the mental health and self-esteem of employees participating in EAPs in the United Kingdom. (Interestingly, however, in this study there was no significant change in levels of job satisfaction and organizational commitment.)

Finally, as with secondary interventions, the introduction of an EAP or some other tertiary intervention may be beneficial to employees and may be viewed by managers as cost-effective, yet still may not confront workplace stressors themselves, in which case the benefits may be short-lived. Organizational stress researchers continue to assert that most organizational interventions fall short because they offer a partial solution and place the onus on the individual to change his or her coping mechanisms, rather than acknowledging and modifying structural variables (at the job or organizational level). Though considerable emphasis is given to secondary and tertiary level interventions, primary strategies that encompass actual reduction in stressors are comparatively rare.

Research on Stress Management Interventions

Despite recognition that levels of employee strain and the costs to organizations of job-related strain may be increasing significantly, only a small number of studies assessing *organizational* interventions have been published (Dollard & Winefield, 1996; Murphy, 1995; O'Driscoll & Cooper, 1996). In the first major review of SMIs, Newman and Beehr (1979) concluded that there was a lack of systematic evaluation of SMI effectiveness and that only 6 of the 52 studies they reviewed entailed any direct empirical evaluation of intervention effectiveness. The large majority (32) relied solely on professional opinions about whether the intervention in question had generated positive results.

Ivancevich, Matteson, Freedman, and Phillips (1990) found only four evaluations where organization-level interventions had been targeted. Three of these interventions, all at the primary level depicted in Table 7.1, were designed to increase levels of employee control or autonomy, which has already been highlighted here as an important issue in stress management. For instance, Jackson (1983) conducted an evaluation of participative decision making in an outpatient hospital setting, observing that increased participation led to more perceived influence and lower emotional distress. In another investigation, Pierce and Newstrom (1983) observed that having more flexible work schedules (flextime) also produced positive benefits for employees, including a reduction in psychological strain. Having greater autonomy in choosing how to complete job tasks was explored by Wall and Clegg (1981), who conducted a longitudinal study of the effects of job redesign, in which increases in work group autonomy were linked with significant improvements in employee mental health. Finally, Murphy and Hurrell (1987) explored the effects of introducing an employee representative committee whose function was to develop recommendations on stress management from surveys of employees. The implication of these findings is that interventions designed to increase worker control over important aspects of the work environment may have a significant impact on reducing psychological strain due to work-related stressors.

Burke (1993) summarized research on several organization-level stress management programs, including (in addition to those reviewed by Ivancevich and his associates) goal setting (to enhance role definition and clarity), use of problem solving to resolve work-related difficulties, reducing the amount of conflict between job demands and family responsibilities, and increasing communication and information sharing between management and employees. With the exception of problem-solving groups, the above interventions appeared to yield positive benefits for employees. Burke suggested that in the study involving problem-solving groups, the intervention was not implemented as planned, which may have undermined its potential beneficial effects. Burke's overall conclusion about the generally positive outcomes of organizational interventions has been challenged, however, by Briner and Reynolds (1999), who suggested that the research reviewed by Burke contained "a rather odd selection of studies of varying methodological rigor and mixed outcomes and whose results do not appear to fully justify the conclusion drawn by Burke" (p. 656).

Perhaps one of the best designed evaluations of an SMI is a field experiment conducted by Ganster, Mayes, Sime, and Tharp (1982). The intervention consisted of a (secondary-level) stress management training program delivered over an 8-week period to 79 employees of a public agency in the United States. Ganster et al.'s evaluation included random assignment of employees to either a treatment or a control group (the members of which did not receive the training during the period of the study). To reduce the potential negative effects of resentment for not being selected for the training program, employees in the control group were informed that it was not possible to include all of them in the program at one time. A further strength of this study was the measurement of three distinct types of strain responses—psychological (anxiety, depression, and irritation), physiological (levels of epinephrine and norepinephrine in urine), and somatic complaints (a 17-item symptom checklist). These measures were collected at three points in time—before training, after training, and at a 4-month follow-up of the treatment group—to assess (relatively) long-term effects of the training program.

Ganster et al. found that employees who underwent the stress management training exhibited significantly lower post-training levels of epinephrine and depression than did control group employees and that these effects did not return to pretraining levels at the 4-month follow-up. Effects of the training on other indexes of strain were less definitive. Moreover, the effects of the training were not replicated when the control group also underwent the training, suggesting a potential lack of generalization. On the basis of their findings, Ganster and his colleagues concluded that the evidence was not sufficiently strong or clear-cut to recommend the use of stress management training to alleviate the impact of workplace stressors. It could also be argued that stress management training is effectively an individual-level, rather than organization-level, intervention (see Briner & Reynolds, 1999).

Another example of a well-designed field experiment using a longitudinal design was an evaluation conducted by Schweiger and DeNisi (1991). As we observed in Chapter 2, to increase their market share, rationalize their operation, or simply improve efficiency, over the past decade numerous organizations have either merged or been taken over by other companies. Although these mergers and acquisitions may be advantageous for employers and for the organization as a whole, they can generate considerable strain for employees, who perceive that their positions and roles in the organization are threatened (Kozlowski, Chao, Smith, & Hedlung, 1993). Schweiger and DeNisi studied the ameliorating impact of a realistic merger preview introduced by a light manufacturing firm that was undergoing a merger with a similar company. The preview, which could be regarded as a secondary-level intervention, consisted of a two-way communication program designed by the researchers to give information to employees on how the merger would affect them and to provide a mechanism for employees to communicate their questions and reactions to management. This communication program was implemented in one plant, with another plant of the same company serving as a control. Surveys including measures of psychological strain and other responses (attitudes toward their job and the organization) were administered on four separate occasions, and absenteeism and turnover data were collected from company records.

Following announcement of the merger, significant increases were found in psychological strain and reductions in positive work attitudes in both the experimental and control plants. Further analyses illustrated that, compared with reactions immediately after the merger announcement, at the final survey administration period employees at the plant that had received the communication program exhibited significantly lower strain and uncertainty and showed higher levels of job satisfaction and organizational commitment. Schweiger and DeNisi (1991) concluded that "a realistic merger preview seems to function at least as an inoculation that makes employees resistant to the negative effects of mergers and acquisitions" (p. 129).

The above studies represent examples of well-designed and well-executed evaluations of SMIs. However, the interventions in both of these investigations were aimed at enhancing workers' coping capacities. As noted earlier, removal or reduction of stressors is "the most direct way to reduce stress since it deals with the source" (Burke, 1993, p. 85). There is mounting evidence that job redesign interventions (especially those that increase employee control and autonomy), adoption of more consultative or participative management styles, development of clearer role descriptions, and use of more effective goal-setting and performance feedback systems can all enhance employee well-being and alleviate work-related strain. Though these approaches may entail greater immediate costs for the organization and require higher commitment and effort from management, research suggests that these will be offset by long-term benefits not only for individual employees but also for the organization as a whole. For a contrary view, however, see Briner and Reynolds (1999), who argued that there is not necessarily an association between organizational SMIs and individual outcomes, such as enhanced well-being.

Overall, it would appear that there has been little systematic use of organizational interventions (especially at the primary level) that might bring about significant reductions in psychological strain among employees. From a managerial standpoint, it may be more convenient to focus SMIs on individual perceptions and behaviors than on organizational or job redesign. Programs such as stress management training and EAPs may be viewed as less costly and more readily implemented than long-term restructuring or major changes in work practices and procedures and, may also serve to keep management from accepting greater responsibility for excessive strain experienced by their employees.

Problems in Evaluating Intervention Effectiveness

A number of difficulties associated with the evaluation of SMIs have already been alluded to. Of particular concern is the infrequent use of well-constructed empirical research that builds upon sound theoretical conceptualizations of intervention effects, incorporates longitudinal designs, and uses multimethod approaches to measurement of outcomes. With a few notable exceptions, such as the studies cited above, most investigations of intervention effectiveness have been unsystematic and based predominantly on ad hoc judgments or viewpoints of observers whose impartiality might be questioned.

Several critiques of evaluation methodology and practice have been published in recent years, and our intention is not to reiterate all of the criticisms raised by these reviewers. Instead, we focus on a few critical issues relating to the evaluation of stress management interventions within work settings. A primary concern is the validity of findings obtained from an evaluation. In a comprehensive overview of factors affecting the validity of SMIs, Beehr and O'Hara (1987) differentiated between three types of validity issues: (a) internal validity, (b) construct validity, and (c) external validity.

Internal Validity

Beehr and O'Hara (1987) noted that many factors (e.g., historical events occurring between pretraining and posttraining measures of an outcome variable, changes within respondents that occur solely due to the passage of time, and employees' own personal characteristics, such as hardiness) may all influence the outcomes of an intervention program and are frequently not assessed or taken into account when evaluating such programs. Fortunately, use of one or more randomly assigned control groups can offset these threats to internal validity, but often researchers may not be able to employ a research design that includes control groups, either because it is simply not possible to randomly assign workers to an experimental or control group or because the organization is unwilling to permit such allocations. In addition, ethical considerations associated with withholding an intervention from certain members of the organization, even for a limited time period, may call into question the justification for assigning some study participants to a control group. An approach similar to that adopted by Ganster and his colleagues might be valuable in this context.

Similarly, in many cases it may not be possible to gather measures of the outcome variables both before and after the implementation of an SMI. Because of this constraint, several intervention evaluations have relied upon a postintervention only design, which severely limits conclusions that can be drawn from the evaluation. A technique known as *retrospective degree of change* (Peterson, 1993) might be used to (at least partially) overcome this problem. In a retrospective design, respondents are asked to reflect upon changes that have occurred since the intervention was implemented. For example, in a merger situation, employees might be surveyed after the merger has occurred and be asked to compare their present perceptions, attitudes, and feelings (about the job and the organization) with these same reactions prior to the merger. This enables the researcher to analyze perceived changes directly without having to rely on pretest/posttest comparisons. Two limitations of this technique, however, are that (a) it relies upon respondents' ability to make valid comparisons of their "then" versus "now" reactions, and (b) it assesses only the extent of change and not actual levels of reactions at different times. Nevertheless, the retrospective-degree-of-change approach may be applicable in circumstances where collection of preintervention data is not feasible.

Construct Validity

The issue of construct validity is, of course, relevant to all research in that valid measurement of constructs is a prerequisite for generalizable conclusions. In the case of SMIs, construct validation relates to both the assessment of outcomes (psychological strain in particular) and the intervention strategy (is it actually directed at reducing psychological strain?). A critical question for many SMI evaluations is whether the indicators that are being assessed (psychological, physiological, somatic, or behavioral) truly reflect levels of strain experienced by recipients of the intervention. Although there is some evidence of convergence between these indicators (Hendrix, Ovalle, & Troxler, 1985), unfortunately the correspondence between self-reports and physiological indexes of strain has not been consistently demonstrated (Pennebaker & Watson, 1988). As outlined earlier in this volume (see Chapter 4), further comparisons using multimethod procedures would help to alleviate concerns about the construct validity of particular measures.

External Validity

Along with the above forms of validity, a further critical issue for stress researchers is whether an intervention implemented in one setting and time period will also be effective in another context or under other circumstances. Although a particular organization may be interested solely in reducing levels of strain among its own members, for consultants and researchers generalization beyond the immediate setting is an important criterion for assessing the validity of stress management interventions.

Beehr and O'Hara (1987) examined three major threats to the external validity of an SMI. The first of these is what they referred to as *subject-by-treatment* interaction, which occurs when an intervention is effective with one group of participants but not with others. For instance, a stress management program may reduce levels of strain among certain occupational groups (e.g., professionals) but have no impact, or even have a deleterious effect, on other groups (e.g., office workers). This issue requires researchers to examine the demographic and personal characteristics of participants in an SMI to determine whether any of these variables might operate as a moderator of the relationship between the intervention and criterion variables.

A second threat described by Beehr and O'Hara is a *treatment-by-setting* interaction, in which the intervention works well in one environment but not in another. This can occur even within a single organization. For example, the culture and climate of one unit or department may be highly conducive to the introduction of participative decision making (which was observed by Jackson, 1983, to reduce strain), whereas another section of the same organization may function more effectively and harmoniously with hierarchically organized decision processes. In the latter, participative decision making (PDM) may be viewed by participants as an unwanted intrusion upon their (already heavy) role responsibilities.

Finally in this category, a *history-by-treatment* interaction suggests that an intervention may be effective at some time periods but not at others. Using the above illustration, participative decision-making schemes are effective only when there is adequate time for preparation and involvement of employees. At peak periods, when role demands are high or deadlines loom large, less rather than more participation in decisions (at least in certain areas) may be desired by employees. Involvement in PDM under these circumstances may become a stressor itself rather than a mechanism for stress reduction.

Other difficulties associated with the systematic evaluation of organizational interventions have also been discussed by various authors, including Beehr and O'Hara (1987), Ivancevich et al. (1990), and Murphy (1988). For instance, Beehr and O'Hara noted that expectancy and placebo effects may occur, the former when participants anticipate that the intervention should have some beneficial outcomes and the latter when any intervention (not just the specific intervention implemented) would have some influence on levels of strain. Expectancy effects represent an instance of self-fulfilling prophecy and may be difficult to control for in an evaluation. Similarly, as noted by Beehr and O'Hara (1987), "Disentangling specific treatment effects from non-specific placebo is a major challenge facing stress reduction researchers" (p. 92).

Ivancevich et al. (1990) have referred to the difficulty of preventing relapse to preintervention levels of strain. Relapse may be especially problematical if the intervention does not modify the workplace environment and hence no real change occurs in the occurrence or level of stressors for workers. A stress management training program may provide individuals with some awareness of stressors and perhaps with some skills and confidence to tackle these stressors, but, as noted earlier, some environmental stressors (e.g., excessive workload) may not be amenable to change by the individual and may require more systemic alteration (by management). One implication for research in this area is that the time frame for evaluations should extend well beyond the completion of the intervention because immediate postintervention assessment may not detect relapse.

A final difficulty (Murphy, 1988) is that of gaining entry into organizations to study SMIs. Often upper-level managers are wary of researchers investigating changes within their organization, particularly if those changes have political and/or legal ramifications. As noted earlier, employers and management tend to favor an individual-oriented approach to stress management and are frequently resistant to approaches that entail structural change by way of either job or organizational redesign. Organizational change researchers can therefore face difficulties in gaining access to the organization and its employees, especially if management suspects that an evaluation may shed unfavorable light on their change efforts. This resistance poses serious problems for the conduct of systematic research on SMIs.

Guidelines for Evaluation Research

The above discussion illustrates that, as with other evaluations in organizational settings (such as assessment of the impact of training on the job performance of personnel), considerable difficulties may arise in the evaluation of organization-level stress management interventions. Many of these difficulties stem from limited access to individuals or groups who are receiving the intervention, inability to collect data at appropriate time periods, lack of management support for evaluation of organizational change programs, and practical problems associated with carrying out the research. It is clear that evaluation research can be fraught with complexities that are not typically confronted by researchers in other areas of organizational behavior.

Nevertheless, strategies for conducting such research are available and have in fact been used, although admittedly in a small proportion of studies. Here we outline a few major procedures and designs that are recommended for consideration. More detailed descriptions of research designs referred to here can be found in Cook and Campbell (1979), whose primer on applied research in field settings remains the definitive reference on this topic. Examples of these designs have also been provided by Beehr and O'Hara (1987) and Ivancevich and Matteson (1987).

Ivancevich and Matteson outlined several key principles for carrying out valid evaluations of stress management interventions:

- Diagnosis of the nature of stressors in the workplace environment and the extent to which workers are experiencing strain
- Use of experimental research designs, where possible, to ascertain the effects of specific interventions

- Conducting longitudinal evaluations to examine effects over a period of time and to test their persistence
- Assessment of more than one measure of strain to avoid method bias (see the Ganster et al., 1982, and Jackson, 1983, studies referred to earlier for illustrations of the advantages of using multiple outcome measures).

In many cases, use of fully experimental designs involving independent experimental and control groups may simply not be possible, and some variant of quasi-experimental design will be the most feasible approach. Of these, two stand out: the *nonequivalent control group* (NECG) design and *time-series* designs. The major difference between these two approaches is that in the nonequivalent control group design differences between the experimental and control groups are analyzed, whereas time-series designs entail within-person comparisons over a period of time. These two designs can be represented diagrammatically as follows:

Nonequivalent control group design

$$O_1 \quad X \quad O_2 \quad \text{Experimental (intervention) group}$$
$$O_3 \qquad O_4 \quad \text{Nonequivalent control group}$$

Time-series design

$$O1 \quad O2 \quad X \quad O3 \quad O4$$

Each of these approaches has certain advantages. The NECG design is very practical to implement when it is not possible to obtain a control group that is equivalent (identical) to participants in the intervention program or to randomly assign employees to conditions. For example, a stress management training program may be devised for delivery within an organization that has separate units or departments. However, the personnel across these departments may not be identical in terms of their jobs, the structure of the departments, or perhaps even their qualifications and experience. The extent to which the intervention and control groups differ from each other on relevant variables is an index of their nonequivalence. The more equivalent they are, the stronger the design and the more generalizable the conclusions that may be drawn from the evaluation.

Clearly, however, the NECG design has the inherent problem that differences between the two groups may be attributable to factors other than the intervention. For instance, the intervention and control groups may vary on variables that are relevant to the success of the intervention, such as job tenure (which can relate to experience with the stressors) or even a variable such as hardiness (which may function as a resistance factor—see Chapter 5). Hence, the intervention may be effective for some groups but not others. Techniques such as analysis of covariance can be used to statistically partial out the effects of between-group differences on relevant variables when these cannot be controlled for experimentally. Nevertheless, differences between the intervention and control groups may restrict the researcher's ability to conclude that the intervention was effective in reducing strain under all conditions.

Beehr and O'Hara (1987) recommended the assessment of more than one control group to strengthen conclusions from an evaluation. Inclusion of several control groups will serve to offset the limitation of the basic NECG design in that comparisons can be made between changes in strain in the intervention group with those in a variety of control groups, increasing the researcher's ability to conclude that observed differences are generalizable. A variant of this strategy is what Beehr and O'Hara referred to as a *cohort design*, in which all groups get exposed to the intervention but at different time periods. Again, however, this strategy may not always be feasible, and the availability of several groups (sections, units, or departments) to serve as control groups may be restricted. There is also the potential problem of contamination, which would occur if current control groups were to gain information about the intervention that might influence their behavior. For example, members of a control group might learn stress management strategies from their colleagues in the intervention group, which would function to negate their role as "controls."

Another recommendation from Beehr and O'Hara, as well as Ivancevich and Matteson (1987), is the inclusion of more than one experimental group. For instance, researchers can make comparisons between different interventions or even different combinations of interventions, rather than simply examining changes among participants in a single intervention compared with those in a control group. This approach has the distinct advantage of ascertaining the relative strengths and limitations of various intervention strategies. A limitation might be that interventions can vary not only with respect to their content but also in terms of the intensity, duration, and quality of their delivery, all of which could influence their effectiveness. In addition, some stress management programs may incorporate a variety of separate interventions, such as seminars, written communications, and actual stress management training. Under these circumstances, it may be difficult to determine whether individual components are effective in reducing strain or whether the total package is required.

An alternative to the NECG design is the time-series design, which is typically used in single-subject research, especially in clinical psychology and related fields. As illustrated in the diagram on page 202, time-series designs entail the collection of data at several time periods, ideally both before and after the intervention has been implemented. Typically, at least four data points are included, two before the intervention and two afterward, to enable plotting of trends in the data and to ensure that changes are not due to random fluctuation in participants' responses.

A major advantage of time-series research over NECG designs is that participants function as their own controls. Each individual is studied as a discrete source of data; hence, there is no need to examine between-groups variance, and the issue of equivalence between groups is circumvented. On the downside, because data are collected over several time periods, events other than the intervention may also influence the person's level of strain. For example, in the Schweiger and DeNisi (1991) investigation discussed earlier, the researchers could have used a single-subject time-series design to examine the impact of the communications program devised to reduce the strain experienced by employees within the merging organization, rather than using one plant as the intervention group and a second plant as the control group. A time-series approach would eliminate the possibility that postintervention changes in levels of strain were due to between-plant differences. However, it is also possible that, in addition to the communications program, other events (such as a change in management style) could have occurred in the intervention group that could have an impact upon employee strain. With a single-subject time-series design, it would be difficult to separate out the effects of the intervention from any changes resulting from other events.

As discussed in some detail in Chapter 3, one final methodological issue that needs to be considered is the use of multiple indicators of strain. Irrespective of whether the research design is experimental or quasi-experimental, selection of appropriate measures of strain is vital to ensure that the outcomes of SMIs are indeed strain related and that method bias does not overshadow the true effects of an intervention. Most research to date has relied predominantly on self-report measures of psychological strain, which reflect just one element of the constellation of strain characteristics. Stronger conclusions about the impact of interventions can be drawn if evaluations extend beyond the measurement of psychological strain to include behavioral, physical, and even physiological indexes of the strain construct. Although more difficult to carry out, multimeasure assessments of strain will provide a more comprehensive account of the effects of SMIs on individual employees and the organization.

Guidelines for Implementing SMIs

To conclude this chapter on organizational interventions, we consider how best to implement such efforts, along with some practical issues that impinge upon the effectiveness of stress management programs. As has already been noted, several factors place constraints on the types of programs that might be introduced within an organization and on how stress management is carried out. The concern is to ensure that strategies used are effective in terms of outcomes and have a high benefits-to-costs ratio.

Earlier, we discussed the need to begin by ascertaining existing levels of strain among members of the organization. This can be done systematically using questionnaires, interviews of selected employees, and other means to determine the relative levels of strain experienced. Coupled with this is the need to identify relevant stressors in the workplace in what is sometimes referred to as a *stress audit*. A stress audit can also be conducted via self-report questionnaires, such as the Occupational Stress Indicator, devised by Cooper, Sloan, and Williams (1988) or the Occupational Stress Inventory (Osipow & Spokane, 1988), both of which were developed to explore the types of stressors that workers confront, as well as providing measures of psychological strain. Alternatively, individuals may be asked to keep a log or diary of events, recording over some period of time those that they found especially stressful. The diary approach is particularly useful for identifying events, situations, or people that might be described as "hassles," episodic stressors that may occur once or several times during the course of a working week. Although these events may not be as intense as some persistent and inherent role-related stressors, such as work overload or role ambiguity and conflict, they can nevertheless be quite stressful and have a significant impact on an individual's well-being (DeLongis, Coyne, Dakof, Folkman, & Lazarus, 1982). Record keeping, by way of diaries or logs, enables the organization to pool information and to identify sources of strain that may be pervasive.

The target of intervention is the next major consideration required. Earlier in this chapter, we described three levels of intervention (primary, secondary, and tertiary) to deal with strain and its consequences. From the research and other information presented here, it is clear that the large majority of interventions concentrate on strain *management* rather than strain *prevention*. This emphasis is associated with the prevalent assumption, among managers in particular, that training individuals to cope with workplace strain is the most viable approach. In addition, as observed by Daniels (1996), many managers still maintain a belief that job-related strain poses a low risk of serious harm or detriment; hence, they display a tendency to underestimate the potential impact of strain on the organization overall. They focus attention on the enhancement of individual coping skills and strategies rather than addressing the actual sources of strain, whether these are located in job roles or organizational processes. This is not to undermine the importance of individual coping strategies in the stress-coping process (see Chapter 6) but simply to acknowledge that at times individual efforts may not be sufficient to ameliorate the impact of stressors, and a more direct approach may be needed. As commented by Briner and Reynolds (1999), the crux of successful intervention is accurate identification of the sources of strain (i.e., the stressors), along with the implementation of stressor-specific interventions.

A key factor in the development of more systematic (and hence more effective) organizational interventions is the extent of commitment from all layers of the organization—employers, management, unions, and employees—to alleviating the impact of stressors. This may require more open communication and a dismantling of organizational norms and expectations that promote, rather than help to reduce, strain among employees: for instance, norms that encourage individuals to work excessively long hours and to take work home with them or that create feelings of guilt about arriving at and leaving work "on time."

The commitment to address stress issues will stem from a supportive organizational climate, one that recognizes that strain is inherent in the workplace and that the experience of strain by workers is not a sign of personal weakness or incompetence. In many organizations, there would still appear to be a "blame the victim" response, in which the individual is perceived as the source of his or her own problems (Dewe, 1997; Dollard & Winefield, 1996).

As we outlined in Chapter 2, new forms of employment contracts and relations may blur the boundaries between workers' job responsibilities and their off-the-job (home) life, creating another form of strain due to conflict between the two domains (De Frank & Ivanevich, 1998; O'Driscoll, 1996). For example, the rapid development of new computer technologies in the 1990s has led to considerable changes in job conditions for many workers. An increasing number of individuals are now employed on a contractual (rather than "permanent") basis and perform their job responsibilities from home or other nonoffice settings. Although the psychosocial effects of these changes have been given some consideration, there is a dearth of empirical evidence on their long-term implications for individuals and their families. More systematic exploration of the interplay between job and off-job conditions and experiences is essential for the development of work conditions that do not create another form of stressor for workers.

The importance of increasing the involvement of workers themselves in designing workplace interventions has been highlighted by many researchers and practitioners (e.g., Jackson, 1983; Murphy, 1995; Schurman & Israel, 1995). For example, the SMIs described by Murphy and Hurrell (1987) and Schurman and Israel (1995) illustrate the critical role of employee participation in stress management processes for the effectiveness of organizational efforts to address strain-related issues. Murphy (1995) has cogently argued that the process of stress management (i.e., how it is done) is as important as what is actually implemented.

Ultimately, as we have emphasized in this volume, it is important to consider stress from a transactional perspective. Several practical implications emerge from this perspective. First, the transactional approach provides an integrated framework for understanding the complexities of the stress-coping process. Traditional definitions of stress have failed to acknowledge that it does not reside solely in the individual or solely in the external environment but is a transaction between the two. For stress management programs, this means that the emphasis must be on the relationship between the individual and the environment; hence, these programs must be designed to capture the processes that link individuals and their environments. Individuals' interpretations of events and their coping resources (both personal and within the organizational context) are key design factors. Little can be gained from stress management programs that provide individuals with a wider range of coping skills and opportunities but fail to recognize that these are of little use if appropriate environmental resources and supports are not available (Dewe, 1997).

In conclusion, organizational interventions to remove stressors or at least reduce their impact will be more effective if a number of steps are carried out. These include (a) identification of factors that may be functioning as potential sources of strain; (b) thorough assessment of the levels of strain experienced by employees, including a range of strain indicators; (c) implementation of interventions that aim to resolve the problem(s) rather than simply dealing with the symptoms; and (d) use of focused evaluation criteria that examine a variety of specific outcomes, not just an aggregate improvement in overall well-being. The challenge is to persuade employers and managers of the long-term benefits of this approach to stress management, both for their employees and for the organization as a whole.

References

Beehr, T., & O'Hara, K. (1987). Methodological designs for the evaluation of occupational stress interventions. In S. Kasl & C. Cooper (Eds.), *Stress and health: Issues in research methodology* (pp. 79-112). New York: John Wiley.

Berridge, J., & Cooper, C. (1993). Stress and coping in U.S. organizations: The role of the Employee Assistance Programme. *Work and Stress, 7,* 89-102.

Briner, R., & Reynolds, S. (1999). The costs, benefits and limitations of organizational level stress interventions. *Journal of Organizational Behavior, 20,* 647-664.

Burke, R. (1993). Organizational-level interventions to reduce occupational stressors. *Work and Stress, 7,* 77-87.

Cartwright, S., Cooper, C., & Murphy, L. (1995). Diagnosing a healthy organization: A proactive approach to stress in the workplace. In L. Murphy, J. Hurrell, S. Sauter, & G. Keita (Eds.), *Job stress interventions* (pp. 217-233). Washington, DC: American Psychological Association.

Cook, T., & Campbell, D. (1979). *Quasi-experimentation: Design and analysis issues for field settings.* Chicago: Rand McNally.

Cooper, C., & Cartwright, S. (1994). Healthy mind; healthy organization: A proactive approach to occupational stress. *Human Relations, 47,* 455-471.

Cooper, C., & Sadri, G. (1991). The impact of stress counselling at work. *Journal of Social Behavior and Personality, 6,* 411-423.

Cooper, C., Sloan, S., & Williams, S. (1988). *Occupational Stress Indicator: The manual.* Windsor, Canada: NFER Nelson.

Daniels, K. (1996). Why aren't managers concerned about occupational stress? *Work and Stress, 10,* 352-366.

Davis, A., & Gibson, L. (1994). Designing employee welfare provision. *Personnel Review, 23,* 33-45.

De Frank, R., & Ivancevich, J. (1998). Stress on the job: An executive update. *Academy of Management Executive, 12*(3), 55-66.

DeLongis, A., Coyne, J., Dakof, G., Folkman, S., & Lazarus, R. (1982). Relationship of daily hassles, uplifts and major life events to health status. *Health Psychology, 1,* 119-136.

Dewe, P. (1994). EAPs and stress management: From theory to practice to comprehensiveness. *Personnel Review, 23,* 21-32.

Dewe, P. (1997). *The transactional model of stress: Some empirical findings and implications for stress management programmes* (Working Paper Series 97/1). Palmerston North, New Zealand: Massey University, Department of Human Resource Management.

Dollard, M., & Winefield, A. (1996). Managing occupational stress: A national and international perspective. *International Journal of Stress Management, 3,* 69-83.

Edwards, J., & Cooper, C. (1990). The person-environment fit approach to stress: Recurring problems and some suggested solutions. *Journal of Organizational Behavior, 11,* 293-307.

Elkin, A., & Rosch, P. (1990). Promoting mental health at the workplace: The prevention side of stress management. *Occupational Medicine: State of the Art Review, 5,* 739-754.

Ganster, D. (1995). Interventions for building healthy organizations: Suggestions from the stress research literature. In L. Murphy, J. Hurrell, S. Sauter, & G. Keita (Eds.), *Job stress interventions* (pp. 323-336). Washington, DC: American Psychological Association.

Ganster, D., Mayes, B., Sime, W., & Tharp, G. (1982). Managing occupational stress: A field experiment. *Journal of Applied Psychology, 67,* 533-542.

Hendrix, W., Ovalle, N., & Troxler, R. (1985). Behavioral and physiological consequences of stress and its antecedent factors. *Journal of Applied Psychology, 70,* 188-201.

Ivancevich, J., & Matteson, M. (1987). Organizational level stress management interventions: A review and recommendations. *Journal of Organizational Behavior Management, 8,* 229-248.

Ivancevich, J., Matteson, M., Freedman, S., & Phillips, J. (1990). Worksite stress management interventions. *American Psychologist, 45,* 252-261.

Jackson, S. (1983). Participation in decision making as a strategy for reducing job-related strain. *Journal of Applied Psychology, 68,* 3-19.

Kozlowski, S. W. J., Chao, G. T., Smith, E. M., & Hedlung, J. (1993). Organizational downsizing: Strategies, interventions and research implications. *International Review of Industrial and Organizational Psychology, 8,* 263-332.

Murphy, L. (1984). Occupational stress management: A review and appraisal. *Journal of Occupational Psychology, 57,* 1-15.

Murphy, L. (1988). Workplace interventions for stress reduction and prevention. In C. L. Cooper & R. Payne (Eds.), *Causes, coping and consequences of stress at work* (pp. 301-339). New York: John Wiley.

Murphy, L. (1995). Occupational stress management: Current status and future directions. In C. Cooper & D. Rousseau (Eds.), *Trends in organizational behavior* (Vol. 2, pp. 1-14). New York: Wiley.

Murphy, L., & Hurrell, J. (1987). Stress management in the process of organizational stress reduction. *Journal of Managerial Psychology, 2,* 18-23.

Newman, J., & Beehr, T. (1979). Personal and organizational strategies for handling job stress: A review of research and opinion. *Personnel Psychology, 32,* 1-43.

O'Driscoll, M. (1996). The interface between job and off-job roles: Enhancement and conflict. *International Review of Industrial and Organizational Psychology, 11*, 279-306.

O'Driscoll, M., & Cooper, C. (1996). Sources and management of excessive job stress and burnout. In P. Warr (Ed.), *Psychology at work* (4th ed., pp. 188-223). New York: Penguin.

Osipow, S., & Spokane, A. (1988). *Occupational Stress Inventory.* Odessa, FL: PAR.

Pennebaker, J., & Watson, D. (1988). Self-reports and physiological measures in the workplace. In J. Hurrell, L. Murphy, S. Sauter, & C. Cooper (Eds.), *Occupational stress: Issues and developments in research* (pp. 184-199). New York: Taylor & Francis.

Peterson, D. (1993, April). *Measuring change: A psychometric approach to evaluating individual training outcomes.* Paper presented at the annual meeting of the Society for Industrial and Organizational Psychology, San Francisco.

Pierce, J., & Newstrom, J. (1983). The design of flexible work schedules and employee responses: Relationships and processes. *Journal of Occupational Behaviour, 4*, 247-262.

Richardsen, A., & Burke, R. (1995). Models of burnout: Implications for interventions. *International Journal of Stress Management, 2*, 31-43.

Schurman, S., & Israel, B. (1995). Redesigning work systems to reduce stress: A participatory action research approach to creating change. In L. Murphy, J. Hurrell, S. Sauter, & G. Keita (Eds.), *Job stress interventions* (pp. 235-264). Washington, DC: American Psychological Association.

Schweiger, D., & DeNisi, A. (1991). Communication with employees following a merger: A longitudinal field experiment. *Academy of Management Journal, 34*, 110-135.

Smith, D., & Mahoney, J. (1989, August). McDonnell Douglas Corporation's EAP produces hard data. *Almanac*, pp. 18-26.

Wall, T., & Clegg, C. (1981). A longitudinal study of work group design. *Journal of Occupational Behaviour, 2*, 31-49.

8 Methodological Issues in
Job Stress Research

Previous chapters have illustrated the variety of research designs, methods, and measures that have been used in job stress research to date. A fundamental question is whether current methodologies satisfactorily assess the complex and dynamic nature of the stress process represented by the transactional model of stress coping. Here we consider some critical issues in the debate over appropriate methodologies and examine arguments that have been proposed for broadening the approach taken in job stress research to include a greater range of assessment procedures and to adopt convergent methodologies. There is no doubt that stress research can only benefit from the careful and thoughtful application of the transactional approach (Harris, 1991). Nevertheless, this approach requires significant changes to traditional measurement practices and to the way in which job stress is conceptualized and investigated. Researchers must avoid treating the arguments for change "positively but casually rather than taking them to heart in their own research" (Lazarus, 1997, p. 159) or regarding them as an inconvenience (Coyne, 1997), an irritant, or an interesting but irrelevant complication that can best be avoided by simply continuing to seek refuge in conventional data analysis and interpretation.

As discussed earlier in this book, the person-environment (P-E) fit conceptualization of stress is at the core of many approaches to work stress research and represents an important advance in our thinking because it provides a structural framework for understanding the stress-coping process. Unfortunately, however, this framework does not explicitly describe the processes through which the person and the environment are linked. A number of limitations can be identified. The first is that it does little to clarify the complexity of the relationship between the person and the environment. Application of the P-E fit model is limited because it presupposes that most factors can be easily classified as either person or environment and does not give full cognizance to the role of the social context within which an encounter takes place. As a result, there is little guidance from this approach on how to fully explore the "tangled influences" of each of these factors on one another (Revenson, 1997).

Lazarus (1991) has drawn attention to three factors that suggest that the P-E fit idea portrays an essentially static relationship. The first of these is the assumption that adaptation is always synonymous with good fit and maladaptation with misfit. This tends to overlook the fact that the process changes over time and between encounters. The second factor is an apparent assumption that some people always function well whereas others always function badly—an assumption that fails to recognize that individuals may effectively cope with one encounter but not with another. The third factor is a tendency to view some environments as essentially "good" and others as essentially "bad," which implies that individuals will always respond in the same way to the same (or similar) situations. The point of noting these limitations is to highlight that the notion of a transaction should extend beyond simply identifying what are considered to be the key structural aspects of any encounter. Researchers must recognize that the stress-coping process "transcends the separate interacting variables of person and environment" (Lazarus, 1991, p. 3) and is the mechanism by which the two are linked. The focus of research must therefore be directed toward exploring those characteristics that define the process and that represent the essence of the P-E transaction.

Traditional research methods, based predominantly on cross-sectional designs using self-report questionnaires to assess stressors, strains, and coping mechanisms, have been taken to task for not capturing the dynamics of the process they are purporting to investigate (Spicer, 1997). As noted in Chapter 1, though avowedly espousing the transactional framework, much job stress research can in fact be depicted as reflecting an interactional model of stress, where the various components (stressors, strains, and coping) are treated as static constructs and as having unidirectional effects. In contrast, the transactional model suggests that research needs to explore the ongoing interplay among these components over time and to examine the possibility of multidirectional (mutual) causality.

Methodological Approaches in Stress Research

Spicer and others (e.g., Magnusson & Törestad, 1993; Somerfield, 1997a) have drawn a distinction between *variable-based* and *person-based* methods in research on stress. Variable-based designs formulate research questions around a set of constructs that reflect certain aspects of how individuals function, but they tend to reduce the dynamics of the stress process "to patterns of empirical relationships [between variables] which can be accommodated in multivariate statistical analysis" (Spicer, 1997, p. 168). Person-based methods, on the other hand, position the individual (rather than variables) as the central focus of analysis. Methodologies using this approach can yield rich descriptive data about individuals and how they function. The need for variable-based research when investigating work-related stress is not disputed. Rather, it is contended that variable-based methods, which have been fundamental to much research on work stress, may have a more limited role to play in exploring the dynamics of the stress process than was previously assumed (Somerfield, 1997a). For a growing number of researchers, person-based (especially qualitative) methods offer a number of advantages for understanding and encapsulating the contextual richness of the stress process (Somerfield, 1997a; Spicer, 1997; Thoits, 1995).

Combining variable-based and person-based methods entails clearing several hurdles. However, there are several arguments in favor of searching for a middle ground that merges aspects of qualitative (person) and quantitative (variable) methods, identifying how each can be used to support rather than compete against the other—a stance that Rosenthal and Rosnow (1991) have referred to as methodological pluralism. Two general issues emerge. The first (Lazarus, 1997) is that there is a need for a period of "quiet reconstruction," the aim of which should be to review where current methods are taking us and what alternative methods can provide. The second is to agree that change is preferable when it is inspired by the thoughtful application of new approaches rather than driven by the "conspicuous lack of meaningful findings" (Somerfield, 1997b, p. 180) from the continuing reliance on a single methodological perspective.

A concern that current (variable-based) research methods have assumed an identity of their own, somewhat divorced from the phenomena they are purporting to measure, has led to a questioning of the structured reality imposed by such methods (Van Maanen, 1979). When confronted by questions like "Whose reality are we measuring?" or "Are our measures measuring what we think they are?" or "Do our measures impose an outsider's view rather than allow the insider's view to emerge?" stress researchers are being nudged toward confronting whether there is a need to search for more vivid and enriched descriptions of processes in qualitative (person-based) as well as quantitative (variable-based) terms (Bhagat & Beehr, 1985). As Spicer (1997) has suggested, this entails progressing from simple acceptance of "systems concepts" to recognizing that we must now also think in terms of "systems methods," exploring those techniques that capture shared meanings and beliefs that interpret, legitimate, and validate individual actions.

It is also important to recognize that, as the complexity of theoretical models increases, the measurement of certain aspects of those models may require the use of qualitative methods (Hari Das, 1983), or at the very least a combination of methods. Inferring the process of the individual's interpretation—a requirement frequently imposed by quantitative methods—in place of capturing the meaning from the person making it fails to facilitate any understanding of those contextual issues fundamental to making meaningful progress toward an understanding of the stress process. Again, the need is for a more balanced approach that recognizes the usefulness of data generated by different methods (Pfeffer, 1990).

Table 8.1 delineates some of these contrasting approaches. Disagreements between researchers over the approach to be used can "lead to neglect of common interests and misunderstanding on both sides" (Morley & Luthans, 1984, p. 28). Quantitative and qualitative approaches both represent legitimate methodologies for work stress research. They should not be considered mutually exclusive (Morley & Luthans, 1984). Many issues need to be explored when considering the type of method to be employed, and sole reliance on a single method may result in an inability to explore certain dimensions of the stress experience (Morgan & Smircich, 1980). Table 8.1 not only highlights important differences between quantitative and qualitative approaches but also emphasizes "the important relationship between theory and method" (Morgan & Smircich, 1980, p. 491).

Table 8.1 illustrates several points. For example, when selecting the measures to be used in research on job-related stress, investigators should consider whether these measures do in fact capture the reality of those who will complete them. This requires consideration of instrument validity versus relevance (Bhagat & Beehr, 1985). Has the focus on ensuring that measures have high reliability meant that, by emphasizing the robustness of these measures, item relevance and significance (to the target individual) are largely overlooked? Similarly, quantifying the amount of variance accounted for in a criterion variable (strain) by a set of predictors (stressors) may not by itself provide much information to explain the stress process (Mohr, 1982). Note that we are not suggesting that there is a single "best way" of conducting research on job stress. However, we would suggest that research on this important topic needs to move beyond the mere identification of different components in the stress process to more in-depth exploration of that process itself, especially the dynamic interplay between those components. In short, there is an urgent need to consider how best the process should be investigated and to use all the tools at our disposal to conduct meaningful research on stress in the workplace. Furthermore, if progress is to be made, future research must endeavor to close the gap between methodologies by (a) identifying common pathways along which research should now be directed and (b) reviewing whether current measurement practices actually reflect what we are trying to measure.

In summary, a number of specific issues have been identified above and need attention from researchers in the field of job-related stress. First, there is now growing acceptance that stress should be defined as relational in nature, involving transactions between the person and the environment. The transactional framework provides an organizing concept around which future theory and research can develop. Second, theoretical models of stress share the idea of a process and a sequence of events,

Table 8.1 Bridging the Gap: Forging a Rapprochement Between Research Orientations

Research Orientation		Source	Contrasting Approaches
Quantitative	*Qualitative*	*Source*	*Contrasting Approaches*
Mechanistic	Contextual	Lazarus (1990)	**Mechanistic** view is traditionally causal and analytic and centered on the objective environment. **Contextual** in contrast emphasizes transaction and process and is meaning centered.
Concrete structures	Social construction	Morgan & Smircich (1980)	**Concrete structures** emphasizes a concern for objective knowledge that specifies the precise nature of the relationship. **Social construction** emphasizes the importance of understanding the process through which individuals construct their social reality.
Reality imposed	Reality emerged	Morley & Luthans (1984)	**Reality imposed** implies that it is the "outsider's" view about how constructs are organized that is being imposed on participants. **Reality emerged** suggests that it is the "insider's" meanings and interpretations about how constructs are organized that is being captured. Is the "reality" of the research something that is imposed on the participant or is it a product of the cognitions of the participant?
Group centered	Individual centered	Morley & Luthans (1984)	**Group centered** uses standardized, controlled environmental contexts and quantitative methods to establish general laws. **Individual centered** uses naturalistic contexts and qualitative methods to recognize the experience of the individual.

Term		Source	Description
Validity	Relevance	Bhagat & Beehr (1985)	**Validity** refers to the internal consistency and robustness of measures consistent with the idea of scientific rigor. **Relevance** is concerned with the utility of scientifically based rigorous knowledge if it is not conceived and communicated to practitioners in a manner relevant to their problems. Has the validity criterion been overemphasized to the exclusion of a relevance criterion?
Primary	Subordinate	Buchanan (1992)	**Primary** refers to the belief that the test of valid and reliable knowledge is gained only through quantitative, hypothesis-testing experiential research design. **Subordinate** refers to the idea that because qualitative research is regarded as explanatory, descriptive, or hypothesis generating, it has a subordinate role because the scientific rigor argument of the quantitative approach tends to inhibit its use, producing a hierarchy of acceptable methods that relegates qualitative methods to a subordinate role.
Variance	Process	Mohr (1982)	**Variance** refers to the fact that the basis of explanation is causality. It is a general statement about the occurrence of a phenomenon. If the phenomenon is Y, then the idea is to explain the variation in Y. **Process** refers to explaining how something comes about. The emphasis here is on interpretation being more important than the objective nature of the phenomenon.
Analysis	Synthesis	Lazarus (1997)	**Analysis** refers to the idea that "science" is defined only in terms of analysis. It concerns the impact of reducing complex processes to separate causal variables. **Synthesis** refers to the need to recognize that "components" need to be considered in terms of the context of the system from which they have been drawn. The failure to resynthesize the components limits understanding.

identifying in a variety of ways the evaluative processes that best express the relational-transactional nature of work stress. However, this agreement tends to manifest itself predominantly at the conceptual level, and empirical studies of job stress are still largely influenced and guided by the interactional nature of stress, where the emphasis is on investigating the interaction between the different components to the transaction rather than on the transaction itself. Useful as it is in identifying the critical constructs that any predictive model should deal with (Dewe, 1991), the interactional perspective makes no real effort to facilitate our understanding of the stress process or to explain, other than by inference, those constructs that best express the essential ingredients of that process. Investigating stress as a transaction places both conceptual and empirical demands that are substantively different from those required when exploring stress from an interactional perspective (Somerfield, 1997a).

There is also a need to adopt methods of research that are congruent with the theoretical platform upon which the research is based in the first place. Conventional methods of data collection, analysis, and interpretation may limit our ability to validly assess the dynamics of the stress-coping process. We do not advocate simply replacing these techniques with others; rather, we advocate questioning the directions in which current methods might take us and asking what alternative methods might offer. As noted earlier, a combination of qualitative and quantitative methods may enable investigators to develop research strategies that benefit from the strengths of both types of approach and that provide more insight into the transactional stress-coping process.

Finally, it is important to ask, "Whose reality are we measuring when we measure stress?" How comfortably does the concept of validity fit with the concept of relevance, and have we overemphasized one at the expense of the other (Bhagat & Beehr, 1985)? Change must come from constructive debate, thoughtful application of new approaches, and the reconsideration and refinement of conventional measures. It should not, as a number of researchers have made clear, emerge from under the "weight of dull and obvious conclusions" (Coyne, 1997, p. 155).

Where Do We Go From Here?

A number of opportunities present themselves. There is no doubt that most reviews of the "where do we go from here?" type emphasize that if progress is to be made in understanding stress-coping processes, researchers must now give considerable thought to how best to "fit" the method to the theory. The ability of conventional methods to adequately unravel the stress process has been intensely debated, and the case for exploring alternative methods is gathering momentum. If understanding the stress process is best advanced by exploring individual meanings and appraisals, then researchers *must* consider methods that capture the richness of the process and the idiographic nature of the experience. This logic does not mean that one methodology should be replaced by another, nor does it mean that one methodology should be regarded as subordinate to another. Nevertheless, as a first step, several "midrange" proposals can be advanced.

A midrange strategy identifies ways in which conventional measurement practices can be reconsidered within the transactional context. At the same time, it explores how alternative methods can provide a framework for redeveloping current measurement practices. Two types of approach can be identified within this context. The first can be described as the *measurement refinement* approach. This approach, though accepting the difficulties inherent in conventional self-report measures, claims that research can still benefit from examining how such measures can be refined to ensure a precision in measurement that continues to reflect our understanding of the different elements of the stress-coping process.

The second approach focuses on process issues and is linked closely with qualitative methodologies. This approach points to the complexity of the stress process and the fact that conventional measures may be too blunt to capture this complexity. Measurement practices, if they are to contribute to our understanding of the stress process, should be free of the structural limitations imposed by traditional conventions. Only in this way can the essence of the stressful experience be truly examined.

These two approaches are not mutually exclusive. Qualitative techniques may represent the primary method of analysis when exploring the subtlety and richness of the stress-coping process. On the other hand, when the focus is on refining measures (which we turn to below), qualitative and quantitative techniques may best be used in combination to capture the reality of the situation and individuals' coping behaviors. Several steps can be taken to facilitate this convergence. These include, for example, (a) reviewing the nature and type of items to be measured; (b) determining the appropriateness of different response categories; (c) examining the way in which response scales are scored—that is, reconsidering the traditional linear additive model; and (d) evaluating the specificity of the stressor-strain relationship under consideration.

Refining Measures of Stressors, Strains, and Coping

Self-report measures of perceived work stressors (such as role ambiguity, conflict, and overload) have long been available, and psychometric evaluation of these measures suggests high construct validity and continuing usage. Paradoxically, however, the accessibility of such measures to some extent has diverted attention from the fact "that the explanatory potential of such measures must lie in developing a better understanding of the constructs themselves" (Dewe, 2000, p. 14). One concern is with the items that make up those scales and a potentially inherent bias (Glowinkowski & Cooper, 1985). By failing to take into account the considerable social and economic change that has occurred since the measures were first developed, researchers may now overemphasize the importance of some events (Glowinkowski & Cooper, 1985), ignore the presence of others (Fineman & Payne, 1981), and fail to consider the significance of other salient events in the working lives of respondents (Brief & Atieh, 1987). Despite these claims, such measures are continually used because they continue to exhibit satisfactory internal reliability. Yet if researchers were to consider whose reality is being measured, perhaps discussion would extend beyond the psychometric properties of such measures to a more systematic appraisal of the events that significantly impinge on the well-being of individuals: that is, how workers themselves describe the demands of their working lives and how these demands can best be identified.

An illustration of the above is provided by items that have traditionally been used to assess variables such as work overload and role conflict. Measures of these variables typically include items such as "There is too much work to do in the time available," "No matter how hard I work there always seems to be as much work at the end of the day as there was at the beginning," and "Conflicting demands make it very difficult to get the work done." However, empirical studies of these variables only infrequently have explored whether these sorts of events or pressures are ones that research participants themselves would identify as actual demands in their particular work setting. Recent research has shown, for instance, that other stressors may have a more salient impact on individuals in the current work environment and hence are more likely to reflect the reality of their working lives, such as the constant amount of change, the threat of job loss, and having to deal with competing demands from work and family (Cooper, 1998; O'Driscoll & Cooper, 1996). We need to consider, therefore, whether concern over the reliability of measures has taken precedence over their relevance to individuals' lives. Use of qualitative approaches (such as critical-incident interviewing) may assist in the development of taxonomies of work-related stressors that reflect the reality of those whose working lives are being investigated and comparison of these stressors with those most often studied in job stress research.

Another concern that has emerged when work stressor measurement is being considered is the way in which stressor measures are scored. The issue here is that although researchers conceptualize work stressors in terms of demand, most studies use self-rating scales that "imply" demand rather than measure it (Dewe, 1991). This has led to oversimplification in the assessment of stressors (De Frank, 1988). Most scales simply ask respondents to indicate whether an event is present in their job and then assume that presence equates with demand, rather than directly assessing the extent of demand created by specific events or people.

Similarly, it is important not only to consider measurement (rather than inference) of demand but also to examine various aspects or dimensions of an event, such as its frequency, duration, intensity, and meaning. To illustrate this point, consider the following agree/disagree response format, which is frequently used in the assessment of perceptions of job stressors:

Example Item	*Strongly Disagree*			*Strongly Agree*	
There are many conflicts	1	2	3	4	5
in my job					

Strong agreement with this item (e.g., scoring 4 or 5 on the above continuum) would typically be considered an indication of high demand or pressure. However, agreement that there are "many conflicts" does not, by itself, provide any information on how demanding the workplace is for the individual because we cannot assume that these conflicts are, in fact, demanding. To obtain information on the perceived level of demand or pressure, more direct assessment of this dimension is required. Using the above example, this could easily be accomplished by replacing the agree/disagree response format with one that reflects the extent of demand (pressure), such as (1) *very little demand/pressure* to (5) *very high demand/pressure.*

In short, there is a tendency in job stress research to make inferences about individuals' experiences that may not be justified on the basis of the variables that are actually measured. Similarly, critical dimensions of those experiences are often left unassessed, such as the frequency of the experience, its intensity, and its duration. To obtain more comprehensive, and hence more valid, depictions of stressors in the workplace context, researchers may have to move beyond simplistic measurement practices to ones that incorporate the critical dimensions of workplace experiences. As noted above, these issues are not unfamiliar to job stress researchers, but to date relatively little attention appears to have been given to them in empirical studies of job-related stressors.

One potential reason for the absence of more complex assessments of stressors is confusion over what to do with the information once it is obtained. Again, using the above illustration, how should frequency, intensity, and duration responses be combined to derive an estimate of the overall extent of demand or pressure exerted by a particular stressor? For instance, should these responses be added (summative model) or multiplied (multiplicative model) in generating an overall demand score for each person, or should each be treated as a separate response dimension? Questions such as these continue to confound researchers searching for the most appropriate and relevant measures of workplace stressors.

A further issue to consider is whether assessments of stressors should focus on perceptions of the same or similar work stressors across occupational groups and organizational contexts or on occupation- or organization-specific stressors. The first approach enables comparison across groups and settings and therefore enhances the generalization of research findings. On the other hand, assessing stressors that are directly salient within the specific context being investigated provides a more ecologically valid account of the demands and pressures actually experienced within that context and may better describe the effects of different work environments, as well as assisting with the development of targeted interventions to alleviate job-related strain within the particular context.

Another issue of concern from a methodological standpoint is the meaning of different stressors to individuals and whether some types of stressors are more salient or important than others. Typically, research on job-related stressors has used a linear additive model of stressors, combining them (or computing a mean score) to represent the total (or average) amount of stressors being experienced. This total or mean stressor score is then used as a predictor of strain. For instance, it is not uncommon in studies of role stressors to combine responses to the role ambiguity, conflict, and overload measures in a single index labeled "role stressors" (see, e.g., O'Driscoll & Beehr, 1994). Even within the separate variables, items that represent separate (albeit related) aspects of the stressor are combined. Such an approach simplifies further statistical analyses by reducing a potentially large array of stressors into more usable and convenient "bundles," perhaps even a single combined category. However, considerable information about individual stressors is lost when this procedure is adopted because total or mean scores give no indication of the patterns of responses that make up a "score." In fact, use of a total or mean score may divert attention from the different ways in which that score can be achieved and the different patterns of responses that individuals may exhibit. This approach may lead to the erroneous conclusion that individuals who manifest the same score have a common experience of the stressor, when in fact their experiences may vary considerably.

Dewe and Brook (2000) provide an illustration of this point. These investigators used *sequential tree analysis* to explore different patterns of scores on a predictor variable (stressor) when respondents obtained the same overall mean score on the criterion variable (job-related tension). Table 8.2 shows score profiles on the stressor measure of two groups of respondents who obtained the same mean tension score (3.23 on the 5-point scale). The stressor investigated in this study was "time demands and a constant sense of urgency" and was measured with 15 items. Inspection of the pattern of scores established through the tree analysis showed that, although having the same mean tension score, the time demands items that contributed to job-related tension were somewhat different for the two groups. Though both groups scored highly on Item 1 of the time demands measure ("Being unable to keep on top of your job without difficulty"), they differed markedly with respect to their responses to four other items. Group 1 reported pressure from

Table 8.2   A Comparison of Stressors for Two Groups With the Same Mean

Group 1	Group 2
Being unable to keep on top of your job without difficulty	Being unable to keep on top of your job without difficulty
Other people not involved putting pressure on you	Feeling that all tasks have a sense of urgency
Knowing that no matter how hard you work there always seems to be just as much to be done at the end of the day	Having to get the job done without a sufficient or a satisfactory workforce

other people and work overload as stressors, whereas Group 2 obtained high scores on items that reflected time urgency and lack of an adequate workforce.

The important point is that, although both groups exhibited the same tension score, their experience of the stressor was different, and simply using the mean stressor score as the index of these experiences would overlook this difference. Furthermore, a stress management intervention based on the generic time demands scores would be likely to fail because the two groups varied considerably on certain dimensions of that stressor. The need to understand score profiles will, of course, depend on the research objectives, but certainly such analysis would lead to more focused interventions and may help to explain why at times relationships between stressors and strains are not always as predicted. It is also interesting to note that although there were 15 items in the "time demands" scale, in each group only 3 of those items had a significant impact on tension scores.

Also frequently missing from stressor measurement is primary appraisal: that is, the way individuals interpret and give meaning to demanding events. One reason for this is that researchers have, as Newton (1989) suggested, been concerned with asking "How much is there of X?" rather than "Why is X a problem for you?" In short, measurement techniques have failed to differentiate between the occurrence of events (demands) and the individual's appraisal of their significance for his or her well-being (Dewe, 1993). Lack of assessment of appraisal mechanisms results in omission of a major step in the stress-coping process and hence in failure to examine the impact of appraisal on the experience of strain. One outcome of this omission is that the subjective meaning of events, which may be an even more salient predictor of strain responses than their occurrence, is often overlooked and effectively discounted in job stress research.

An example illustrating the difference between the meaning that individuals give to events and the events themselves was provided by Dewe (1993). When asked to describe the meanings associated with various work stressors, individuals described their appraisals in terms of "losing credibility" (e.g., feeling they may not meet expectations or feeling they would lose the respect of someone important to them), "being seen as a difficult person" (e.g., appearing difficult to get on with; appearing in the wrong), "feeling they may not achieve" (e.g., feeling they may not achieve an important goal; failing to meet their own expectations), and "being made to feel responsible" (e.g., being made to take the blame; feeling hostility from others). These appraisals are sufficiently different from the sorts of events identified as stressors (such as "too much work to do in the time available," "not having enough resources to do the job," and "having to deal with conflicting demands") to establish the importance of primary appraisal and its role in the stress process as one that should be investigated further.

Of course, the observations above assume that quantitative self-ratings represent the best way to capture the character and essence of demanding events. As we noted earlier, however, qualitative methodologies expose meaning rather than impose it, and they make no a priori assumptions about the nature of the data collected. Another reason for considering alternative approaches is what Bartunek, Bobko, and Venkatraman (1993) described as the "value-added" requirement. That is, researchers need to show how a methodology generates knowledge or moves the field forward in ways that other methods do not. In essence, the requirement is to get researchers to consider what various methods have to offer and not to overstate the contribution of any single methodology. Finally, alternative approaches can expand the traditional definition of data (Bartunek et al., 1993). From their review of different methodological approaches, Bartunek and her colleagues discovered that enormously varied and rich sources of data are frequently left untapped in organizational research. Traditional research approaches have tended to adopt a rather narrow interpretation of "measurement." Measurement, however designed, should expand our knowledge rather than limit the possibilities for understanding the phenomena under investigation. We suggest that this observation applies especially to the field of job stress research.

Job stress researchers are certainly not unfamiliar with qualitative techniques (Erera-Weatherley, 1996; Oakland & Ostell, 1996, O'Driscoll & Cooper, 1994). But from use of different methods (e.g., critical-incident technique, structured interviews, open-ended questions), the general conclusion appears to be that the potential of such approaches needs to be further explored and that this must "arguably, be better than adhering uncritically to ... quantitative measures" (Oakland & Ostell, 1996, p. 153). Other researchers have explored the difficulties involved in trying to combine qualitative and quantitative methods (Buchanan, 1992). The motivation for this sort of research has been to develop a familiarity with the goals, assumptions, and standards of qualitative methods, as well as to acknowledge that they offer valuable insights into the stress-coping process that may not be obtainable via other research strategies.

The potential of qualitative approaches can be illustrated in a number of different ways. Using a critical-incident technique, O'Driscoll and Cooper (1996) asked respondents to describe in detail a specific event that had occurred in their work environment over the past 6 to 12 months and had caused them considerable difficulties or problems (p. 124). The content analysis of responses identified 10 different categories of work stressors. What is interesting is to compare the results that emerged from this sort of analysis with the more commonly used role overload, conflict, and ambiguity scales. Though 53.7% of responses reflected traditional role issues, the remaining responses were sufficiently different to confirm that traditional stressor measures may not be capturing the work experience of those being researched.

For example, O'Driscoll and Cooper (1996) identified, in addition to the work stressors mentioned above, such stressors as "unavailability of or lack of control over resources," "conflict with people outside the organization," "technological problems," "communication problems," "perceived wage inequity," "skill deficit," and "work/nonwork conflict" (p. 125). The clear indication from this sort of approach is that relevance is as important as validity. Such results should prompt researchers to look at how their measures of work stressors may be refined and developed to reflect the reality of the different working experiences. They also point to how qualitative and quantitative approaches can be used to support one another. It would be possible to use these results to redevelop work stressor scales and then to use more traditional psychometric approaches to consider the utility, validity, and internal coherence of these newly refined measures. In this way, relevance and validity would work together, and through this process would come a more robust set of measures for exploring the stress process.

Similar conclusions can be drawn regarding research on coping resources and strategies. The debate surrounding how coping should be measured is as intense as that pertaining to job stressors and strains (see Chapter 6). Again, the major issue has centered on whether current measurement strategies are fulfilling their intended function and the identification of areas for improvement. In the context of "Whose reality are we measuring?" and "Do our instruments measure what we think they are measuring?" it is clear that there is considerable scope for rethinking how coping items should be derived, how they should be classified, whether frequency ratings best capture the underlying coping response, and how responses should be scored (e.g., do mean scores obscure the real nature of coping?). This latter point also draws attention to the use of internal reliability statistics to validate coping scales. In any specific encounter, use of a particular coping strategy may obviate the need for, or even exclude the use of, other forms of coping. If this occurs, a coping "scale" may exhibit relatively poor internal consistency, even when aspects of that scale represent valid indexes of coping strategies. Scale scores may, therefore, not accurately reflect an individual's actual coping behaviors.

In summary, questions have been raised about whether the reliance on quantitative self-ratings of coping activities can adequately capture the dynamics of the coping process (Oakland & Ostell, 1996; Thoits, 1995). Thoits (1995), for example, has suggested that researchers should develop alternative techniques that are more "faithful to the dynamic, unfolding nature of the phenomena under investigation" (p. 63). These alternative techniques include critical-incident interviewing (O'Driscoll & Cooper, 1994, 1996), semistructured interviewing that in certain respects "parallel[s] the diagnostic approach of a therapist building a model of a client's problem situation" (Oakland & Ostell, 1996, p. 142), open-ended questions using content analysis followed by axial coding (Erera-Weatherley, 1996), and daily diary or panel survey methods (Thoits, 1995). There is also a need to consider the extent of control that the person can exert over the situation, along with the coping resources (both personal and structural) available to the individual in the workplace setting and outside of it.

Drawing on the qualitative work of Oakland and Ostell (1996), it is possible to gain insights into the "tremendous diversity and complexity of coping behaviours and the dynamic nature of a process" (p. 151). Using a set of open-ended questions ("What did you do initially to deal with the situation?" "What was it about the situation that made you feel angry, guilty, anxious, etc.?" "What, if anything, did you do when you felt angry, anxious, etc.?" "Did the chosen coping strategies work or were they effective? If not, why not?") these researchers were able, from their content analysis, to establish a number of issues surrounding coping not altogether easily established from self-report coping questionnaires. For example, determining a strategy for coping involves taking into account the goals and earlier actions of other people and revising sometimes radically such a strategy depending on how others respond.

Second, it was clear from the Oakland and Ostell analysis that to cope with some issues individuals have to acquire certain knowledge and skills (e.g., expertise relating to a work problem) that may take time to acquire and that consequently during that time other coping strategies (e.g., emotion focused, because the problem-focused skill isn't there) may have to be used. Finally, it was clear from their data that how someone copes often results in additional problems being generated—something that is not easily established with quantitative measures. Paraphrasing the Oakland and Ostell (1996) data to illustrate this point: "I talked in a reasoned way—she got very upset—there was a dreadful atmosphere— and things just went from bad to worse" (p. 150). The important point from this sort of analysis is that if we are to better understand the coping process, not only are there ways that qualitative techniques can advance this understanding, but such findings should prompt researchers to consider the utility of traditional quantitative approaches and whether from such information alternative approaches can be devised, perhaps through more longitudinal studies to explore these sorts of issues. As suggested earlier, it is not a question of replacing one method with another but of using the methods individually and in conjunction to build on each other's strengths and to support research that continues to advance our understanding of complex process such as how people cope.

The social context in which coping occurs is frequently ignored in stress-coping research. Indeed, Handy (1988) argued that most research models focus solely on the individual level of analysis and therefore divert attention from serious examination of the social order within organizations. Consequently, traditional models of work stress have paid little attention to whether the different functions and structures of organizations "constrain individuals to think and act in particular ways" (p. 352). Further, according to Handy, researchers have underestimated the importance of investigating (a) the proactive efforts of individuals to influence organizational structures and functions, (b) the fact that individuals may act in pursuit of their own goals, and (c) the fact that behavior in organizations is more likely to be dependent on a "negotiated order" between individuals that differs from that expressed in formal organizational charts. Finally, models of work stress may overemphasize the level of consensus in organizations and fail to adequately consider issues of power and conflict when considering the resources individuals may have in managing stress. In sum, Handy and others have clearly articulated that greater attention must be given to the development of methods that explore the social experiences that individuals encounter in their workplaces and the meaning of these experiences for their well-being.

Conclusion

Several important themes concerning research strategies and methodologies have been discussed in this chapter. These can be broadly grouped under two headings: (a) refinement of measures and (b) assessment of the stress-coping process.

Refinement of Measures

Two strategic issues emerge under this heading. The first is concerned with establishing *whose reality is being measured* and the question of reliability versus relevance. As mentioned earlier, this requires that existing measures be evaluated in terms of (a) the content of items, (b) the scoring of responses, and (c) the manner in which internal reliability is established. Second, the issue of *measure confounding* needs serious consideration by job stress researchers. Confounding occurs when instruments that purport to assess one construct (e.g., a stressor) in reality tap into another (e.g., a strain). Researchers may inadvertently introduce confounding into their measurement procedures. For instance, instructions to respondents to indicate "the extent to which each of the following produces stress for you" inextricably confound the "causes" of strain with the strain itself. Research strategies must clearly distinguish between dependent and independent variables and avoid measurement overlap (Dewe, 2000), considering a range of measurement strategies (e.g., self-ratings; qualitative, physiological, and physical indicators of strain; and peer observations). Searching for more meaningful ways to measure different variables may help us not only to better understand the problem of confounding but also to better capture the reality of the experience being investigated.

Assessment of the Process

Process issues cannot be easily separated from measure refinement, simply because sound measures are the cornerstone of any attempt to understand stress coping. The fundamental question concerns how the process might be most effectively studied. Given the dynamic nature of stress-coping transactions, longitudinal data collection would appear to represent an effective research strategy because it provides the opportunity to clarify causal relationships that are otherwise indeterminable through cross-sectional analysis (Kahn & Byosiere, 1992). Whether longitudinal research is best operationalized through standard multivariate analysis or through qualitative techniques is part of the current debate, but the inclusion of techniques such as qualitative time diaries and multiple measurement procedures would certainly expand the scope of research investigations and generate a richer understanding of stress coping.

This chapter has been concerned with how empirical research on job stress and coping is conducted, and it has raised some issues relating to measurement (of stressors, strains, and coping behaviors) and the design of stress-coping studies. As we have noted, a critical concern is to ensure that research in this field makes progress toward an understanding of the contextual richness of the stress-coping process. To achieve this understanding, it is important for researchers to confront two primary questions: "Whose reality is being assessed?" and "Do our measures actually focus on the key components of stress transactions?" Here we have examined some of the major issues that surround these questions and have suggested that multiple approaches to the assessment of stress are required to enable the construction of comprehensive theories and models of stress coping. In the final chapter, we turn attention to some elements of work and employment relationships in the 21st century, highlighting the potential effects that new kinds of work arrangements may exert on individuals' lives and the consequences for their experience of stress and their overall well-being.

References

Bartunek, J. M., Bobko, P. P., & Venkatraman, N. (1993). Toward innovation and diversity in management research methods. *Academy of Management Journal, 36,* 1362-1373.

Bhagat, R., & Beehr, T. (1985). An evaluation summary and recommendations for future research. In T. A. Beehr & R. S. Bhagat (Eds.), *Human stress and cognition in organizations: An integrated perspective* (pp. 417-431). New York: John Wiley.

Brief, A. P., & Atieh, J. M. (1987). Studying job stress; Are we making mountains out of molehills? *Journal of Occupational Behaviour, 8,* 115-126.

Buchanan, D. R. (1992). An uneasy alliance: Combining qualitative and quantitative research methods. *Heath Education Quarterly, 19,* 117-135.

Cooper, C. (1998). Introduction. In C. Cooper (Ed.), *Theories of organizational stress* (pp. 1-5). New York: Oxford University Press.

Coyne, J. C. (1997). Improving coping research: Raze the slum before any more building! *Journal of Health Psychology, 2,* 153-155.

De Frank, R. S. (1988). Psychometric measurement of occupational stress: Current concerns and future directions. In J. J. Hurrell, L. R. Murphy, S. L. Sauter, & C. L. Cooper (Eds.), *Occupational stress: Issues and developments in research* (pp. 54-65). New York: Taylor & Francis.

Dewe, P. J. (1991). Primary appraisal, secondary appraisal and coping: Their role in stressful work encounters. *Journal of Occupational Psychology, 64,* 331-351.

Dewe, P. (1993). Measuring primary appraisal: Scale construction and directions for future research. *Journal of Social Behavior and Personality, 8,* 673-685.

Dewe, P. (2000). Measures of coping with stress at work: A review and critique. In P. Dewe, M. Leiter, & T. Cox (Eds.), *Coping, health and organizations* (pp. 3-28). New York: Taylor & Francis.

Dewe, P., & Brook, R. (2000). Sequential tree analysis of work stressors: Exploring score profiles in the context of the stressor-stress relationship. *International Journal of Stress Management, 7,* 1-18.

Erera-Weatherley, P. I. (1996). Coping with stress: Public welfare supervisors doing their best. *Human Relations, 49,* 157-170.

Fineman, S., & Payne, R. (1981). Role stress: A methodological trap. *Journal of Organisational Behaviour, 2,* 51-64.

Glowinkowski, S. P., & Cooper, C. L. (1985). Current issues in organisational stress research. *Bulletin of the British Psychological Society, 38,* 212-216.

Handy, J. A. (1988). Theoretical and methodological problems within occupational stress and burnout research. *Human Relations, 41,* 351-369.

Hari Das, T. (1983). Qualitative research in organisational behaviour. *Journal of Management Studies, 3,* 301-314.

Harris, J. R. (1991). The utility of the transactional approach for occupational stress research. *Journal of Social Behaviour and Personality, 6,* 21-29.

Kahn, R. L., & Byosiere, P. (1992). Stress in organizations. In M. D. Dunnette (Ed.), *Handbook of industrial and organizational psychology* (pp. 571-648). Chicago: Rand McNally.

Lazarus, R. S. (1990). Theory-based stress measurement. *Psychological Inquiry, 1,* 3-13.

Lazarus, R. S. (1991). Psychological stress in the workplace. *Journal of Social Behaviour and Personality, 6,* 1-13.

Lazarus, R. S. (1997). Hurrah for a systems approach. *Journal of Health Psychology, 2,* 158-160.

Magnusson, D., & Törestad, B. (1993). A holistic view of personality: A model revisited. *American Review of Psychology, 44,* 427-452.

Mohr, L. B. (1982). *Explaining organizational behavior.* San Francisco: Jossey-Bass.

Morgan, G., & Smircich, L. (1980). The case of qualitative research. *Academy of Management Review, 5,* 491-500.

Morley, N. L., & Luthans, F. (1984). An EMIC perspective and ethnoscience methods for organizational research. *Academy of Management Review, 9,* 27-36.

Newton, T. (1989). Occupational stress and coping with stress: A critique. *Human Relations, 42,* 441-461.

Oakland, S., & Ostell, A. (1996). Measuring coping: A review and critique. *Human Relations, 49,* 133-155.

O'Driscoll, M., & Beehr, T. (1994). Supervisor behaviors, role stressors and uncertainty as predictors of personal outcomes for subordinates. *Journal of Organizational Behavior, 15,* 141-155.

O'Driscoll, M. P., & Cooper, C. L. (1994). Coping with work related stress: A critique of existing measures and proposal for an alternative methodology. *Journal of Occupational and Organisational Psychology, 67,* 343-354.

O'Driscoll, M. P., & Cooper, C. L. (1996). A critical incident analysis of stress-coping behaviours at work. *Stress Medicine, 12,* 123-128.

Pfeffer, J. (1990). Management as symbolic action: The creation and maintenance of organizational paradigms. In L. L. Cummings & B. M. Staw (Eds.), *Information and cognition in organizations* (pp. 1-52). Greenwich, CT: JAI.

Revenson, T. A. (1997). Wanted: A wider lens for coping research. *Journal of Health Psychology, 2,* 164-165.

Rosenthal, R., & Rosnow, R. (1991). *Essentials of behavioral research: Methods and data analysis.* New York: McGraw-Hill.

Somerfield, M. R. (1997a). The utility of systems models of stress and coping for applied research. *Journal of Health Psychology, 2,* 133-151.

Somerfield, M. R. (1997b). The future of coping research as we know it: A response to commentaries. *Journal of Health Psychology, 2,* 173-183.

Spicer, J. (1997). Systems analysis of stress and coping: A testing proposition. *Journal of Health Psychology, 2,* 167-170.

Thoits, P. A. (1995). Stress, coping and social support processes: Where are we? What next? [Extra Issue]. *Journal of Health and Social Behaviour,* pp. 53-79.

Van Maanen, J. (1979). Reclaiming qualitative methods for organizational research: A preface. *Administrative Science Quarterly, 24,* 520-526.

9 The Changing Nature of Work

IMPLICATIONS FOR STRESS
RESEARCH

In this book, we have outlined and discussed critical features of the stress-coping process as it manifests itself in work organizations. Specifically, we have used the transactional model of stress developed by Lazarus (1966) and his colleagues to examine the nature of stress in the workplace, some of the more salient sources of stress (*stressors*), along with individuals' responses or experiences (*strains,* including burnout), and possible outcomes of strain, such as increased absenteeism and turnover within the organization, decrements in performance, and the overall diminution of personal well-being. We have also reviewed potential moderators or buffers of stressor-strain relationships. Finally, we have considered how job-related strain might be counteracted at both the individual level (personal coping) and the organizational level (stress management interventions).

Throughout the previous chapters, we have emphasized methodo-logical issues surrounding research on job stress and have provided illustrations of well-conducted studies, as well as pointing to some of the limitations inherent in stress research. Clearly, knowledge about stress-coping processes and how to alleviate strain is fundamentally dependent upon the quality of research that is carried out. As we have illustrated, however, there is considerable room for enhancing the design and execution of workplace stress research; hopefully, the issues raised in this volume and the examples discussed will contribute to critical thinking and debate, as well as sharpening the focus of research in this arena. In this final chapter, our intention is twofold: first, to draw together the threads of information, knowledge, and suggestions that have been outlined in previous chapters; and second, to advance some reflections and recommendations about directions for future research on job stress.

In addition to other factors that have been referred to as sources of work-related strain, a further issue that is highly relevant for stress research, and that numerous commentators have reflected upon in recent years, is the changing nature of work and careers as we embark upon the 21st century. The last half-century has seen enormous changes in the nature of society, and of the workplace in particular, and we must consider the implications of these developments for the experience of strain. The general thrust of these changes has been summarized by Kevin Murphy (1999), who depicted the new environment as the "postindustrial workplace," and by Gowing, Kraft, and Quick (1997), who referred to it as the "new organizational reality." Patricia Murphy and Susan Jackson (1999), for example, have suggested that work no longer comes in neatly packaged bundles of prescribed tasks, as was the case until very recently. Instead, future job descriptions "will be fluid rather than fixed, abstract and general rather than a detailed picture" (Murphy, 1999, p. 297). There have even been suggestions that the job, as we currently know it, either will no longer exist at all (Bridges, 1994) or will exist for only a small proportion of the workforce (Gowing et al., 1997; Murphy, 1999; Parker & Inkson, 1999).

Several environmental, economic, political, and sociocultural forces can be identified as shaping the way in which work arrangements (and hence jobs) are being restructured. One major reason for the emergence of new forms of working is the rapid development and implementation of new technologies (Hesketh & Neal, 1999), especially computer-based communication systems, which now pervade virtually every workplace. These new technologies have revolutionized ways of working, as well as the structure and functioning of organizations themselves. Although computerization has affected the world of work for almost three decades, and some of the dramatic changes witnessed in the 1990s were already beginning to surface in the previous decade, the exponential rate of technological change observed more recently (Martin & Freeman, 1997) has, we would argue, outstripped efforts to develop sociotechnical perspectives that integrate human needs and values into the management of jobs and organizations. In short, we suggest that work today is driven predominantly by the technological imperative rather than by holistic perspectives that also take account of personal, social, and cultural issues within societies.

A second major force, equally as powerful, is the emergence of the global marketplace. Globalization of trade has had several significant effects on organizations and workplace arrangements. One prominent effect has been the impact of globalization on the sheer number of workers (employees) needed to perform critical functions. Together with increased technological capability, global competition has led to substantial reductions in workforce size in an array of industries, especially manufacturing (production of goods), which has traditionally been a major employer in many societies.

Finally, there is the dual issue of unemployment and underemployment, generated by economic and structural transitions within societies. Increased rates of unemployment were recorded in the 1980s in many societies (Burke & Nelson, 1997), and although this trend abated to some extent in the 1990s in some more "developed" countries, when coupled with the introduction and development of new technologies that require less human input to achieve the same level of work output, the flow-on effects into the 1990s were considerable. Simultaneously, for many workers who retained jobs, the actual amount of work time available declined (Sullivan, 1999), and the scope of their work has diminished as technology has assumed increasing responsibility and control over outputs (Quick, Gowing, & Kraft, 1997). These forms of *underemployment* have been found to be both pervasive and significant in their impact on the psychosocial well-being of individual employees (Burke & Nelson, 1997; Gowing et al., 1997; Sullivan, 1999).

Burke and Nelson (1997) noted that, as a result of the forces described above, three major types of change within organizations have been observed over the past decade: mergers, acquisitions, and downsizing. Marks (1994) developed the acronym *MADness* to depict these events. Together, they represent efforts on the part of organizations worldwide to improve their chances of survival in a competitive global environment and to increase their productivity (and hence profitability). The impacts of mergers and acquisitions are sometimes considered together (see, e.g., Cartwright & Cooper, 1990), in particular their effect on the number of workers employed and the social and psychological outcomes of organizational restructuring. Bereavement in itself is considered to be a universally stressful life event, and a merger or acquisition can be a form of organizational bereavement. However, at the same time that employees may be dealing with feelings of loss, they have to cope with the uncertainty associated with major organizational change. Cartwright and Cooper (1990), for instance, found that mergers and acquisitions have a profound impact on the psychological well-being of employees involved and their families, and Schweiger and DeNisi (1991) noted that employees were affected even in a "friendly" or uncontested acquisition, let alone a hostile one.

Schweiger and DeNisi observed that emotional detachment and the attendant anxiety experienced by employees are manifested in four immediate concerns. First, because the acquisition or merger marks the death of the organization as its members know it, there is a noticeable feeling of "loss of identity." Second, almost all mergers are clothed in secrecy concerning future job prospects, reward systems, role changes, staffing changes, and so on, which creates "uncertainty stress." Third, maintaining one's existing personal status, prestige, and power can assume the highest priority for individuals and may even override organizational goals—hence, sheer survival can become a psychologically destructive obsession. Finally, work-related anxieties, particularly if they concern the financial implications of an uncertain job future or the possibility of relocation, spill over into family life and lead to replication of the stressor-strain cycle.

Perhaps the most discussed phenomenon in the occupational environment of the 1990s has been the downsizing of organizations, especially the shedding of managerial and professional workers, as well as other members of the labor force. Downsizing has been a response to several coacting forces (Martin & Freeman, 1997), especially those mentioned above. The decline of manufacturing jobs, along with the *delayering* of organizations, entailing a reduction in the number of managers in particular, has resulted in heavy job losses in many occupational sectors and hence a substantial increase in the amount of psychological strain due to job insecurity and unemployment (Harnisch, 1999). For the first time, employees in positions that were traditionally considered quite stable and secure, such as managerial-level jobs, began to experience the uncertainty and strain associated with either actual loss of their position (and career!) or at least the possibility of redundancy. For instance, Burke and Nelson (1997) cited job loss figures in the 1980s from a variety of "developed" countries, including the United States, Canada, Europe, and Japan, as being in the millions, noting that "changes such as these over the past 10 years are challenging workers' traditional expectations of career advancement" (p. 22). They also challenge the validity and generalizability of traditional theories about career choice and development (Sullivan, 1999).

New Forms of Work Arrangements

As a result of the internal and external forces impinging upon organizations in the 1990s and now into the new century, several new forms of employment relationships have emerged. The outcomes of these new relationships, especially for individuals directly affected by them, are only just beginning to be researched and understood. One of the key agendas for future stress research will be to explore these effects more systematically and to generate viable suggestions for counteracting the potential negative impact they exert on individuals and their families, as well as on employing organizations. Here we will highlight some of the more evident, and perhaps more influential, changes in organization-worker relationships that have surfaced over the past 10 years or so. First, we briefly overview the nature of these changes; then we discuss their likely implications for the health and well-being of individuals and society as a whole.

In addition to restructuring (especially downsizing) of the workforce, another reaction from many organizations to the changed economic climate has been to move toward a two-tiered workforce of *core* and *contingent* employees (Murphy, 1999). According to Murphy,

> [A] key assumption of the post-industrial workplace is that the turbulent external environment faced by organizations (such as the need to change products or services frequently in response to market demands or competitors' innovations) will lead to the need for frequent changes in workers' responsibilities, tasks and work relationships. (p. 297)

As a result, fewer permanent or "core" positions are required by organizations to fulfill their goals and objectives. Instead, many tasks (particularly those requiring specific technical skills but perhaps less knowledge of the organization as a whole) are now being outsourced to individuals or groups who may complete work on contract for several organizations rather than being employed by a single entity. These workers are typically referred to as "contingent" employees because their relationship with the organization depends on the availability of tasks that they have the expertise to complete.

In the United Kingdom, for instance, more than one in eight workers is self-employed, and part-time and short-term contracts are growing faster than permanent full-time positions. The number of males in part-time employment has almost doubled over the past decade; at the same time, the number of people working in companies that employ more than 500 people has declined to just over one third of the total workforce (Cooper & Jackson, 1997). Similar trends have been observed in other countries (Kompier & Cooper, 1999).

Cooper and Jackson (1997) have predicted that most organizations in the developed world in the first decade of this new millennium will have only a small core of full-time, permanent employees working from a conventional office. They will buy most of the skills they need on a contract basis from either individuals working at home and linked to the company by computers and modems (teleworking) or by individuals hired on short-term contracts to do specific jobs or carry out specific projects. In this way, companies will be able to maintain the flexibility they need to cope with rapidly changing organizational realities. Much of this change is already happening. For instance, British Telecom, a large telecommunications company in the United Kingdom, has claimed that more than 2.5 million people are already working wholly or partly from home, and they predict this number to rise to 4 million early in the 21st century. There is also a significant rise in the provision to industry of senior management by management agencies on a project management basis. All the trends are in the direction of the "contingent workforce" or contract working, which clearly influences the employment relationship between individuals and organizations (Cohen & Mallon, 1999).

More generally, there has been a pronounced reduction in the job security of workers worldwide. An International Survey Research (ISR) survey of 400 companies in 17 countries, published in 1995, indicated that the employment security of workers throughout Europe significantly declined between 1985 and 1995: in the United Kingdom from 70% in 1985 to 48% in 1995, in Germany from 83% to 55%, in France from 64% to 50%, in the Netherlands from 73% to 61%, in Belgium from 60% to 54%, and in Italy from 62% to 57%. In addition, part-time working has increased: in the United Kingdom, for example, the number of men working part time has doubled over this same period (ISR, 1995).

Potential Effects of the New Work Arrangements

The shifts and changes in employment patterns and practices high-lighted above have far-reaching consequences, not just in terms of how organizations function but (more importantly from the perspective of job stress research) also on the lives of individual workers and their families. It could be anticipated, therefore, that some of the stressors discussed in Chapter 2 and the strains discussed in Chapter 3 may be experienced more strongly and by a greater proportion of the workforce than has previously been observed. For instance, one significant conse-quence of contingent employment contracts is that individuals working under these arrangements become totally responsible for managing their own career development and advancement (Murphy & Jackson, 1999), rather than this being (at least partially) the organization's responsibility. Hall and Moss (1998) have referred to this type of career progression as the *protean career* (see Chapter 2) in that individuals must personally "seek out opportunities to develop, practice, and exploit their knowledge, skills and abilities" (Murphy & Jackson, 1999, p. 350), whereas previously many of these opportunities would have been provided for them by their employing organization. This increased responsibility for professional development can produce considerable ambiguity and insecurity, and hence strain, for persons who have received no training or coaching in this area and who previously depended sub-stantially on organizational support for advancing their professional careers.

Employee expectations about job/career security have also, of necessity, shifted in recent times. Individuals must now focus less on employment security over a long term within a single organization, or even a single occupation, and concentrate more on their "employability" (Parker & Inkson, 1999), which relies heavily on both flexibility (in terms of job or career preference) and versatility (of skills and knowledge). Arthur and Rousseau (1996) have called this the *boundaryless career* because it is not centered on, or bounded by, development and advancement within a particular organizational context. A similar notion is that expounded by Handy (1994) of the *portfolio career:* "The portfolio is a collection of different bits and pieces of work for different clients. The word 'job' now means a client" (p. 175).

For many individuals, particularly those who have been employed by, and have invested themselves in, a single organization for a long time, this shift in both attitudes and capabilities can be extremely threatening. More research is needed on the extent of psychological strain resulting from this massive orientation shift, both for individuals themselves and for their families, as well as on effective strategies for managing the transition from an approach to career progression based on the expectation of lifetime employment (whether within a single organization or in a single career path) to one that requires flexibility and versatility, and where change is the norm. For example, Cohen and Mallon (1999) identified the absence of a regular income, lack of employment security, problems with maintaining a professional identity, and absence of a ready-made "structure" for one's working week as salient stressors in a sample of managers and professionals who had voluntarily moved out of organizational employment into portfolio working. In situations entailing involuntary career moves, we predict that these stressors would have even greater impact on individuals.

A related phenomenon, also referred to earlier (see Chapter 2), is that of career *plateauing,* which occurs when individuals are unable to advance further within their organization (Burke & Nelson, 1997). Increasingly, both managerial and other employees within organizations are encountering constraints on their career progression, and there has been an erosion of the traditional expectation of a (linear) hierarchical career path that is traversed over a long time period. Plateauing can have serious detrimental effects on individuals who have been socialized to perceive upward advancement as the hallmark of career success and personal achievement. The challenge for many organizations is to identify and implement alternative reward structures for high achievers. Organizational researchers and practitioners have begun to examine possible alternatives, including refocusing on lateral (or sideways) career development (Langan-Fox, 1998; Sullivan, 1999), but as yet none of these alternatives has been clearly demonstrated to carry the same reward value as hierarchical career progression.

Even for individuals who remain within the same organizational setting or continue to develop their career incrementally within the same occupation, there have been sizable shifts in role responsibilities as organizations have changed their modi operandi to meet the demands of the current economic environment and to remain competitive. These role shifts have been particularly significant for middle managers, whom some regard as an "endangered species" (Jaffe & Scott, 1997), in that there has been a considerable reduction in the numbers of workers employed in that role. Further, those who have retained middle-management status have been required to make significant modifications to their way of operating. Due to downsizing and a general flattening of organizational structures, in many organizations the need for supervisory personnel has declined considerably, and the nature of supervision has been radically altered (Jaffe & Scott, 1997). Overall, there is consistent evidence that levels of work-related stressors for middle managers have increased and that this group of employees often experiences as much, or even more, strain than other occupational categories (O'Driscoll & Cooper, 1996), as well as having to confront the uncertainty of potential job loss (Harnisch, 1999). Job stress researchers need to reexamine the notion of organizational roles in light of these changes and to assess the likely impact of such role shifts on employees' affective experiences at work. As noted earlier, they should also adopt perspectives that endeavor to develop alternative approaches to the design of workplace roles and contexts, ones that contribute positively to individual well-being rather than creating strain and perhaps leading to burnout. To date, stress research has been more reactive (to existing conditions) than proactive in this respect.

One other change that has been noted in the way in which organizations function is the increasing reliance on teamwork and team-based performance and productivity. Following the lead, in particular, of Japanese organizations in the 1960s and 1970s, during the 1990s managers in the United States and many European and other countries came to regard the use of teams as a mechanism for improving productivity and hence organizational effectiveness. However, as noted by many researchers (see, e.g., Cohen & Bailey, 1997; Kivimaki & Elovainio, 1999), effective teamwork is critically dependent upon a number of personal and situational factors, including an organizational climate that fosters and facilitates team functioning and a collectivistic orientation that values group or team outcomes (performance) over and above individual outcomes. For instance, it has been suggested that the reason for the relative lack of success of quality control circles in many U.S., U.K., and European organizations, compared with Japanese companies, is that the effectiveness of quality control circles hinges upon a collectivistic value orientation, and in Western countries individuals are socialized to value, and are rewarded for, individual achievement (Agrell & Gustafson, 1994).

The introduction, therefore, of team-based approaches (such as quality control circles) into Western organizations may generate a variety of stressors for individuals not accustomed to functioning in such an environment and not previously rewarded for contributions to team outputs. For example, the use of teams requires placing more emphasis on social skills (such as communication, negotiation, group decision making, and conflict resolution) and enhanced sensitivity to others. Traditionally, these are not skills that have been universally taught and rewarded, and they will require major adjustment on the part of many employees.

Not only this, but many organizations are now moving toward the utilization of "virtual teams" where group members do not actually interact face to face but communicate via computers and other technologies. From an organizational perspective, virtual teams open up new possibilities for teamworking that are unimpeded by time and space contraints. However, they also pose new and special challenges for individual employees, especially with respect to developing their interpersonal relations skills.

> At this point, very little is known about the skills, personality characteristics, and so on that are most likely to be critical for functioning effectively in jobs where telecommuting, virtual teams, electronic brainstorming, and so forth are part of the landscape. (Murphy, 1999, p. 304)

Similarly, our knowledge about the unique stressors that arise from functioning in such systems is also very limited.

Finally, to round off this discussion of job-related stressors in the 21st century, whether they be newly emerging or simply more pronounced, we also need to consider the impact of new forms of employment relationships and work organization on individuals' lives off the job. Each of the changes identified above has the potential to significantly influence workers' family lives, relationships with spouses/partners and children, leisure activities, and what is often referred to as "home-work" balance. With increasing numbers of people working from home or having contingent employment relationships, we anticipate that it will become increasingly difficult for individuals to separate their job/career from their lives off the job; hence, there will be a further blurring of boundaries between these two domains. Technological innovations are already making it possible for people to be "at work" virtually any time, anywhere. Although these innovations certainly create flexibility and may even enhance productivity at both an individual and organizational level, less attention has been given to their possible negative impacts on individuals' lives more generally (O'Driscoll, 1996).

As noted earlier, we are becoming a technologically driven society, and there is a distinct danger that sociocultural values will be subordinated to technological and economic imperatives. Although many organizations are beginning to implement family-friendly initiatives, such as flextime and provision of child care facilities, little attention has been devoted to the more fundamental issue of how employment contracts and the very structure of work itself affect individual and family well-being. Many years ago, Rosabeth Moss Kanter (1977) debunked the myth of separate (job and family) worlds, yet by and large job stress research has continued to assess stressors and strains in the workplace separately from other life domains and has ignored the inherent interplay between various life domains, including work. We suggest that stress researchers need to adopt a more holistic perspective, moving away from examination of work-related stressors and stress management in isolation from other (e.g., family) contexts to a model where work experiences (both positive and negative) are considered along with family and other domains as part of a gestalt. Recent studies of interdomain (especially job-family) spillover represent an example of a research paradigm that endeavors to take an approach to identifying the stress-coping process from a more holistic perspective.

Finally, growth in the proportion of women entering the workforce over the past 15 to 20 years has highlighted further critical issues to consider with respect to job stress. First, the career expectations of women have changed markedly during this time, such that many women are now seeking the same kinds of rewards, including career advancement, as their male counterparts (Langan-Fox, 1998). However, despite the rhetoric that has developed about equal opportunities and affirmative action in the workplace, these expectations are in many cases thwarted by bureaucratic systems that are controlled by traditional thinking and have failed to keep pace with broader societal value and attitude shifts. The personal strain that this incongruence creates for career-oriented women is often not dealt with effectively by their employing organizations.

At the same time, there has been little change in societal expectations of women's roles in the household and family, and by and large women still perform the bulk of household chores and shoulder primary responsibility for child rearing and other family activities (Kroska, 1997). Although evidence that women report more job → family conflict than men is mixed (O'Driscoll, 1996), there is no doubt that women are more often confronted by demands from both occupational and family demands that may be experienced as conflictual. Two potential explanations have been proffered for the apparent contradiction in research findings comparing male and female levels of interdomain conflict. The first is that, although there continue to be disparities in the extent of male versus female responsibility for family and household activities, men and women actually experience about the same amount of inter-role conflict overall but not the same kinds of conflict. It may be that males encounter more family → job interference, whereas females experience more of the converse (job → family interference). The second explanation is that, although women may experience more inter-role conflict, their appraisal of the degree of conflict varies from men's appraisals. For instance, though many men may perceive having to attend to the illness of a child as a major source of interference with their job responsibilities, for women this may be viewed as "par for the course" and hence not regarded as a major stressor—it is simply one of life's events that has to be dealt with. Similarly, it is likely that women (in general) have developed more effective strategies for coping with such events and therefore do not report the same level of strain as their male partners/spouses. This is not to say that they do not *experience* strain but simply that they *report* it as being at a lower level.

There has also been a considerable rise in the proportion of dual-income households, where both partners/spouses are in paid employment. Early research on this phenomenon focused predominantly on dual careers (see, e.g., Higgins, Duxbury, & Irving, 1992), where both partners are in managerial or professional occupations and seek to advance themselves within those occupations. The emphasis of much of this research has been on the types and extent of job-family conflict that partners report (e.g., Higgins et al., 1992; Milkie & Peltola, 1999), their respective levels of both job and family (or marital) satisfaction and functioning (e.g., Aryee & Luk, 1996; Burley, 1995; Mauno & Kinnunen, 1999), and the level of psychological strain experienced by each person (e.g., Parasuraman, Greenhaus, & Granrose, 1992). Research on dual-career couples has also focused on two forms of "stress contagion," the first occurring when the strain experienced by an individual in one domain (such as employment) spills over into the other (family), and the second ("crossover"), where one partner's strain gets transmitted to the other partner (Chan & Margolin, 1994; Jones & Fletcher, 1993). The latter occurs especially when there is substantial job $\rightarrow$ family conflict for one individual in the relationship.

More recently, due to the downturn in the economy of many countries and the accompanying shifts in employment relationships discussed earlier, in the late 1990s many couples have been forced into the dual-earner situation, where having both partners employed is not a (career) choice but a financial necessity. Frequently, one or even both individuals are employed in short-term, perhaps even part-time, contracts that hold little if any prospect for career advancement. The stressors encountered under these circumstances, and therefore the kinds of strain experienced, are likely to differ considerably from those confronted by dual-career couples. To date, however, research has not systematically compared (and contrasted) these markedly different situations. Along with our previous injunction about more "integrated" empirical studies of job stress, we suggest that the job-family interface will become increasingly important in stress research and that various employment and family circumstances need to be more carefully differentiated so that studies of the stress-coping process can better describe the types of stressors and strains, as well as examining implications for stress management at both the individual (or couple) level and the organizational level.

A range of future research topics is evident in the area of job-family balance. Lewis and Cooper (1999) suggested the following. First, because jobs are becoming more contingent and short-term contract, hence intrinsically more insecure, what is the impact of these changes on the interface between work and the family? Second, as more and more women pursue careers and not just jobs, what will be the impact of this on work culture and on home life, and how will men cope in the future without their identity as primary breadwinner intact? Third, if the two-earner family encourages flexible working arrangements, how effective are they? Are some flexible working arrangements more successful than others, or does there have to be a match between family circumstances and the particular arrangement (e.g., compressed work week, teleworking, hot-desking)? Fourth, as jobs become more insecure and individuals are expected to work longer and more unsocial hours, what will the impact of these hours be on personal health, on the family, and on productivity? Finally, will changing gender patterns of employment and consequent shifts in home-work balance encourage the emergence of virtual organizations, and, if so, what will be the consequences for the health and well-being of individuals and their families?

Agendas for Job Stress Research

The issues and phenomena that we have surveyed above pose major challenges for job stress researchers. To conclude this chapter, we suggest some directions for future research in this field. These suggestions are not intended to be exhaustive, nor are they presented in any specific order of importance, but they do highlight some key issues that we believe need to be attended to for research to continue to make a meaningful contribution to theories about the stress-coping process, as well as for the application of empirically based knowledge to the management of stress in the workplace.

Consistent with arguments we have outlined earlier in this volume (see, e.g., Chapters 2 and 3), our first suggestion is that there needs to be more explicit focus on the *context* in which stress coping occurs. Currently, there is a tendency to regard the strains that individuals experience as being the same, irrespective of the setting in which they arise and of the stressors that the person is confronted with. For example, frequently used indexes of strain include variables such as general depression, anxiety, and tension (Kahn & Byosiere, 1992), and popular instruments for assessing psychological strain, such as the General Health Questionnaire (Goldberg, 1972), tap generic indicators of strain (including items such as "felt constantly under strain," "lost confidence in myself," and "felt I couldn't overcome my problems"), without locating these experiences within any specific context. Combined with the tendency to use cross-sectional designs that depend almost exclusively on self-report measures (of both stressors and strains), concentration on these generic variables and measures means that researchers are unable to differentiate between the forms of strain that arise in the workplace, the family environment, or some other setting. Consequently, only limited knowledge has been acquired about various manifestations of strain and the possibility that the kind of strain experienced in one environment may differ from that experienced in another.

Second, and following from the above recommendation, we would argue that stress-coping research should adopt a holistic perspective that takes into account the totality of an individual's life space rather than simply assessing one domain in isolation from others. For instance, as noted earlier in this chapter, despite acknowledgment of the dynamic interplay between various life domains, there has been a tendency for researchers interested in job stress to study only what happens in the work setting and to ignore other areas (such as family domain). Hence, though a particular study might uncover statistically significant relationships between (for example) workplace stressors, such as role ambiguity and conflict, and psychological (or other forms of) strain, we cannot be certain that these are the only, or even the primary, determinants of strain for the individuals under investigation. It may be that family pressures or personal relationship problems are major predictors of an individual's affective reactions at the time of measurement. Furthermore, personal (dispositional) characteristics may also be contributing to the nature and extent of strain experienced. In sum, implementing the transactional perspective on stress coping requires a joint approach that incorporates contextual factors and dispositional variables and examines the total set of stressors impinging upon a person.

A third recommendation, also discussed earlier in this chapter, is that job stress research could be more "proactive" in its approach. The typical stress study examines predictors (stressors) and outcomes (strain responses) after they have occurred. This is necessary for us to establish putative cause-effect relationships between stressors and strains as they unfold in the workplace. But although this line of research is important, we suggest that it would be also be valuable now to move beyond these post hoc approaches. Specifically, we advocate the use of research designs that examine theoretically driven stress management systems (at both the individual and organizational level) that may yield positive benefits for workers, their employing organizations, and ultimately society as a whole. In short, we believe it is time to become more innovative, "experimental," and forward looking in our approaches to research on stress management, rather than continuing solely with "after-the-fact" investigations that simply attempt to replicate previous findings concerning the predictors of workplace strain.

Fourth, and emerging from our discussion of the impact of new technologies and changing employment conditions, more needs to be done to counteract the detrimental effects of strain induced by the new organizational realities. As mentioned previously, to a large extent these realities are driven by economic and technological forces, and less importance has been attached to personal, social, and societal outcomes, including disruption of individuals' personal and family lives. Although there have been some investigations of (individual) coping mechanisms and (organizational) stress management interventions (see Chapters 6 and 7), generally speaking much less is known about how to effectively combat the kinds of strain brought about by the massive organizational transformations that have been occurring in the past decade, and that every indication suggests will become increasingly pervasive in the foreseeable future. We endorse the view, also expressed by various other commentators (see, e.g., Adkins, 1997; Burke & Nelson, 1997; Cooper & Cartwright, 1994), that the development, implementation, and evaluation of effective stress management mechanisms, at both individual and organizational levels, represents a critical agenda item for job stress researchers over the next 10 years.

Some Implications for Methodology

In addition to the above general issues concerning the nature of future job stress research, some specific recommendations about methodological refinements are appropriate at this juncture. Other chapters in this volume have addressed some of the critical issues concerning the design and execution of research on job stress (see especially Chapter 8), so we will not repeat these issues in detail here. Rather, the following discussion focuses on four additional areas that we believe should be considered.

Earlier, we discussed the need to expand our perspectives on the nature of job-related strain to encompass a broader range of strains and to differentiate between types of strain that may be experienced in various contexts. To achieve this objective, it is necessary for researchers to examine a greater range of affective reactions in their research designs and to assess the specific strains that are experienced in reaction to particular stressors. At a very simple level, we need to ask, for example, whether stressors such as role ambiguity and conflict induce the same kinds of strain as other stressors, such as work overload. Similarly, is the strain experienced in response to workplace stressors the same kind of strain as that encountered in other environments (e.g., the family) or as a result of interdomain (e.g., job-family) conflict? As yet, these questions have been given scant research attention, so there has been little attempt to specify the nature of strain that is created by different stressors.

Allied with the above notion is the need to move away from total reliance on self-reports of stressors and strains. Gathering data on individuals' perceptions of the environment and their affective reactions is clearly important and yields valuable information on subjective interpretations of life experiences. However, to generate knowledge that can be used to develop effective stress management interventions, we must tap sources of data that complement (and supplement) self-reports, including physical reactions (e.g., recordings of physiological processes) and behavioral responses (including those perceived by significant others). Furthermore, as we have suggested in Chapter 7, although psychology may be the study of individual behavior, it is important to move beyond the study of individual coping to analysis of stress management at the organizational and occupational levels in order to determine whether certain organizational and workplace conditions create strain for people, irrespective of their (different) subjective responses. Put another way, stress researchers have a unique opportunity to assist with the construction of "healthy organizations" (Cooper & Cartwright, 1994) that contribute to individual well-being rather than inducing or exacerbating levels of strain.

A third recommendation is that there needs to be greater triangulation of research methodologies or perspectives to enhance our ability to obtain comprehensive and generalizable findings. Typically, job stress research falls into one of two camps: deductive (based on a priori hypotheses) and inductive (exploratory), and these approaches tend to be mutually exclusive. Deductive research is normally carried out using structured questionnaires or interview schedules, and the data are subjected to statistical analysis (e.g., multiple regression) of predictor and criterion variables. Such research is useful for testing hypotheses concerning relationships between known entities. Inductive research, on the other hand, tends to use more open-ended interview questions and is usually designed to "discover" entities or to explore particular areas of interest in depth. For instance, O'Driscoll and Cooper (1994, 1996) illustrated the use of Flanagan's critical-incident method, a form of interviewing based on identification of antecedent conditions, behavioral responses, and outcomes, in the study of individual coping strategies.

We suggest that a convergence of methodologies would substantially advance our knowledge of the stress-coping process and would provide a more detailed account of stressor-strain relationships than is possible using either methodology alone. Deductive and inductive methods both have advantages and limitations, and each generates information that is not readily obtainable using the other approach. Although it may not always be practical or feasible to combine these approaches, we recommend that a convergent strategy be adopted wherever possible.

Finally, by its very nature, the term *stress* conveys a negative connotation of workplace experiences and life in organizations. This is perhaps best exemplified by a quote from Studs Terkel's (1972) classic ethnographic account of workers in various occupational settings:

> This book, being about work, is, by its very nature, about violence—to the spirit as well as to the body. It is about ulcers as well as accidents, about shouting matches as well as fistfights, about nervous breakdowns as well as kicking the dog around. It is, above all, about daily humiliations. (p. xi)

For many workers, the reality of working life may well be reflected in Terkel's comments. On the other hand, we also need to acknowledge the benefits of working, the advantages that accrue to individuals in paid employment, and the positive contributions that jobs and careers make to individuals' overall well-being (Danna & Griffin, 1999; Warr, 1999). Again, it is time for organizational research to adopt a broader perspective that incorporates the variety of experiences—both positive and negative—that individuals encounter in their jobs and to develop research designs that capture the depth and richness of those experiences, rather than focusing simplistically on relationships among a limited subset of variables.

Ultimately, the value of job stress research will be judged by its contribution to the enhancement of individual well-being, as well as organizational productivity and effectiveness. The responsibility rests with researchers themselves to ensure that their empirical studies provide "added value" to the expanding body of knowledge about stress-coping processes and interventions. Work can create strain and lead to ill health and reduced well-being (Cooper, Liukkonen, & Cartwright, 1996), which incur economic costs and productivity losses for organizations (Cooper, 1998). The onus rests with stress researchers to conduct research that contributes to the development of more "healthy" working environments (in the fullest sense of that expression), and that enables individuals and organizations to alleviate the negative effects of stressors when they cannot avoid them altogether. We believe that the future for stress research is exemplified in the following excerpt from the Tokyo Declaration Work-Related Stress and Health in Three Postindustrial Settings (1998), which suggests that the overall thrust of such research is toward "improving the health and well-being of the labour force . . . the productivity and economic wellbeing of organizations and the economic system, the participation of workers in the democratic process, and the enhancement of social capital at work and outside it" (quoted in Levi, 1999, p. 395).

The Tokyo Declaration seems to be reinforcing what has been urged by many over the last several decades, that an individual employee's health depends on how he or she is managed at work. Indeed, over 30 years ago, Kornhauser (1965) explored the mental health of the American worker and suggested,

> Mental health is not so much a freedom from specific frustrations as it is an overall balanced relationship to the world, which permits a person to maintain a realistic, positive belief in himself and his purposeful activities. Insofar as his entire job and life situation facilitate and support such feelings of adequacy, inner security, and meaningfulness of his existence, it can be presumed that his mental health will tend to be good. What is important in a negative way is not any single characteristic of his situation, but everything that deprives the person of purpose and zest, that leaves him with negative feelings about himself, with anxieties, tensions, a sense of lostness, emptiness, and futility. (p. 15)

The challenge is there for stress researchers to strive toward having a significant practical input into the health and well-being of individuals, organizations, and ultimately the societies in which they live and function. We believe, and hope, that the issues and recommendations presented in this volume contribute to the ongoing development and enhancement of research in this important field of investigation.

References

Adkins, J. (1997). Base closure: A case study in occupational stress and organizational decline. In M. Gowing, J. Kraft, & J. Quick (Eds.), *The new organizational reality: Downsizing, restructuring and revitalization* (pp. 111-141). Washington, DC: American Psychological Association.

Agrell, A., & Gustafson, R. (1994). The Team Climate Inventory (TCI) and group innovation: A psychometric test on a Swedish sample of work groups. *Journal of Occupational and Organizational Psychology, 67,* 143-151.

Arthur, M., & Rousseau, D. (1996). The boundaryless career as a new employment principle. In M. Arthur & D. Rousseau (Eds.), *The boundaryless career* (pp. 3-20). New York: Oxford University Press.

Aryee, S., & Luk, V. (1996). Balancing two major parts of adult life experience: Work and family identity among dual-career couples. *Human Relations, 49,* 465-487.

Bridges, W. (1994, September 19). The end of the job. *Fortune,* pp. 62-74.

Burke, R., & Nelson, D. (1997). Mergers and acquisitions, downsizing and privatization: A North American perspective. In M. Gowing, J. Kraft, & J. Quick (Eds.), *The new organizational reality: Downsizing, restructuring and revitalization* (pp. 21-54). Washington, DC: American Psychological Association.

Burley, K. (1995). Family variables as mediators of the relationship between work-family conflict and marital adjustment among dual-career men and women. *Journal of Social Psychology, 135,* 483-499.

Cartwright, S., & Cooper, C. (1990). The impact of mergers and acquisitions on people at work: Existing research and issues. *British Journal of Management, 1,* 65-76.

Chan, C., & Margolin, G. (1994). The relationship between dual-earner couples' daily work mood and home affect. *Journal of Social and Personal Relationships, 11,* 573-586.

Cohen, L., & Mallon, M. (1999). The transition from organisational employment to portfolio work: Perceptions of "boundarylessness" *Work, Employment & Society, 13,* 329-352.

Cohen, S., & Bailey, D. (1997). What makes teams work? *Journal of Management, 23,* 239-290.

Cooper, C. (1998). Introduction. In C. Cooper (Ed.), *Theories of organizational stress* (pp. 1-5). New York: Oxford University Press.

Cooper, C. L., & Cartwright, S. (1994). Healthy mind, healthy organization: A proactive approach to occupational stress. *Human Relations, 47,* 455-471.

Cooper, C., & Jackson, S. (1997). Introduction. In C. Cooper & S. Jackson (Eds.), *Creating tomorrow's organizations: A handbook for future research in organizational behavior* (pp. 1-4). New York: John Wiley.

Cooper, C. L., Liukkonen, P., & Cartwright, S. (1996). *Stress prevention in the workplace: Assessing the costs and benefits to organizations.* Luxembourg: European Union.

Danna, K., & Griffin, R. (1999). Health and well-being in the workplace. *Journal of Management, 25,* 357-384.

Flanagan, J. (1954). The critical incident technique. *Psychological Bulletin, 51,* 327-358.

Goldberg, D. (1972). *The detection of psychiatric illness by questionnaire.* New York: Oxford University Press.

Gowing, M., Kraft, J., & Quick, J. (1997). A conceptual framework for coping with the new organizational reality. In M. Gowing, J. Kraft, & J. Quick (Eds.), *The new organizational reality: Downsizing, restructuring and revitalization* (pp. 259-268). Washington, DC: American Psychological Association.

Hall, D., & Moss, J. (1998, Winter). The new protean career contract: Helping organizations and employees adapt. *Organizational Dynamics*, pp. 22-36.

Handy, C. (1994). *The empty raincoat: Making sense of the future.* London: Hutchinson.

Harnisch, K. (1999). Job loss and unemployment research from 1994 to 1998. *Journal of Vocational Behavior, 55,* 188-220.

Hesketh, B., & Neal, A. (1999). Technology and performance. In D. Ilgen & E. Pulakos (Eds.), *The changing nature of performance: Implications for staffing, motivation and development* (pp. 21-55). San Francisco: Jossey-Bass.

Higgins, C., Duxbury, L., & Irving, R. (1992). Work-family conflict in the dual-career family. *Organizational Behavior and Human Decision Processes, 51,* 51-75.

International Survey Research. (1995). *Employee satisfaction: Tracking European trends.* London: Author.

Jaffe, D., & Scott, C. (1997). Rekindling work commitment and effectiveness through a new work contract. In M. Gowing, J. Kraft, & J. Quick (Eds.), *The new organizational reality: Downsizing, restructuring and revitalization* (pp. 185-205). Washington, DC: American Psychological Association.

Jones, F., & Fletcher, B. (1993). An empirical study of occupational stress transmission in working couples. *Human Relations, 46,* 881-903.

Kahn, R. L., & Byosiere, P. (1992). Stress in organizations. In M. D. Dunnette (Ed.), *Handbook of industrial and organizational psychology* (pp. 571-648). Chicago: Rand McNally.

Kanter, R. (1977). *Work and family in the United States: A critical review and agenda for research and policy.* New York: Russell Sage.

Kivimaki, M., & Elovainio, M. (1999). A short version of the Team Climate Inventory. *Journal of Occupational and Organizational Psychology, 72,* 241-246.

Kompier, M., & Cooper, C. L. (1999). *Preventing stress, improving productivity.* London: Routledge.

Kornhauser, A. (1965). *The mental health of the industrial worker.* New York: John Wiley.

Kroska, A. (1997). The division of labor in the home. *Social Psychology Quarterly, 60,* 304-322.

Langan-Fox, J. (1998). Women's careers and occupational stress. In C. Cooper & I. Robertson (Eds.), *International Review of Industrial and Organizational Psychology, 13,* 273-304.

Lazarus, R. (1966). *Psychological stress and the coping process.* New York: McGraw-Hill.

Levi, L. (1998). Stress in organizations: Theoretical and empirical approaches. In C. L. Cooper (Ed.), *Theories of organizational stress* (pp. v-xii). New York: Oxford University Press.

Levi, L., Sauter, S. L., & Shimomitsu, T. (1999). Work related stress-it's time to act. *Journal of Occupational Health Psychology, 4*(4), 394-395

Lewis, S., & Cooper, C. (1999). The work-family research agenda in changing contexts. *Journal of Occupational Health Psychology, 4,* 382-393.

Marks, M. (1994). *From turmoil to triumph.* New York: Lexington.

Martin, R., & Freeman, S. (1997). The economic context of the new organizational reality. In M. Gowing, J. Kraft, & J. Quick (Eds.), *The new organizational reality: Downsizing, restructuring and revitalization* (pp. 5-20). Washington, DC: American Psychological Association.

Mauno, S., & Kinnunen, U. (1999). The effects of job stressors on marital satisfaction in Finnish dual-earner couples. *Journal of Organizational Behavior, 20,* 879-895.

Milkie, M., & Petola, P. (1999). Playing all the roles: Gender and the work-family balancing act. *Journal of Marriage and the Family, 61,* 476-490.

Murphy, K. (1999). The challenge of staffing a postindustrial workplace. In D. Ilgen & E. Pulakos (Eds.), *The changing nature of performance: Implications for staffing, motivation and development* (pp. 295-324). San Francisco: Jossey-Bass.

Murphy, P., & Jackson, S. (1999). Managing work role performance: Challenges for twenty-first century organizations and their employees. In D. Ilgen & E. Pulakos (Eds.), *The changing nature of performance: Implications for staffing, motivation and development* (pp. 325-365). San Francisco: Jossey-Bass.

O'Driscoll, M. (1996). The interface between job and off-job roles: Enhancement and conflict. *International Review of Industrial and Organizational Psychology, 11,* 279-306.

O'Driscoll, M. P., & Cooper, C. L. (1994). Coping with work related stress: A critique of existing measures and proposal for an alternative methodology. *Journal of Occupational and Organizational Psychology, 67,* 343-354.

O'Driscoll, M., & Cooper, C. (1996). Sources and management of excessive job stress and burnout. In P. Warr (Ed.), *Psychology at work* (4th ed., pp. 188-223). New York: Penguin.

Parasuraman, S., Greenhaus, J., & Granrose, C. (1992). Role stressors, social support and well-being among two-career couples. *Journal of Organizational Behavior, 13,* 339-356.

Parker, P., & Inkson, K. (1999). New forms of career: The challenge to human resource management. *Asia Pacific Journal of Human Resources, 37,* 76-86.

Quick, J., Gowing, M., & Kraft, J. (1997). Introduction. In M. Gowing, J. Kraft, & J. Quick (Eds.), *The new organizational reality: Downsizing, restructuring and revitalization* (pp. xv-xix). Washington, DC: American Psychological Association.

Schweiger, D., & DeNisi, A. (1991). Communication with employees following a merger: A longitudinal field experiment. *Academy of Management Journal, 34,* 10-35.

Sullivan, S. (1999). The changing nature of careers: A review and research agenda. *Journal of Management, 25,* 457-484.

Terkel, S. *Working.* New York: Avon.

Warr, P. (1999). Well-being and the workplace. In D. Kahneman, E. Diener, & N. Schwarz (Eds.), *Well-being: The foundations of hedonic psychology* (pp. 392-412). New York: Russell Sage.

Index

About the Authors

Cary L. Cooper is BUPA Professor of Organizational Psychology and Health in the Manchester School of Management and Deputy-Vice-Chancellor (External Activities) of the University of Manchester Institute of Science and Technology (UMIST) United Kingdom. He is the author of over 80 books (on occupational stress, women at work, and industrial and organizational psychology), has written over 300 scholarly articles for academic journals, and is a frequent contributor to national newspapers, TV, and radio. He is currently Founding Editor of the *Journal of Organizational Behavior*, coeditor of the medical journal *Stress Medicine*, and coeditor of the *International Journal of Management Review*. He is a Fellow of the British Psychological Society, the Royal Society of Arts, the Royal Society of Medicine, and the Royal Society of Health. He is the President of the British Academy of Management, is a Companion of the (British) Institute of Management, and is one of the first UK-based Fellows of the (American) Academy of Management (having also won the 1998 Distinguished Service Award for his contribution to management from the Academy of Management). He is the Editor (jointly with Professor Chris Argyris of Harvard Business School) of the international scholarly *Blackwell Encyclopedia of*

Management (12-volume set). He has been an advisor to the World Health Organisation and the International Labour Office and has recently published a major report, entitled "Stress Prevention in the Workplace," for the European Union's European Foundation for the Improvement of Living and Working Conditions.

Philip J. Dewe is Professor of Organizational Behaviour and head of the Department of Organizational Psychology at Birkbeck College, University of London. He graduated with a master's degree in commerce and administration from Victoria University in Wellington, New Zealand, and with an MSc and PhD (in organizational psychology) from the London School of Economics. After a period of work in commerce in New Zealand, he became a Senior Research Officer in the Work Research Unit of the Department of Employment (United Kingdom). In 1980, he joined Massey University in New Zealand and headed the Department of Human Resource Management until joining Birkbeck College in 2000. His research interests include work stress and coping, human resource management issues, and the employment of the older worker. He is a member of the editorial board of *Work and Stress* and the *International Journal of Selection and Assessment.* He has written widely in the area of work stress and coping.

Michael P. O'Driscoll is Professor of Psychology at the University of Waikato, Hamilton, New Zealand, where he teaches courses in organizational psychology and organizational research methods. He has a PhD in psychology from the Flinders University of South Australia. His primary research interests are in the fields of job-related stress and coping, and the interface between job experiences and people's lives off the job (especially family commitments and responsibilities), including conflict between job and family commitments. More generally, he is interested in work attitudes and behaviors and the relationship between work and health. He has published empirical and conceptual articles on these and other topics in organizational and social psychology. He has served as an editorial consultant for several academic journals and in 2001 will assume editorship of the *New Zealand Journal of Psychology.*

Lightning Source UK Ltd.
Milton Keynes UK
07 September 2009

143446UK00001B/59/A